MEDIEVAL AMERICAN ART

MEDIEVAL AMERICAN ART
Masterpieces of the New World before Columbus

BY

PÁL KELEMEN

Third Revised Edition

IN TWO VOLUMES

Volume One

Dover Publications, Inc., New York

Published in Canada by General Publishing Company, Ltd.,
30 Lesmill Road, Don Mills, Toronto, Ontario.
Published in the United Kingdom by Constable and Company, Ltd.,
10 Orange Street, London WC 2.

This Dover edition, first published in 1969, is an unabridged
and revised republication of the second edition (Macmillan,
1956) of the work originally published by The Macmillan Company, New York, in 1943. The alterations made in the present edition are explained in detail in the author's new Preface to the
Dover Edition (see especially page xiii).

International Standard Book Number: 0-486-21993-3
Library of Congress Catalog Card Number: 68-28248

Manufactured in the United States of America

DOVER PUBLICATIONS, INC.
180 Varick Street
New York, N. Y. 10014

TO THE MEMORY
OF THE HEROIC NINETEENTH CENTURY PIONEERS
OF PRE-COLUMBIAN ARCHAEOLOGY

Preface to the Dover Edition

SINCE the last appearance of this work, archaeological investigations in the pre-Columbian field, that is, of America before the Conquest, have revealed more of the historical sequence, especially in the Mexican and Maya areas. It now appears that the Olmec culture, centered in the states of Tabasco and Vera Cruz, Mexico, was higly developed as early as 900 B.C. The Olmecs had a calendar and a system of writing which later great cultures—Teotihuacán, Zapotec, and Maya — developed further according to their individual talents and needs. Teotihuacán's Temple of the Sun is believed to date within a century of the birth of Christ. The comparatively serene and well-organized theocratic community of Teotihuacán spread its influence over a vast area until it fell, toward the end of the seventh century of our era, to the warlike Toltecs. Tula was the Toltec capital, full of turbulence and intrigue. Around the end of the tenth century one group of Toltecs under an exiled leader (who bore the name of the god Quetzal-cóatl) moved into the Maya territory of Yucatan; and when, some two hundred years later, the still more warlike barbarous Chichimecas broke their power, there seems to have been a mass migration of Toltecs into Yucatan. Research by Mexican and American scholars within the past decade has also brought out the importance of the Mixtecs in the region of Puebla-Cholula before their expansion southward toward the turn of the millennium. This people is especially remarkable for its technically and visually sophisticated work in gold.

Though investigations in South America are not so coordinated, they have shown that the Chavín culture of northern Peru probably played a role in the Andean area somewhat parallel to that of the Olmec culture in Middle America in the centuries before Christ.

Regardless of new revelations and fluctuating theories, the master monuments shown here stand fast in testimony to the talent and individuality of these diverse peoples. The great art period in pre-Columbian America coincides in time with those of medieval Asia and Europe and equals them often also in quality.

The increasing appreciation of pre-Columbian art continues to be, as sketched in my previous Foreword (1943) and Preface (1956), mainly the work of connoisseurs, artists, writers, collectors, art dealers, and some museum personnel.

< ix >

More art museums have ventured into the field lately, spurred by the gifts of outstanding collectors. The archaeologist and the art historian are not yet making their full contribution toward the esthetic evaluation of this subject.

The archaeologist with a leaning toward science is trained to deduce facts from an aggregation of material, to summarize them, and to publish them. He has often specialized too soon to acquire the cultural background necessary for the presentation of an alien art that was developed in isolation. There have, however, been archaeologists of God-given talent who could discern the art among the tables of statistics. George C. Vaillant and Wendell C. Bennett—all too early departed—were outstanding. Above all, Ralph Linton, possessed of an uncanny eye although he modestly called himself merely an ethnologist, had the perception of a dozen "professional" art historians. These names, with that of the late Alfred V. Kidder, should be added to the dedication at the opening of this book as worthy followers of the great pioneers.

For art historians, our subject practically did not exist before World War II. When our country entered that war and the Good Neighbor policy was especially timely, the *Art Bulletin* solicited an article on pre-Columbian metalwork which was checked by George C. Vaillant and highly recommended. It never appeared in print. Indeed, to this day not a single Americanistic study, whether on pre-Columbian or colonial Latin American art, has been published in the *Art Bulletin,* although seventy learned institutions now contribute toward the expenses of this official prestige publication. These educators have rejected the opportunity to present a new and American art field to world scholarship.

But the blame does not fall on this group alone. In 1945, while the war was still in progress, a Conference for Studies in Latin American Art was convened in the Museum of Modern Art in New York. Administrators and educators were invited to participate. Some half-dozen art historians had concluded work or reported work in progress on one branch or another of Latin American art. The conference produced a series of lengthy resolutions covering all phases of the subject. It appeared after the conference as if the arts of Latin America would finally have their own forum. However, this never came to pass. Atrophy set in, and in *The Visual Arts in Higher Education,* a study prepared by the College Art Association of America (1966), we read that, while in more than six hundred colleges and universities art history is now a standard course, and while three hundred fifty courses are offered on Gothic, Renaissance, and related art subjects, there are only twelve on the Latin American arts, covering pre-Columbian, colonial, folk, and contemporary art.

Yale is one of the few universities where the art of the Americas is being taught on the graduate level, and yet the 1967 *Yale Course Critique* says: "History of Art No. — is good only for those people specifically interested in Latin America . . . since many of the paintings and buildings covered require a special love if their eccentricities are to be appreciated." From the majestic Maya temples to the rustic beauty of *mestizo* churches in the Andes, from the intricate cast gold jewelry of the Mixtecs to the work of the great muralists of our own age—all are looked on as "eccentricities."

The head of the Carnegie Institution of Washington, a mathematician, dealt our subject a great blow when, in 1955, with the theorist's myopic view of the humanities, he stopped all archaeological activity and withdrew the relatively small sum allowed for it. The public was deprived of the Institution's lucidly written publications; the scholar, even in Latin America, was baffled.

As early as the 1940's, even before the demise of some of the great personalities in our field, and more and more noticeably in the 1960's, the climate of Academe was changing. Method was becoming emphasized over matter. Footnotes were collected for footnotes' sake. Scathing book reviews appeared, sometimes unsolicited, obviously inspired by personal antagonism, causing one distinguished English scholar to write that the methods of the Blitzkrieg had been introduced into the American campus. It was openly recommended by some that quotes and bibliographical material from books published in Latin America and Europe be used without mention of the actual source. Again, some educators not financially needy have obtained not one but sometimes several fellowships for the sake of prestige; but have turned thumbs down when less fortunate scholars' applications came to their desks. Small wonder that suspicion and reluctance have invaded the field.

In addition, the 1966 study on higher education mentioned above states (page 39), under the heading "The High Mortality Rate of Graduate Students in Art History":

A high percentage of the graduate students who come to the large Eastern universities have not risen from the undergraduate programs of these schools, but have come from far away—from the Midwest, the South, the West. They represent a great variety of backgrounds and a wide range of competence. They also may reflect the provincialism of their own original milieux. Poorly oriented, conscious of their inadequacies, torn between remedial undergraduate courses and the highly specialized graduate work, overwhelmed by a sudden *embarras de richesses,* they easily become discouraged. Even those who persevere may never acquire a harmonious and coherent education in the history of art but may go on to become one-sided and over-specialized teachers.

Such anomalies on the one hand and my fortunate position on the other confirmed in me the decision to remain independent. Before the war, living in a *villino* in Florence under San Miniato, I could study the Codex Florentino of Aztec picture-writing in the Laurentian Library and could enjoy an occasional stimulating visit with Bernard Berenson, before he came to world fame. Doyen of art historians in the field of Italian painting, Berenson had enthusiasm and sharp perception also for pre-Columbian art. At the same time I could observe the narrowing of the field of art-historical specialists. (When later many were admitted to the United States—whose humanistic climate they seldom approached with humility—all too few attempted to broaden their scope to the global orientation of this continent.)

In my native Budapest, during a lecture tour of Central Europe, I had the opportunity to visit another native of that city, Sir Aurel Stein. He spoke of his explorations in Inner Mongolia and on the Kirghiz steppes. (From these regions in prehistoric times migrating tribes had moved in the direction of the New World also, until bellicose nations and changing topography turned them toward the West.) Stein was strongly in favor of academic independence and adhered to his own, up to his eighty-second year, when he died in Kabul, Afghanistan, preparing for another independent expedition.

In 1956, when the present work was going into its fourth printing and my volume devoted to the highlights of the colonial epoch of the same areas was being widely distributed (*Baroque and Rococo in Latin America,* 1951; Dover reprint, 1967), the State Department invited me to go on a lecture tour of Europe. This was the first time and, to my knowledge, the only time to date that the subject of the art of the American continent—pre-Columbian, Hispanic colonial, and folklore—was presented to European audiences under an official aegis. The countries visited were Portugal, Spain, Italy, Greece, and Turkey. The reactions were diverse and illuminating.

In harbor cities, accustomed to products of distant continents, an elasticity of comprehension, even an enthusiastic response, was encountered. In Trieste, then recently wrenched from the Yugoslav dictator's grasp, this glimpse of a new subject was taken as a gift from the Western Hemisphere, a message of encouragement from the great American democracy.

< xii >

As for the land-locked capitals: in Madrid our effort served to illuminate and glorify the Conquest of the Spaniards. In Rome the society of impoverished aristocrats showed its indifference toward the achievements of a "parvenu" nation. In Athens, where the Acropolis constitutes the hub of the universe, Maya art could not have much effect.

It was not until I spoke at the National University in Istanbul, where the audience stood deep in the corridors, that the excited gasp occasioned by my slides betokened an unbiased response. Next afternoon, in the villa of our host professor at the edge of the Bosporus, it became clear that these students were working on Persian pottery, Turkish book illumination, rug patterns of Turkestan, the architecture of old Iran. Here we had an audience for whom the Greco-Roman ideal of beauty was just one chapter in the many-volumed history of art. They were free of Western European academism and could breathe the beauty of this New World unhampered by the intellectualization of art.

Homeward bound, we spent some time at Thessaloniki, returning there after trips to Mt. Athos and a survey of Byzantine murals in Macedonian churches. Resting, we spent many hours with the Director of Macedonian-Byzantine (not Greek!) Antiquities. Sitting on the quay, looking across the blue Aegean to the snow on Mt. Olympus, we talked of the various nationalities who worked in his field. He said: "Perhaps we needed the Germans—but they dried up the garden."

The art of the Americas grew out of American soil. It represents a different psychology and cannot be measured with the meter-sticks and methods worked out for the Classical world. The art historian will have to develop a more elastic instrument and produce more than technical manuals and exercises in palaeography. He must be concerned with the illumination and evaluation of pre-Columbian art and, above all, with the education of vision.

The present edition, like the first (1943), is divided into two volumes, but this time each volume contains part of the text and part of the illustrations, Volume One including the preliminary matter and the first five chapters with the plates discussed therein, and Volume Two the remaining material. The Catalogue of Illustrations, formerly located after the plates, has now become the List of Illustrations, divided between the two volumes (the Register of Museums and Collections appears in both volumes); the opportunity has been taken in this edition (at the end of the Register of Museums) to indicate the change of ownership of several items in recent years, principally pieces that have been acquired by the Cleveland Museum of Art and the Dumbarton Oaks Collection from the Brummer Gallery and John Wise, Ltd. Within the text itself a very few passages

< xiii >

have required revision in the light of recent research, which has, for instance, cast doubt on the authenticity of two or three pieces. The second part of the Preface to the Second Edition (1956), which describes the items illustrated on Plates 307 and 308 (new in that edition), now forms an Addenda section on pages 382–386 in Volume Two. The area map that formerly appeared on the endpapers is now located on pages xlii and xliii of Volume One.

It was the connoisseur mainly who brought before the general public the arts of Egypt, Persia, China, and Japan, and he is doing the same also for the art of the Americas. In 1932 this author had to explain the purpose of his project in the face of considerable skepticism. Today, after four printings totaling 15,000 copies, always retailed at a high price, his work is available to those of modest means. This is due to the connoisseurship of Hayward Cirker, President of Dover Publications, and to the enthusiasm of his staff.

Pál Kelemen

Norfolk, Connecticut, May, 1968

< xiv >

Preface to the Second Edition

THE story of how this book came into being is told in the Foreword. What has happened since in the appreciation of the art which it surveys is another and challenging story.

When I first visited the United States, in the autumn of 1932, and commenced work on this survey, only seven universities and colleges had permanent facilities for the study of the history of art. The pioneers in the subject came from other fields—the classics, linguistics, philosophy, architecture, history, newspaper work. The late 1930's saw a rapid enlargement, with the influx of many European refugee scholars. They brought with them the European orientation, not only with its valuable assets but also, frequently, with an overemphasis on the art of a few countries, such as Italy and France; further, their method was inelastic and often pedantic and they failed to realize the different preparation and requirements of the students in this country.

Humanistic studies were devoted almost exclusively to the values of the Greco-Roman civilization and what developed from it, commonly known as the Western World. The great artistic manifestations of Asia and Africa had a few champions and a limited audience. But the art of the Americas was in limbo. Slowly, sporadic interest turned to the civilization which flourished here before Columbus. This occurred through the medium of archaeology, which because of its proximity to science had dignity and could not be derided as effeminate.

Not until the clouds of World War II gathered was this country forced to grow up into a world power. The initiation of the Good Neighbor policy brought the realization that, besides trade and industrial relations, the cultural tie also constitutes a real and vital factor. Some hold that our soldiers, returning from service at far points of the globe, did more to change the general attitude towards art than many a professor. They experienced how big the world is, how varied the arts of its many peoples, and reacted intelligently to them. Now that the United States accepts global responsibility in the tactical, political, diplomatic, and social spheres, our humanistic education is faced with the responsibility of preparing students for the expanded horizon.

< XV >

PREFACE TO THE SECOND EDITION

Pre-Columbian art, product of the civilization that flourished in the New World before Columbus, has been brought to public attention through the enthusiasm of connoisseurs, artists, collectors, art dealers, and museum directors. By now a number of museums have fine collections; some colleges include the subject in classes on art history; some even present special courses on the three epochs of the art of the Americas (the pre-Columbian, the colonial, and the modern). Unfortunately some of our younger educators who try their hand at the art of pre-Columbian America have a desiccating touch; they lack the broad view and the clear style of presentation without which this art, not developed according to the canons of Greco-Roman esthetics, can be neither understood nor interpreted.

As Henry Adams says in his Autobiography: "Nothing in education is so astonishing as the amount of ignorance it accumulates in the form of inert facts." A hodge-podge of data collected from books, presented in an undigested form, its publication financed by subsidies, is little more than exercise in the mechanics of scholarship and is critically viewed by scholars abroad, sometimes with concern, sometimes with malicious glee. Our professional art historian is all too often prepared in a vacuum. His highly specialized knowledge, narrow and petrified, would be inadequate even in a humanistically more refined society than ours. We are producing "experts" who, even in their own fields, are untrustworthy because they have never developed a sense of proportion; and since they are increasingly influential in the granting of scholarships, their myopia affects the orientation of the youngest generation.

Recently the museums, in dire need of qualified curators, have been trying to bring the budding art historian into their workrooms. Here he can establish a living connection with the art works and recognize that the love and experience of art take precedence over the technique of collecting mountains of footnotes and miles of bibliography. Alas, up to now he seldom has been able to make contact with the great audience that goes into the museum seeking to know more about art.

Even business and industry are complaining that executive capacity has not been sufficiently developed in our college graduates, that is, the ability to make far-sighted decisions and to distinguish quality. That academic circles also recognize this minor bankruptcy in our educational system is evident from the calling up of a committee by one of our most famous universities which published its report earlier this year. It finds that disproportionately few students of high calibre are attracted to the study of art history and deplores the dearth of crea-

< xvi >

tive scholarship in the writings of graduate students. It admits also the lack of attractiveness of the courses and a general apathy in the student body towards this idealistic subject of the liberal arts college. One reason might be that too many teachers have attained their position, not through talent, but through political or social connections and financial contributions; too many have arrived by the "bicycle technique," bending above cajolingly and treading downwards ruthlessly. Without a drastic change in the present set-up, no improvement can be expected. The real educator in the humanities has to have the ability to inject his subject with life and make it appealing as a spiritual asset for the student's later years.

While the great originality of the artistic civilizations of Asia and Africa is now accepted and enjoyed, some people are reluctant to allow the same status to the art of pre-Columbian America. The hobby-horse of the Atlantis admirer has lost its vigor. Now, however, a mirage has arisen that projects the importing of the pre-Columbian civilization across the Pacific Ocean; balsa rafts are traveling to and from the South Seas and beyond. Few who have studied the past and present of the American Indian would argue against the proto-Mongolian (earliest Asian) ancestry of the ancient Indian tribes. But valid evidence has yet to be offered against the autochthonous origin of the arts covered in this book. Man's existence in America at the end of the Pleistocene Age recently received new proof, with the discovery of his traces as a hunter of mammoth in the Valley of Mexico. Chinese sources have just recently thrown light on the question whether certain typical American plants were actually indigenous. They present weighty linguistic evidence that the plants reached China *after* the discovery of America, with Portuguese or Spanish boats.

If, from the botanical to the linguistic, from the paleontological to the religious, the evidence does not suffice, the character of the art itself presents a convincing case for its originality. However, here again, the lack of ability to see and the marshaling of arguments towards a preconceived goal obfuscate the mind. Many people, emotionally immature and artistically insensitive, write professionally about art, who would not venture, with similar equipment, to put their pens to problems of poetry or music. The difficulty for the serious student lies, not in works which through their flamboyant and extravagant statements appear questionable even on the surface but in those publications which contain truths, half-truths, and manipulated "facts" presented under the dignified cloak of scientific method. All this junketing with American art and archaeology

< xvii >

makes entertaining reading. But as long as the student is offered blurry comparisons, distorted in proportion and omitting concomitant details, or hand-drawn sketches with arbitrary shading that produces false emphasis—the statements of Chapter XII are fully valid.

Just a few years ago, a method of dating in archaeology was developed. A by-product of studies in atomic physics, it is known as the radio-carbon or Carbon[14] method of dating. For this, only human, animal, or plant remains qualify. Since many masterpieces are of stone, pottery, jade, or metal, and are in collections—lifted out of context, as it were—this new method of dating cannot be applied to them. From the freaks which have occurred in its calculations and from the vastness of areas still unexplored, as well as unexplorable, it is clear that it is too early to discard for this new method a chronology which was evolved through decades by painstaking and often cross-checked research.

This survey is so constructed that, by perusing the introductory and concluding paragraphs of each chapter, the reader can get a satisfactory general picture and can go at will into further detail by picking out the description of the particular illustrations that catch his eye. The new edition offered the opportunity to replace certain photographs with more recent ones, taken on our various field trips by my wife. *Plates 307, 308* are new, the artistic merit of their subjects warranting inclusion in this volume. For technical reasons their description is given here [now on pages 382–386 of Volume Two].

On paging through the book, it will become evident that the many cultures delineated their own distinct physical types in various manners. All have considerably alien flavor for the man educated in the artistic climate of the Western World. To those who are able to discard their esthetic prejudices, each style will offer a rewarding artistic experience.

September, 1956

P. K.

< xviii >

Foreword

*All attempts to reduce art to science are in vain.
Science is not art, and, if a work of art can legiti-
mately convey scientific information, that is because
its material includes matters of universal scope.*

—Tovey

MY INTEREST in pre-Columbian art and my manner of presenting it
may require a few paragraphs of a personal nature, as well as some
comment on the status of art-history at the time of my early studies.
When more than thirty years ago I attended my first classes in the history of
art, even the leading European universities were limited in their program.
While the painters and sculptors of the Renaissance were abundantly treated, the
masters of the Trecento had still the mist of a delayed sunrise on them. Spanish
art was not yet in the process of being discovered; on Greco no monograph was
yet published, with the exception of Cossío's pioneer work in Spanish. Cézanne
and Gauguin were anathema to every museum, and we were led to admire and
analyze the compositions of Géricault and Delacroix. The art of Byzantium,
together with the tremendous iconographic influence which took its name from
that metropolis, was the little noticed hobby of a few. The archaeology and art-
history of the Far and Near East were in their infancy, primarily because of a
national aloofness but also because of the difficulties of travel in those lands.

The field was then not so highly specialized. Systematized methods had not
been thoroughly established, and the inspiration and poetry of the subject were
still uppermost. Art-history was young, and we approached it through the
broad avenue of the humanities—philosophy, drama, literature, music.

In my native Budapest, the colleagues of Liszt were still holding the bastion
of academic music, but an enthusiastic if sparse audience applauded the compositions of Bartók and Kodály, based on the genuine folk song. After a perform-
ance of Debussy's quintette with the composer at the piano, we listened in breath-
less silence to his defense of his new music. Gordon Craig had just presented his
new ideas of décor and Max Reinhardt had begun his experiments, bringing the
stage out of the frame of the proscenium arch into the three dimensional in vast

< xix >

halls and the open air. Nijinski was not yet a myth, but a young and talented solo dancer. In the home of the aging Auguste Rodin at Meudon Val Fleury, I listened to the sculptor's broad and elastic views on art in general—not only on sculpture—in an interview which made up one of my first published essays. At that time Rodin was far from generally acknowledged; his Balzac statue was refused, even as a gift, by the municipality of Paris.

Great revaluations in art-history and general esthetics were taking place. Salomon Reinach, Henri Bergson, Heinrich Wölfflin—in whose classes I sat— Benedetto Croce, Walter Pater, Bernhard Berenson, with others were reformulating the principles of art criticism. But intellectual life was shaken and disrupted by World War I. In the late summer of 1914, with Croce's "Estetica" in my saddlebag, I rode out as a young cavalry officer.

After the war anything seemed possible in the political arena, and experimentation ran almost as wild in the arts. I was fortunate enough to be able to go on with my studies, but from my original thesis, "Impressionism before the 19th Century," I ventured far, going back into the formative periods of Christian art.

While in pursuit of this subject and studying illuminated manuscripts at the British Museum in 1926, I had my first taste of pre-Columbian art and made some notes on the strange monumental concepts and technical refinement manifest in the specimens on exhibit there. But involved then in my own studies, I did not follow up these impressions. My next contact with it did not come until after I had met and married an American in Italy and, some time later, made my first visit to the United States. Here, in 1932, I intended to study certain phases of Spanish art, so well represented in this country, but the tremendous artistic vitality in the civilization of pre-Columbian America encountered in the various museums soon began to absorb my interest.

By that time a few books had attempted to present the artistic side of this civilization, and an exhibit or two had awakened sporadic interest. I decided to make a comprehensive survey of these cultures from the point of view of art and was encouraged in this undertaking by scholars here. The outline of this work was formulated then and the collection of the material began. The scope of the project continually expanded as I went along.

This survey is planned to introduce to the reader generally interested in art those achievements of the pre-Columbian civilization which demand attention for their beauty and power irrespective of dates and styles.

It would be ideal if the objects could speak for themselves; but, for most people, some effort must be made to bridge the gap of centuries and to offset inherited esthetic standards. In this technological age, the investigation into the material construction of a work of art is threatening to become more important than intimacy with the spirit which created it. A broad new world of human expression cannot be opened by a "proliferation of minutiae"; the approach has to be through the emotional—the one common denominator of man's grasp at art. For centuries the colors of Titian have been enjoyed without analyzing their chemical ingredients, and the canvases of Velásquez have been awarded world renown without a knowledge of the kind of hair he used in his brushes. I have avoided as much as possible the "professional" terminology of the specialist—one cause of the general reader's diffidence toward books on archaeology and art-history—and have tried to present a humanistic subject to him in such a manner that he can perceive the beauty of its moods and follow not so much the intricate and overladen thoughts of an author as the clear and colorful line of the subject itself.

The full grandeur of a building, however, or the delicacy of a jade pectoral cannot be completely transmitted by a photograph. As my work proceeded, the vague reaction of the public to pictures in general, as well as the shortcomings of most of the pictures existing in this field, became increasingly apparent. At best a photograph is only an approximation, and for one who is unfamiliar with an object, it must be made to aid his eye and stimulate his imagination as far as possible. The straight front or exact profile view of anthropological files is not always the best means of bringing out artistic quality effectively. Consequently, the necessity arose for pictures taken from a new angle. The original position of some pieces had to be considered—for instance, a sculpture high in a carved frieze, with the top lighting of a tropical sun. Also those "artistic shots" had to be avoided in which an overlively background or overdramatic lighting reduced the object to a mere vehicle for the photographer. Several trips were undertaken to Spanish America for new photographs and first-hand observation and to Europe for comparative material.

To put into one survey all the manifestations of the artistic development of a wide range of cultures over one and a half millennia is obviously an impossibility. The production of each area is given space according to its artistic importance, proportionate, as I see it, to the general picture. Certain sites and specimens, which to the specialist may appear important, have been omitted because it was my conviction that they would not contribute appreciably to the reader's grasp of this art.

FOREWORD

"Pre-Columbian" as used in this survey stands for the time-span in the Western Hemisphere before cultural contact with the white man. While not entirely satisfactory, because it is not self-explanatory, this term is as good as anything offered so far and has the added advantage of being traditional, carrying with it long-accepted connotations. Columbus is, after all, responsible for the opening of the New World, and as long as his name is not perpetuated in that of the new continent, he deserves at least to be commemorated in the term which defines the civilization that existed here before his enterprise. "Medieval American" has a more restricted meaning and is discussed in the opening chapter.

In arranging the material, a name had to be coined for the Isthmian countries and the adjoining regions; I have called this section the Interlying Area. For the other territories of highest civilization, the accepted designations—Southwest, Mexican, Maya, and Andean—have been used. It will be found that the borders of these areas cannot be strictly adhered to, for cultural limits do not necessarily coincide with boundary lines. In general, a geographical rather than a chronological sequence has been followed, but here also other considerations have occasionally led to a change.

If I had not been warned that further delay would result in an indefinite postponement of publication, due to war conditions, I would have added more detail, elaborated certain ideas, and polished on the style. Data which in certain cases might have weighed down the text have been relegated to the Catalogue of Illustrations, where measurements, other such information, and various credits are recorded. In a few cases, the order of the illustrations within the framework of one page is not followed by the text, for, while the text pursues the logical sequence, the plate was arranged to please the eye. Often the use of a modest magnifying glass will increase the reader's enjoyment of the illustrations. The chronological chart and the map are appended for his orientation and are simplified and generalized to that end.

During the ten years in which the material was collected for this survey, I have received the help of a great number of museum directors, curators, photographers, art collectors, and connoisseurs. To name them all, from Vienna, Austria, to Lima, Peru, would not be possible in the space allowed. I hope that they will accept this general expression of my sincere gratitude.

There is a smaller group whose coöperation in this work was of a more personal kind. Professor Alfred M. Tozzer of Harvard University was the first to whom I went in the autumn of 1932 with my ideas and plans, and he, with the

< xxii >

experience and understanding of a great teacher, put me on the right track; since then, whenever advice has been needed, he has given it unsparingly. Dr. Alfred V. Kidder, Chairman of the Division of Historical Research, Carnegie Institution of Washington, showed early interest in my project, and his far-reaching arm has facilitated my work both in the field and in the museums. The reader will appreciate, I am sure, his generosity in procuring the permission to include here material, as yet unpublished, from the famous Maya site, Uaxactún, excavated under the leadership of A. Ledyard Smith of the same Institution, thus making it known to a different circle. Director Donald Scott of the Peabody Museum, Harvard University, gave me the freedom of the rich collection and magnificent library there; it is through his kindness that it was possible to include the pictures of pottery specimens excavated at Coclé, Panama, the report of which is in press.

The manuscript was read by J. Eric S. Thompson of the Carnegie Institution of Washington. For years he has taken a most helpful interest in my work and, with his erudition and innate gentlemanliness, has stood at my side as a rare friend. Many of his criticisms have been included in the text, and all dates throughout the Maya Area are based on his latest conclusions. Dr. Wendell C. Bennett of Yale University has given much attention to the sections relating to South American cultures, and his nomenclature and chronology for the Andean Area have been used. Miss H. Newell Wardle of The University Museum, Philadelphia, furnished considerable data and identified a number of the Peruvian fabrics. The textile glossary is in great part her work. Kenneth Macgowan of the Office of Coördinator of Inter-American Affairs also has read the manuscript and, with his wide knowledge and connoisseurship, contributed toward the clarification of a number of statements.

Special privileges in handling and photographing the material under their care were given by Sir George Hill, Director of the British Museum, London, who also permitted me to use Maudslay's original photographic plates; Dr. Alfonso Caso, Director of the Instituto Nacional de Antropología e Historia, Mexico; Professor J. Antonio Villacorta C., Secretary of Education of Guatemala; Carlos A. Villacorta B., Director of the Museo Arqueológico of Guatemala; and also Dr. Emeriterio Oscar Salazar of San Salvador. Professor Jorge A. Lines of San José furnished photographs of unpublished rare material from Costa Rica. Professor Verle L. Annis of the University of Southern California, Los Angeles, placed at my disposal a great number of his excellent photographs. Frederick C. Orchard of Peabody Museum, Harvard University, and Kenneth

< xxiii >

C. Miller of the Museum of the American Indian, Heye Foundation, New York, gave countless hours and their unlimited patience in making photographs from my angle. The Harvard College Library coöperated in sending their books to me in Norfolk, saving me trips and giving me the opportunity to work in the calm of my study.

To arrange 960 photographs of different character, quality, and size into 306 plates was no light task, and Edward C. Wolf of The Beck Engraving Company, New York, brought to the work his great resourcefulness and good taste. For the last year and a half Helen B. Hartman has helped in the assemblage of the material, in editorial work, and in the typing. Her faithfulness to the cause and her growing enthusiasm were of great assistance to me. The index is principally her work.

Finally, acknowledgment of a more intimate character is due my wife, Elisabeth, my constant collaborator in the various phases of this survey. She has not only accompanied me on all my trips, sharing the frequent discomforts of primitive conditions, but, under most trying circumstances, has taken numberless photographs for me which otherwise could not have been obtained. She has helped also substantially in preparing the manuscript. Her rare artistic sense and unflagging spirit have contributed greatly toward the completion of this work. Throughout the undertaking she has exemplified that fine type of American womanhood—not faddist, not sterilely intellectual, but of constructive mind—which has helped to make and keep this country great and free.

Pál Kelemen

Boston, Massachusetts, October, 1932
  Norfolk, Connecticut, November, 1942

Contents

Illustrations in Volume One

This compilation contains data, measurements, and various credits not included in the text or captions. Measurements denote height unless otherwise stated. When a museum or a collector owns the piece and has also furnished the photograph of it, the name is given only once. The following abbreviations have been used for names which occur most frequently.

AMNH.	American Museum of Natural History, New York
BG.	Brummer Gallery, Inc., New York
CIW.	Carnegie Institution of Washington, Washington, D. C.
DO.	Dumbarton Oaks Collection, Washington, D.C.
EZK.	Elisabeth Zulauf Kelemen
FAM.	Fogg Art Museum, Cambridge, Mass.
FM.	Field Museum, Chicago, Ill.
INAH.	Instituto Nacional de Antropología e Historia, Mexico, D.F.
JW.	John Wise, Ltd., New York
LA.	Laboratory of Anthropology, Santa Fé, N.M.
LAM.	Los Angeles Museum of History, Science, and Art, Los Angeles, Calif.
M.	Museum
MAG.	Museo de Arqueología, Guatemala
MAI.	Museum of the American Indian, Heye Foundation, New York
MAL.	Museo Nacional de Arqueología, Lima, Peru
MARI.	Middle American Research Institute, Tulane University, New Orleans, La.
MFA.	Museum of Fine Arts, Boston, Mass.
MH.	Musée de l'Homme, Paris, France
MN.	Museo Nacional de Arqueología, Historia y Etnografia, Mexico, D.F.
MVBG.	Museum für Völkerkunde, Berlin, Germany
MVBS.	Museum für Völkerkunde, Basle, Switzerland
MVVA.	Museum für Völkerkunde, Vienna, Austria
OSM.	Ohio State Museum, Columbus, Ohio
Ph.	Photograph
PM.	Peabody Museum of Harvard University, Cambridge, Mass.
RC.	Rossbach Collection, Chichicastenango, Guatemala
TM.	Textile Museum of the District of Columbia, Washington, D.C.
UCAL.	University of California Museum, Berkeley, Calif.
UMP.	The University Museum, Philadelphia, Pa.
USNM.	United States National Museum, Washington, D.C.

< xxvi >

Architecture

< xxvii >

ILLUSTRATIONS IN VOLUME ONE

ARCHITECTURE

< xxix >

Sculpture

< xxxi >

< xxxii >

Pottery

POTTERY

< xxxvii >

ILLUSTRATIONS IN VOLUME ONE

< xxxviii >

Register of Museums and Collections

This list shows the location of most of the objects illustrated in this survey. In addition, there are twenty-five private collections represented which are not included here.

American Museum of Natural History, New York, N.Y.
  28b, 33d, 62a, 69b, 89a, 97c, 98b, 101b, 104c, 114b, 115c, 115d, 117a, 118a, 118c, 119a, 134a, 140b, 142d, 150a, 156d, 158b, 162b, 164b, 164c, 165a, 166a, 166b, 167a, 169c, 171c, 172b, 176c, 183b, 185a, 190b, 191b, 191c, 191d, 192b, 196a, 204a, 204b, 207b, 213a, 225c, 229c, 231c, 243b, 245b, 276a, 276e, 289c, 293a, 294a, 294c, 294d, 294f, 296c, 298a, 299b.

British Museum, London, England
  59a, 61a, 76b, 85b, 86a, 90, 111c, 117c, 126c, 131a, 144a, 153c, 174a, 174b, 203b, 205b, 206d, 209d, 210c, 211b, 214c, 217a, 220b, 225b, 238b, 242b, 246a, 255b, 275a, 278a, 278b, 278c, 279a, 292d, 299a.

Brooklyn Museum, Brooklyn, N.Y.
  27b, 30b, 63b, 146a, 151h, 177a, 188a, 214a.

Brummer Gallery, New York, N.Y.
  61b, 68c, 68d, 88c, 94a, 95b, 115a, 116c, 117e, 125a, 131d, 137a, 161a, 207a, 235b, 237c, 237d, 239f, 240b, 241g, 242d, 243c, 247b, 247c, 249b, 251d, 253a, 254b, 256a, 256d, 276c, 282b.

Buffalo Fine Arts Academy, Albright Art Gallery, Buffalo, N.Y.
  135a.

Buffalo Museum of Science, Buffalo, N.Y.
  106e.

Carnegie Institution of Washington, Washington, D.C.
  262a, 263a.

City Art Museum, St. Louis, Mo.
  132a.

Cleveland Museum of Art, Cleveland, Ohio
  117b, 195c, 215a, 253d.

Copan Museum, Copan, Honduras
  82a, 83b.

Cranbrook Academy of Art, Bloomfield, Mich.
  66a, 156c, 199a, 202a.

Dartmouth College Museum, Hanover, N.H.
  88b.

Denver Art Museum, Denver, Colo.
  102b.

Dumbarton Oaks Collection, Washington, D.C.
  66b, 206a, 206b, 206e, 241a, 250b, 250c, 252c, 252d.

Field Museum, Chicago, Ill.
  108b, 109c, 111a, 111d, 111e, 112b, 114a, 114c, 125b, 126a, 133b, 149a, 156a, 156b, 161d, 162f, 184c, 191a, 193a, 193b, 200a, 204d, 230b, 243a, 244a, 258a, 272a, 276d, 277a, 282c, 296f.

Institute of Arts, Minneapolis, Minn.
  64a.

Instituto Nacional de Antropología e Historia, Mexico, D.F.
  264d.

Laboratory of Anthropology, Santa Fé, N.M.
  101c, 102c, 103c, 105a, 105d.

Los Angeles Museum of History, Science, and Art, Los Angeles, Calif.
  101e, 145c, 282a, 285a.

Metropolitan Museum of Art, New York, N.Y.
  63b, 114b.

< xxxix >

Middle American Research Institute, Tulane University, New Orleans, La.
60b, 80d, 86d, 94b, 116d, 126b, 134d, 134e, 140a, 142e, 143a, 145b, 149c, 158c, 163a, 163b, 163c, 163d, 227b, 237a, 245h, 251f, 281b.

Montezuma Castle National Museum, Montezuma Castle, Ariz.
171a.

Musée de l'Homme, Paris, France
113c, 123b, 133a, 133c, 153d, 154c, 155a, 155d, 157b, 158d, 161b, 185b, 185c, 200b, 238a, 250a, 256b.

Museo Arqueológico, Guatemala, Guatemala
72a, 97a, 97b, 127a, 127b, 127c, 127d, 128a, 128b, 128c, 129a, 132b, 134b, 135c, 136a, 136c, 141a, 141d, 145d, 236b, 242c.

Museo Arqueológico Nacional, Madrid, Spain
81a, 214b.

Museo de la Universidad, Lima, Peru
99a.

Museo Nacional, San José, Costa Rica
97d, 148d, 222a, 294e.

Museo Nacional de Arqueología, Lima, Peru
99b, 198a, 198c, 199c, 201a, 202c, 258c.

Museo Nacional de Arqueología, Historia y Etnografia, Mexico, D.F.
58a, 58b, 65a, 65c, 67a, 67b, 67c, 69a, 75b, 78b, 82b, 82c, 84b, 93b, 110a, 110b, 110c, 111b, 111f, 112c, 113a, 115b, 119b, 121c, 122a, 122b, 124a, 124b, 227a, 228d, 233b, 234a, 237f, 241f, 246b, 248d, 249a, 249d, 254a, 257c, 257d, 260a, 260b, 261b, 269, 285b, 285c, 287a, 292a, 292b, 292e, 293c.

Museo Preistorico ed Etnografico, Rome, Italy
219c, 273a.

Museum für Völkerkunde, Basle, Switzerland
148b, 274.

Museum für Völkerkunde, Berlin, Germany
121a, 131b, 273c.

Museum für Völkerkunde, Vienna, Austria
59b, 65b, 68b, 189b, 239b, 240a, 249c, 251b, 286a, 287b, 287c.

Museum of Art, Providence, R.I.
201b.

Museum of Fine Arts, Boston, Mass.
192a, 202b, 216a, 219a, 226a.

Museum of New Mexico, Santa Fé, N.M.
4b, 170a.

Museum of the American Indian, Heye Foundation, New York, N.Y.
86c, 101a, 103f, 108c, 108d, 109b, 109d, 114d, 117d, 123a, 123c, 125c, 133d, 138a, 139d, 143c, 144c, 151e, 154a, 155b, 155c, 157c, 164a, 164d, 178a, 194a, 194b, 194c, 195b, 195d, 197a, 198b, 199b, 200c, 208a, 208b, 216b, 216c, 217b, 217c, 219b, 226b, 226d, 228c, 229a, 231b, 233a, 240c, 240d, 241b, 242a, 245e, 258b, 271a, 272b, 279b, 280a, 280b, 280c, 283a, 283b, 283c, 289a, 289b, 295a, 296e, 297b, 297c, 298b, 298c.

Oaxaca Museum, Oaxaca, Mexico
68a, 123d, 124c, 228a, 229b, 229d, 230a, 230c, 231a, 232a, 232b, 251e, 255a, 257a, 284b, 284c.

Ohio State Museum, Columbus, Ohio
194d, 295b, 295d, 296a, 296b, 296d.

Peabody Museum of Harvard University, Cambridge, Mass.
77a, 78a, 85a, 87, 88d, 89b, 102a, 106a, 106c, 106e, 107, 108a, 109a, 134c, 137b, 142c, 146b, 146c, 146d, 146e, 147a, 147b, 147c, 147d, 147e, 147f, 159a, 161c, 171b, 176b, 189c, 197b, 218c, 221a, 221b, 222d, 224a, 224b, 224c, 225a, 227c, 234b, 238c, 238d, 240e, 240f, 241d, 244b, 248a, 248b, 248c, 259a, 259b, 262b, 263c, 273b, 276f, 284a.

Peabody Museum of Yale University, New Haven, Conn.
148c, 148f, 149b, 205c, 226c, 295c.

Phillips Academy, Andover, Mass.
281a, 281c.

Pitti Gallery, Florence, Italy
288.

Puebla Museum, Puebla, Mexico
59c, 60c, 252a, 256c, 293b.

Rijksmuseum, Leyden, Holland
235a.

Rossbach Collection, Chichicastenango, Guatemala
96a, 136b, 141b, 141c, 208c, 208d, 237e, 241c, 241h.

Southwest Museum, Los Angeles, Calif.
170b.

Textile Museum of the District of Columbia, Washington, D.C.

165b, 175a, 175c. 178b, 178c, 179a, 180a, 182b, 183c, 187, 218b, 222c.

United States Department of the Interior, Park Service, Washington, D.C.

103e, 105b.

United States National Museum, Washington, D.C.

98c, 101d, 103a, 103b, 103d, 105c, 138b. 189a, 204c, 235d, 295e, 295f.

University of California, Berkeley, Calif.

162a, 162d, 162e, 167c, 167d, 175b, 179b, 181b, 183a, 184a.

University of Colorado, Boulder, Colo.

104b, 106b, 106d, 169b, 169d, 170d.

University of New Mexico, Albuquerque, N.M.

259c.

University of Pennsylvania, The University Museum, Philadelphia, Pa.

72b, 73a, 74a, 77b, 83a, 86b, 94d, 95a, 96b, 98a, 100a, 100b, 104a, 118b, 118d, 120, 121b, 129c, 130a, 130b, 130c, 130d, 139b, 149d, 150b, 150c, 150d, 152a, 152b, 154b, 158a, 160a, 167b, 168, 169a, 170c, 174c, 181a, 184b, 201c, 203a, 205a, 210a, 211a, 212, 213b, 215b, 218d, 220a, 223a, 223b, 224d, 228e, 239c, 244c, 245f, 251a, 271b, 272d, 272e, 297a.

Wadsworth Atheneum, Hartford, Conn.

253b.

Walters Art Gallery, Baltimore, Md.

60a, 62b, 222b.

Wise, John, Ltd., New York, N.Y.

176a, 177b, 179c, 180b, 180c, 182a, 182c, 186a, 186b, 190a, 196b, 239a, 241e, 245a, 245c, 275b.

Worcester Art Museum, Worcester, Mass.

157a.

SUPPLEMENT, 1968

The following items are now in the Cleveland Museum of Art: 61b*, 163a, 176a†, 179c†, 186a†, 186b†, 195a, 207a* (scraper and disk at right and necklace), 224c, 235b*, 237d*, 239f*, 240b*, 241g*, 247b*, 247d, 256d*. The items marked with an asterisk were acquired from the Brummer Gallery and should be considered as deleted from the Brummer listing; those marked with a dagger were acquired from John Wise, Ltd.; number 163a was formerly in the collection of the Middle American Research Institute; number 224c was formerly in the collection of the Peabody Museum at Harvard.

The following items are now in the Dumbarton Oaks Collection: 135b, 137a*, 207a* (scraper and disk at left), 213c, 237a, 237c*, 239a†, 243c*, 247c*, 254b*, 282b*. The asterisks and dagger have the same meaning as above; number 237a was formerly in the collection of the Middle American Research Institute. Numbers 241a, 250b, and 250c have been transferred from Dumbarton Oaks to private collections.

Numbers 242d and 253a of the Brummer Gallery listing are now in private collections.

< xli >

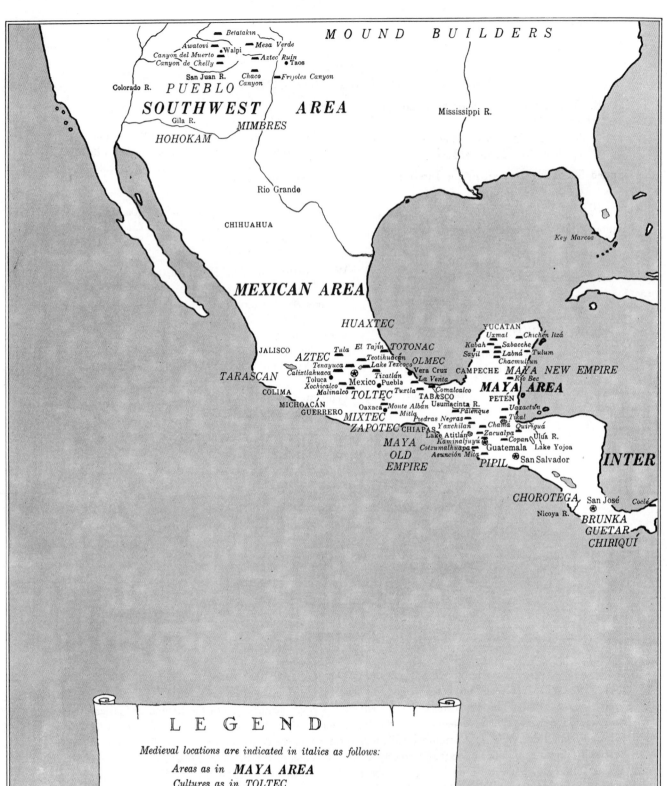
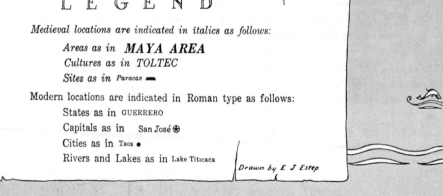

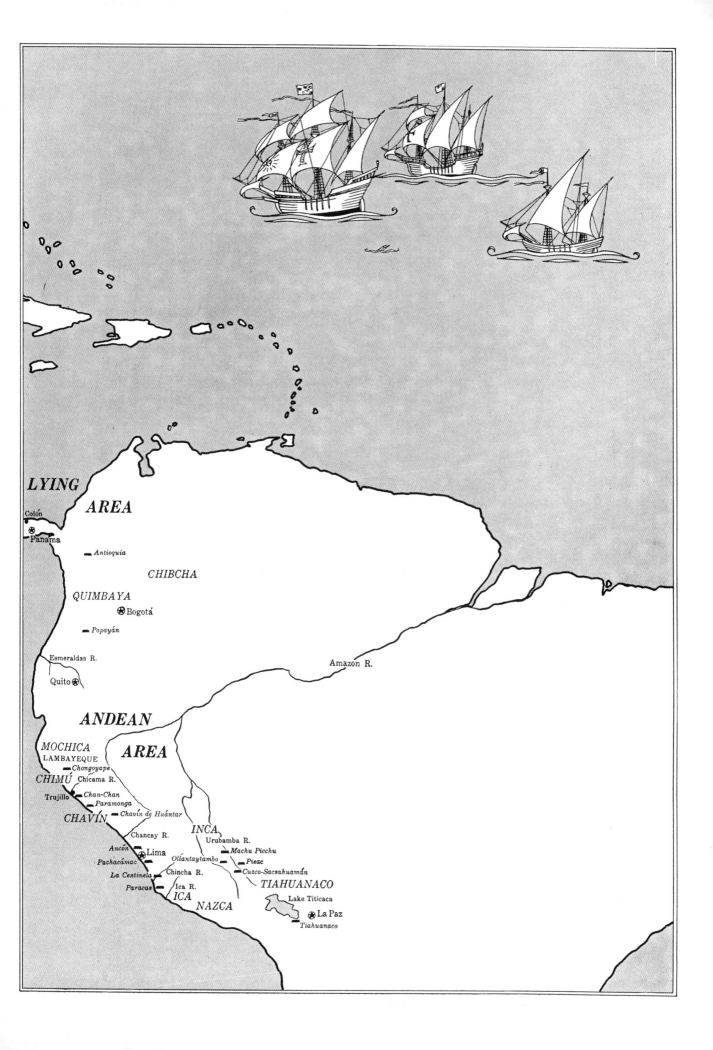

I

Art–History and Medieval American Art

ONE of the most significant events at the close of the Middle Ages of Europe was the discovery of America. The same event marks the end of medieval American civilization. The phrase is not a paradox. As in Europe the nations in the process of formation created great art during these centuries, so also in America certain regions blossomed forth with marked individuality of culture, beginning roughly with our Christian era. Rising from an obscure archaic background, these pre-Columbian peoples went through the phases of agricultural development and subsequent economic expansion, struggled with problems of increasing population, felt the rivalry of belligerent neighbors and the stimulus of trade. With the coming of the white man, the fabulous civilization developed in isolation by the red man came to ruthless destruction. The modern world that has grown out of the transplantation of European culture on ancient American soil is not our subject here, although it has furnished enough color, variety, and material to occupy ethnologists and interest travelers since the beginning of the colonial era. The purpose of this book is to evaluate the artistically important aspects of the aboriginal cultures that made up pre-Columbian civilization.

Europe at the end of the 15th century was carrying on an increasingly rich trade with the Near and Far East. Merchants and travelers had been adding to the knowledge of the globe ever since Marco Polo's fascinating accounts, and by this time a constantly growing group of enlightened men was becoming more and more convinced of the existence of other lands and of other routes to Asia. With the rise of Turkish power, when the caravan termini as well as the eastern Mediterranean harbors, both important in Oriental trade, fell to the troops of the Crescent Moon, geographers, astronomers, navigators, and adventurers speculated on the possibility of a new approach to the Far East. In 1474 a Florentine physician and astronomer, Paolo Toscanelli, wrote to a canon in Lisbon, conjecturing on the lands that might be found in a western crossing of the ocean and giving a map and his opinion on possible weather and water conditions.

There is evidence that this may have reached the hands of Christopher Columbus and strengthened the conviction that drove him for years from one court of Europe to another, seeking support for his expedition. When he at last sailed on his first voyage to the west, he carried with him a letter from the Spanish Court addressed to "the most serene Prince, our very dear friend" and intended for the Great Khan of Cathay, that is, China. On landing on an island, to which the name San Salvador was given, his courageous band believed themselves in the vicinity of the Asiatic mainland, and as long as he lived, Columbus never realized that he had reached a new continent and no mere outpost of India. Certain misnomers from those days still survive among us, by which, for instance, we call the islands of the Caribbean the "West Indies" and designate the American aborigines as "Indians," when the romantic term "redskin" would be more exact.

The Europe of Columbus was just crossing the threshold of the Renaissance with a new impetus toward learning and the arts. Kings and emperors vied with one another as ambitious collectors and patrons of science. Artists were accorded wide respect and recognition. As early as the 1420's, Masolino, teacher of the pioneer Masaccio, is known to have left the Italian field for a time to execute the frescoes in a new palace at Buda (Budapest) for the Hungarian king, Matthew Corvinus. Leonardo da Vinci spent his last years in France at the Court of Francis I, where he died in 1519, the year that Cortés landed in Mexico. Titian (1477–1576) was commissioned by Charles V of the Holy Roman Empire, sovereign of the *conquistadores,* and traveled as far as Augsburg for a sitting for a royal portrait.

Silks from China, rugs from Persia, ivory carvings from India were in demand for the European market. The exotic products of distant lands were prized, however, more for their rarity, their collector's value, than for the creative art which they embodied. It is only in the past century that we have learned to view an art not our own with an interest devoid of condescension. It is significant that those practical objects upon which craftsmen of all countries and all ages have lavished so much skill and imagination are grouped nowadays under the heading "applied art" rather than as "minor arts."

When the *conquistadores* arrived on American soil, they found a highly developed civilization and sent shipments of gold, textiles, feather-work, stone sculpture, and pottery back to the Spanish king in proof of the success and worthiness of their mission. The gifts that Cortés received from Montezuma for his sovereign were publicly exhibited for the admiration of the Spanish Court and people. The presence of extraordinary specimens of pre-Columbian metal-work in Europe can be traced, to a certain degree, in the literature of the period.[122] Aside from the metal, most of which was soon melted down, these gifts from the New World passed into the curio collections of the Medici and Borgia Popes, the House of Habsburg, and aristocrats in their favor, thence to disappear, piece by piece, as the years went on.

Best in a position to appreciate the skill and beauty of this work, which had come from a civilization so different from their own, were the craftsmen, members of the medieval guilds. One of them, Albrecht Dürer, descendant of a line of Hungarian goldsmiths, wrote in his diary in 1520 on the occasion of a visit to Brussels:

"Also I saw the things which were brought to the King from the New Golden Land: a sun entirely of gold, a whole fathom broad; likewise, a moon, entirely of silver, just as big; likewise, sundry curiosities from their weapons, armor and missiles; very odd clothing, bedding and all sorts of strange articles for human use, all of which is fairer to see than marvels.

"These things were all so precious that they were valued at a hundred thousand gulden worth. But I have never seen in all my days what so rejoiced my heart, as these things. For I saw among them amazing artistic objects, and I marveled over the subtle ingenuity of the men in these distant lands. Indeed I cannot say enough about the things which were there before me." [148]

Unfortunately, the soldiers who carried out the Conquest were neither princes of culture nor craftsmen of delicate skill. They were akin to those French cavalrymen who in 1525 stabled their horses in the refectory of a convent near Milan, causing the early ruin of Leonardo da Vinci's fragile masterpiece, *The Last Supper*. Vandalism was even more rampant in the fight among the heathen, and history tells that hand-illuminated Persian and Turkish manuscripts were dumped into the river to serve as a bridge for European wagon trains. How could the New World fare better? Some observations of an astronomical, botanical, and medicinal nature made by the American aborigines were on a par with those of contemporary Europe; but the *conquistadores*—cold-blooded adventurers, some of them criminals released from prison to fill the ranks for this hazardous undertaking—had not braved the dangers of an unknown sea to admire a different civilization. They were after booty. Spain, deep in debt, sought new economic fields, untapped sources of wealth; her religion, new converts.

"The New Golden Land" gratified all these needs in undreamed of abundance. The inhabitants, with their spear-throwers and bows and arrows, were singularly defenseless against the guns and armor of the Europeans. Besides this, they were torn with inner dissension and unwisely sought to use the invaders against their old enemies. It must not be forgotten that the Spanish soldiery of that age was welded into a superb fighting machine comparable to the Roman legions of classic times. Magnificently equipped for those days, they were elastic and independent, resourceful in battle and capable of living off the land for long periods. Some of Prescott's anthropological conclusions may be outmoded, but his descriptions of the historic panorama in his *Conquest of Mexico* and *Conquest of Peru* remain unsurpassed. The orgy of pillage and enslavement continued for centuries in this world of apparently inexhaustible wealth. Millions of dollars' worth of gold was looted from the people. Bizarre and exotic jewelry, ranging from simple bracelets to complicated breast and head ornaments, was melted at once into ingots, the better for shipment. Gold dug from the slave-worked mines of America financed the building of the Armada, as well as England's defenses against it, for the booty of English privateers preying on Spanish galleons helped pay for the Queen's navy. Hundreds of tons went to the bottom of the sea, and still the golden stream poured in upon Spain.

It is difficult even to imagine what has disappeared in architecture, sculpture, and the other arts from the pre-Columbian scene. As the buildings served the rites of pagan gods, their destruction was looked upon as an essential and righteous act. The hand-written and illustrated books of the Maya, Zapotecs, and Aztecs, recording the time-count of the people, the history of their tribes, their ritual, and their legends, were burned by the first priests as works of the devil. Only a few examples now remain. The loss of the books is especially deplorable since these might also have helped to reveal the psychological development of this race which climbed so high through circumstances so different from our own. The spiritual and mental build-up of this world that was systematically devastated and reduced will never be grasped in its true proportions. Only broken bits of the mosaic can be found, which science is now busy trying to piece together into a coherent picture.

Had the *conquistadores* come over some centuries earlier, unfortified by the self-conscious power of the awakening Renaissance, the impact might have been less violent and medieval America might have contributed more to Europe.

There are two chief reasons why medieval American art is so tardily being granted its deserved position in the history of human civilization. In the first place, it developed and flowered in isolation—isolated at least from those contacts with the Eastern Hemisphere which formed the background of the white man's culture and contributed toward the formulation of our esthetic principles. We confront, in the chapter "Evolution or Influence," the various arguments concerning the origins of the race and the possibilities of connection with Asia or the South Sea—whether remote, accidental, or recurrent. In the second place, it was destroyed almost upon discovery, and only the most tenuous of living threads remain to bridge the gap for us across the centuries.

The fabric of Old World archaeology and art-history is like a vast web, stretching from the Roman ramparts of England to the delicately drawn woodcuts of Japan, from the Byzantine icons of the Russian steppes to the wondrous world of the royal tombs of Egypt. It is an enormous territory, which produced amazingly varied manifestations of artistic taste over an enormous period of time—from the fourth millennium B.C. to our present day. Yet remote as certain points lie from one another, as different as are the styles which they produced, nevertheless it is clear that details and even whole ideas were incorporated, adapted, and developed interregionally. When Greek art came to full flourish, about 500 B.C., there were already three thousand years of cultural heritage from which to draw inspiration; highly artistic civilizations had existed in Mesopotamia, China, Egypt, and the eastern half of the Mediterranean with its islands. It might be said that in the cauldrons of all these previous cultures the Hellenistic ideal of beauty was first boiled down which reached forms and expressions that we accept and use today. The three continents, Asia, Africa, and finally Europe, contributed to the concepts, inspiration, and technical accomplishment of the arts of the Greeks, whose architecture and sculpture in turn still predominate in the style of our public buildings and whose precepts remain our general standard of beauty.

The art of awakening Christianity likewise drew upon previous periods. Egypt, through the Coptic, influenced the iconography of the new religion. The style of the Christian church grew out of the pagan basilica. Instead of medallions of the emperors, mosaics of the saints decorated the walls. The fresco was already in existence in the tombs of Egypt, the Hindu temples of India, the grave chambers of Etruria, the synagogue of Dura on the Euphrates. The technical formulae were already set, and the background of tradition was established. Only a new content was necessary to enliven the arts to serve the new faith.

Later Christian architecture underwent a similar development. Structural as well as ornamental elements of the Gothic had their proving-ground in the brick mosques of Persia.[144] What we know as the Renaissance was the revitalizing of the grandeur which had been Rome's a thousand years before.

We can trace back to prehistoric times the various contributions of different races and regions to our present culture, and we find that the art which surrounds us today was developed by cross-fertilization of ideas from other continents. Invisible threads of influence tie together and finally connect the remote corners of our geographical oblong.

The American continent was not in such a fortunate position. It is generally accepted that it was settled by waves of migratory hunters who crossed the Bering Sea from Asia while still in a very primitive state. Dr. Clark Wissler puts the final date of these migrations at the dawn of the Neolithic, or New Stone, Age.[169] But whatever the time, the great achievements of the early Bronze Age in Asia, the domestication of cattle, the cultivation of rice, the application of the wheel in transportation, and the use of the plow were all unknown here. The early Americans had to build up their civilization and art from their own spiritual resources. They had no wandering camel caravans that transported the products of an Orient into remote lands. There were no great galleys to carry obelisks and huge marble slabs incredible distances, to the wonder of an alien populace and the amazement of modern engineers. Nor were there Crusades to bring the glowing art of a tropical climate to a new growth in the north.

Even the three main periods of anthropology—Stone, Bronze, and Iron ages —find no application here. Although the pre-Columbian peoples did not advance technically much beyond the neolithic, yet they constructed architecture on a grand scale. Their tools were primitive, but their carvings are unsurpassed in India, Assyria, or Egypt. The ancient Americans never knew the smelting of iron, and what bronze they had was too soft for general practical use, yet their metal-work excited the admiration not only of Dürer but of jewelers' guilds throughout Renaissance Europe. Although fashioned on a simple hand loom, their textiles were highly complicated, and their pottery manufactured without the use of the potter's wheel can hold its own with the ceramic art of other continents. To appreciate the magnitude of this achievement, we have only to compare it with the accomplishments of the aborigines of other isolated territories, such as Australia.

Because each step of the way had to be invented of their own ingenuity, it is natural that the pre-Columbian peoples developed here a completely individual ideal of beauty, untouched by historical influences such as coöperated throughout the Eastern Hemisphere to form the white man's concept. The approach and attitude of the general observer toward medieval American art is bound to be affected by the ideals of beauty upon which he was reared; he is unable to make himself independent of the standards which he has been taught from youth and will feel the art of another civilization alien and remote. The realism which plays such an important rôle in our art was not a primary aim in medieval American art. It should be kept in mind always that the purpose here was the expression of an idea, often highly complex, in which the imitation of nature may frequently have been irrelevant.

Although there never was a complete break between Europe and Asia, only a few generations ago the arts of Asia, the Near East, and ancient Egypt suffered likewise from the differences in esthetic approach and evaluation. The exotic and bizarre were sought after, the rich and rare, but there was little attempt to grasp the spiritual content. Contact with the Orient has always existed, yet only recently were its styles digested and accepted by Europe.

This leads to the second reason for the tardy reception of medieval American art into the chapters of art-history. Not only is it built on concepts entirely different from our own, but, while the arts of Asia lived on and European eyes gradually acquired a comprehension of them, pre-Columbian civilization met a violent death with the Conquest. Those subtle ties were then destroyed that might have served to bind it to our times and interpret its language more directly to our European-trained minds. Between us and the last living manifestation of medieval American art there is a vacuum of four hundred years. Pre-Columbian America had no Plato to write a philosophy of its art, no Vasari to record the activities of his contemporaries. For a time after the Conquest, certain techniques were still practiced. The Peruvian skill in weaving was applied to imitations of Chinese and Persian fabrics, and a few mitres, stoles, and holy pictures in exquisite feather-work exist in European museums. Pagan symbols found their way into the sculptural ornament of early colonial buildings and appear in embroideries. But the vitality of such work weakened steadily.

This sunken civilization has never ceased, however, to intrigue the imagination of men, sometimes taking the form of pure romance and fantasy. The recently hypothesized Island of Mu now rivals Atlantis as a possible mother of pre-Columbian cultures. And as late as 1934 a pretentious book appeared which traced the Maya to a direct colonization from ancient Egypt. Thus, regardless of the mass of authenticated research now accumulated, misconceptions continue to be promulgated by writers who never saw an ancient American site and who would not think of tampering so arbitrarily with the arts of China or Egypt.

The unique contribution of pre-Columbian art lies in its presentation of the achievements of an isolated continent, in the fascinating mixture of primitiveness and maturity which could have been produced only under the circumstances that prevailed here. Only within the past century has a constructive attempt been made to add up the sum total of this legacy. Several branches of modern science are now coöperating in the task. Ethnology seeks clues to the ancient rites and customs through legends and practices of the living aborigines. The linguist, enlarging the map of languages, adds to the knowledge of the distribution and extension of various tribes and the areas of their influences. The geologist and paleontologist work on the correlation of existing and extinct animals with early man in America. The archaeologist, in surveying the extant material and excavating new sites, is occupied in unraveling the sequence of development in the various cultures and coördinating them in an ever-growing framework. As the most recent in the field, the art-historian endeavors to evaluate the production of these cultures in the light of esthetics, setting it among the arts of the rest of the world.

II

Historical Approach

A LARGE part of the American continents was inhabited when the Spaniards arrived on these shores. Although in north and east North America and in east and central South America the scale of living was still relatively primitive, certain areas—a broad band stretching from the Southwest to northern Chile—ranked high in the lasting character of their architecture and other arts. Without denying the ingenuity or specialized skill of the semi-nomadic peoples, it is clear that their mode of living did not foster development of artistic talent in the same degree as did sedentary life, which, with its settled routine, brought forth an intellectual level capable of producing a civilization of more enduring values. Where city-like settlements were constructed on a grand scale, a high cultural level was achieved.

Outspoken artistic cultures existed especially in five areas of medieval America. Four of them had architecture on a monumental scale. All of them used the true loom, which was known in less than one-fifth of the total territory of the Americas.[169] The first, the Southwest, comprises the region roughly covered by the states of Utah, Colorado, Arizona, and New Mexico. It was given this name by Charles F. Lummis, one of its first explorers, who published a series of books about the country in the late 19th century.[72] The second is the Mexican Area, stretching from the Rio Grande south through the states of Vera Cruz and Oaxaca. The third, or Maya Area, is comprised of the easternmost section of present Mexico, together with British Honduras, Guatemala, and parts of Honduras and El Salvador. We have given the name Interlying Area to those states that lie between the Maya and Andean areas. It includes the rest of Honduras and El Salvador, Costa Rica, Nicaragua, Panama, and Colombia. The Andean Area, the fifth, extends along the west coast of South America, including the lowlands and highlands of Peru and sections of Ecuador, Bolivia, Chile, and the Argentine. There are artistic manifestations outside these areas that warrant attention and will also be considered here, among them copper-work, shell and stone carvings of the Mound Builders, and pottery from Venezuela and Brazil.

Medieval American Art was chosen as title, because it designates the period within which all the objects and ruins presented here were created, paralleling the Middle Ages in Europe. Before the birth of Christ several preliminary phases of civilization must have existed in these areas, however, for some of the earliest pictorial representations that we find are already so highly conventionalized that the layman can recognize their significance only after explanation. It is supposed that many forms, which in later centuries appear in stone, metal, and other durable materials, were first fabricated of wood or leather.

The diverse cultures were generally contemporaneous, although each, in spite of apparently increasing intercourse, retained much of its own ancestral traditions. Our knowledge of commerce in medieval America is far from complete, but present-day research has shown that there was actual trade between various regions, although in some cases probably only sporadic. Adaptation from another culture seems to have occurred only after due consideration. In this, also, medieval Europe offers a parallel. Although her nations were much more closely connected, with wider and more varied fields of commerce, each, nevertheless, showed a distinctive artistic expression.

Geographically the five great areas of pre-Columbian America have a common feature in that at least parts of them were situated at extraordinarily high altitudes. The elevation of the Southwest ranges from 1500 to 8000 feet; the plateau of Mexico is about 7500 feet high. Although Yucatan, in the Maya Area, lies at sea level and some of the famous cities of the Great Period are also in the lowlands, evidence is accumulating to favor the claim that Maya culture first rose in the highlands of Guatemala, which reaches an altitude of 7700 feet. The Cordilleras in Colombia, equally high, had also their thriving settlements. In the Andean highlands there are architectural remains over 12,500 feet above sea level. As the American Indian is undoubtedly a relative of the early Mongolian, it is interesting to note, without enlarging upon theories, that the culture of Tibet flourished at a similarly high altitude, while nowhere in Europe or Africa does such a parallel occur.

The five areas under discussion have another common factor. All cultivated maize, a grain indigenous to America. A number of varieties are known to have been grown, acclimatized to the regional seasons,[87] with systems of artificial irrigation and dry-farming practiced where rainfall was deficient. There is evidence that certain tribes gave up nomadic life and became agriculturalists on the introduction of maize into the Southwest from Mexico.[95] This transformation can best be observed in this area, for in south and central Mexico agriculture had very early beginnings. The cultivation of beans and squash was also widespread, and the Andean Area added to these the potato.

It is natural that the areas which produced the highest cultures were the first to be exploited. The presence of gold, or lack of it, gave impulse, direction, and speed to the Conquest. Really important discoveries of the precious metal were made only in the realms of the Aztec and Inca empires, although valuable finds were taken from the Isthmus and farther south. Cortés established himself as ruler of the Mexican Empire in 1521. In 1535 Pizarro founded Lima as the new capital of his domain, controlling the Andean Area. As early as 1524, Alvarado set up his first headquarters in Guatemala; and in 1540 Montejo broke the resistance of the Maya in Yucatan. Though poor in gold, this area was important for strategic reasons. In 1540 Coronado started with his expedition into the Southwest, a region which yielded them no precious metals in spite of the abundant rumors to the contrary that had led them on. It is ironical that great mineral wealth actually existed there, though the natives were ignorant of it. The difficulties met by all these Spaniards, although not always similar, were everywhere of almost superhuman magnitude.

The four hundred years which have passed since the arrival of the first *conquistadores* have seen innumerable journeyings and expeditions of soldiers, adventurers, missionaries, travelers, and scientists, all of whom have added information to our knowledge.

THE SOUTHWEST

The land of the Southwest is a region of high plateaus, of huge sandstone formations—called *mesas,* or "tables," by the Spaniards—and deep eroded canyons. The earliest culture of which there is accumulated evidence is that of a nomadic people who gradually gathered into camps of circular or oval pit-houses, sunk about three feet into the ground and presumably covered with a shelter of branches and earth. These were the Basket Makers. They began to practice primitive agriculture and used the spear-thrower as their weapon, adopting the bow and arrow only in the last stage of their separate existence. Taking advantage sporadically of the rain-carved caverns of the great canyon walls for living quarters, they began to construct rectangular masonry buildings, also at a late period. Although they made little and crude pottery, they were masters in the weaving of baskets, hence the name given them today.[38]

By the beginning of the 9th century, there are evidences of the infiltration of a new race, who brought with them a more perfected agriculture and a more integrated system of masonry. They established group settlements of adobe and wood, domesticated the turkey, cultivated cotton, and developed a superior type of pottery. Their manner of living, rapidly adopted by neighboring tribes, is called the Pueblo culture from the Spanish word for "village."

Harried by predatory neighbors, they were later forced to scatter, abandoning much of the territory that they had occupied. Many sought shelter in the natural caves or on the mesas, where they erected community houses of stone and sun-dried brick. Others apparently drew together in the valleys, constructing easily defended communal dwellings on the banks of the major rivers.[61]

With the 10th century, a higher architectural form developed, and the cultural achievement of individual localities reached a new height. In addition to the skillfully placed and tastefully executed community houses that nestled in the natural caverns, the objects connected with their daily life demonstrate a ripening artistic talent. The pottery shapes became refined, the ornamentation varied, the weaving ingenious, and the jewelry composite. For three hundred years this development continued.

During the 13th century another migratory movement took place. Between 1276 and 1299 a protracted period of severe drought occurred throughout the region, and for more than twenty years the high mesas and narrow mountain valleys bore an insufficient harvest. Year after year more of the Cliff-dwellers, as they are called, were forced to leave their mountain fastnesses and join their relatives in the valleys of the larger rivers. At the end, the cliff-dwellings were probably deserted, nor were they discovered by white men until the second half of the 19th century. The Indians through the centuries had held the abode of their ancestors in awe and left them undisturbed.

In subsequent centuries, all the sedentary Southwest tribes continuously declined in numbers. The outlying sections were deserted, and a concentration of the population took place in the central regions. Finally, when Coronado and his resplendent band of seventy-five horsemen arrived from Mexico in 1540, they found only about eighty scattered villages, which were in northeastern Arizona and western New Mexico. It is interesting to note that four different languages were spoken, although the culture was relatively homogeneous.[61]

The conquerors entered the Southwest led on by legends of the seven fabulous cities of Cibola. The name seems to be the Spanish version of Shi-wi-nah, by which the Zuñi called their tribal range. The Spaniards visited most of the settlements still in existence at that time, but found no marvels, no wonders, no gold. The houses were constructed of chipped stone, sun-dried brick, and mud. The jewelry consisted of turquoise necklaces with pendants of shell or bone. This disappointing region was left to the zeal of the Franciscan, and later the Dominican and Jesuit, missionaries. Here the invaders did not encounter the armies of powerful allied tribes and war lords; each village fought its own battles and, taken singly, was doubtless easier to overcome.

The Spanish colonial history of the Southwest was as tumultuous as the medieval, but any detailed account of its manifestations is outside the scope of this book. Army posts were created along certain trade routes as these developed, but interest in the region, known as Nuevo Mexico, was not great, and it drew a minimum of white settlers. A political subdivision of Mexico after the break with Spain, this Indian world with its romantic landscape became United States territory in 1846. The Indians remained aloof and even today retain their ancient cultures to a remarkable degree. With the introduction of the horse and sheep, nomadic tribes, among them the Navaho, who now surpass the Pueblos in number, acquired a new cultural impulse.

We owe the establishment of the chronology of the ruins in the Southwest to a recent discovery in another branch of science. Dr. A. E. Douglass, astronomer of the University of Arizona, in studying the effect of sun-spots on the growth of trees, found that tree-ring formations in certain types of wood of the region are never repeated in similar sequence.[32] Thus, the series of rings, varying in width with the growth of the tree during wet and dry years, form a pattern which, although perhaps slightly divergent due to the position of the individual tree, is nevertheless recognizable as a sequence in all the trees of this type which have passed through the same season. If the date of the felling of one tree is known, the calendar of its lifetime can be computed through the cross-section of its rings, beginning with the final outer one. And as this pattern is constant, the calendar can be extended by comparison with the rings of other trees which began or ended at some time within the life-span of the first. Owing to the high dry atmosphere of the region, many of the prehistoric cities contain well-preserved wood which can be incorporated into the study. Sections of the roof beams of the numerous chapels and churches of the 17th century contribute an unbroken series of dates. Even charcoal from ancient fires has been found of use.[47] Thus, through painstaking correlation the tree-ring calendar of the Southwest has already been carried back well into the first century.

MEXICAN AREA

The second area offers one of the most complex pictures of pre-Columbian America. Lying between the lands on the north and the entrance to the Isthmus, it was the repository of various migrations and the scene of cultural metamorphoses. All the multitudes who moved about here during prehistoric millennia and whose circumstances are unknown to us left some imprint on the people and their art during the rotation of cultures. This archaic background is still much of a mystery and doubtless embraces several successive cultural phases that vary with the different regions considered.[151]

One of the earliest and highest cultures, as documented by its ruins, centered around the great temples of Teotihuacán not far from present-day Mexico City. The early site is said to have been occupied about A.D. 700 by the Toltecs, the first comers recognizable in a series of migratory shifts. These "skilled workers," as the Nahua name implies, are generally believed to be members of the Nahua language group. Some authorities, however, think that they may have been indigenous and Otomi-speaking. But whatever their source, the remains of their culture are extremely impressive. Evidences of flourishing trade with the Maya and Zapotecs of that day exist and of the exchange of certain cultural achievements. Sherds of pottery typical of one Toltec phase were excavated as far north as Pueblo Bonito in New Mexico.[61]

About the 12th century, the Valley of Mexico was again overrun by a more virile wave from the north, the Chichimecas, or "fur-wearers." [146] The Toltecs were subdued or driven out of the wide area which they had dominated, and their influence appears on the Late Maya horizon in Yucatan. The newcomers rapidly adapted themselves to the ways of the city-dwelling population, taking over many customs, often with a veneer of their own traditions.

The next arrivals of importance were the Aztecs, also members of the Nahua language group. It is interesting to note that all of these Nahua tribes belong to the Shoshonean linguistic stock which still extends as far north as Oregon and Montana. The early Basket Makers of the Southwest are believed to have been of the same racial entity, and the more cultured peoples with whom they later mingled are thought to have drifted northward from Mexico.[61]

Relatively few in number and primitive in culture, the Aztecs wandered about making contacts with their racial predecessors who were already living a sedentary life. As they were not at first strong enough to acquire any of the fertile agricultural districts, they settled on a marshy island of Lake Texcoco, founding what later became the famous city of Tenochtitlán. The accepted date for this event is 1325, and 1376 is identified as the year that the first Aztec king appeared. Less than one hundred fifty years later, Tenochtitlán became the Christian capital that we know as Mexico City.

Thanks to a tactically protected position, the tribe increased in number, advanced in civilization, and soon felt the urge toward expansion. They allied themselves first with neighboring populations, later with more distant peoples. Throughout the 15th century, they made constant gains in power and possessions, succeeding in subjugating many tribes, or at least in registering them as nominal allies. In the north they counted as tributaries the Otomis; in the east the Totonacs and Huaxtecs; in the south the Zapotecs and Mixtecs, and in the west the Tarascans. These peoples were generally more advanced in culture than the masters, yet were forced to yield to the better fighters. Their arts and crafts, however, retained their distinctive features.

The Aztecs exacted the characteristic products of each district as tribute and acquired a material culture of amazing variety. The market place of Tenochtitlán was, according to an eyewitness, Bernal Díaz, twice as large as that of contemporary Seville. It was surrounded with an immense portico where were sold products of all sorts: brightly colored skeins of cotton thread; pottery of all shapes and sizes, most of which was burnished and painted; ornaments of gold, silver, or semiprecious stones; fruits and vegetables, food, cooked and uncooked. Each kind of merchandise was assigned its own street or its own section. There was an herb street with apothecary shops, barber shops, and restaurants; a street for the sale of game of every known variety; places for furniture and tools; a court for the regulation of measures.

The Aztecs on the Mexican high plateau utilized in architecture the experience of their predecessors. Even though their temples were not the most magnificent in detail work, their imposing effect cannot be denied. Many of their art products were turned out in great numbers and, therefore, in quality could not show true finesse.

Special mention should be made here of the Zapotecs. A proud and self-reliant people, they developed their own system of writing and their own distinctive traditions. Although some of their towns are recorded as paying the Aztecs a tribute or indemnity of blankets, foodstuffs, and cochineal for fine red dye in the last pre-Columbian decades,[129] the extent of Aztec control is unclear and apparently did not affect their freedom in cultural matters. In general, they were able to maintain their independence until shortly before the Conquest, when the Mixtecs, a neighboring and antagonistic tribe, became dominant. Mixtec glyphs are akin to the Aztec, but the Zapotec system, much of which is still indecipherable, is believed by its expert, Alfonso Caso, to be related to the ancient Maya who dwelt south of them.[20] The geographical remoteness of the Zapotec realm may partly explain the amazing difference between their art and that of the Mexican high plateau. All but the most general history of this interesting region is still in shadow.

In 1502 Montezuma II, the ninth Aztec king, became head of a mighty confederacy, stretching from the Atlantic to the Pacific and far to the north and south. It was his fate to live at the time of the landing of the Spaniards, and to die a prisoner in their hands. Many historians and archaeologists have related the story of the conquest of Mexico, and Cortés's advance, so rapid and successful, has been ascribed to several factors. It was a weakness of Aztec rule that it had made no effort to assimilate subjugated tribes and had treated them too ruthlessly. Cortés succeeded in playing these tribes against their masters. The peculiar method of Aztec warfare, which served their religion, also worked to their disadvantage, for it aimed at killing few of the enemy and capturing as many as possible for human sacrifice. Furthermore, they were no match for such superior equipment as the gun, the steel sword, and the horse. After the terrible massacre of natives following the final attack on Tenochtitlán, their empire practically ceased to exist. The greedy search after gold gave the Spaniards unflagging impetus toward the complete subjugation of the Indian.

The tale of colonial Mexico with its quarrels among the Spaniards, battles with the Indians, pseudo-conversion of the natives, intrigues carried to Europe and back covers the viceregal period from 1521 to 1808. Then began the struggle for independence, coinciding with Napoleon's march into Spain. The government shifted back and forth between Spanish-Mexican emperors and republican presidents until 1864, when Maximilian of Habsburg, brother of Franz Joseph of Austria, was crowned Emperor of Mexico through French intervention. Three years later the magic cycle of Habsburg domination in the New World begun by Charles V ended with the execution of Maximilian at Querétaro.

MAYA AREA

The location of the cradle of the Maya is still a matter of conjecture. Their culture is among the oldest and, with its distinguishing characteristics, spans the American Middle Ages. While the other regions experienced considerable change in their population and subsequent alterations in their arts, Maya objects from the earliest sites bear the marks of their Maya origin. Even those from the last period before the Conquest in Yucatan show clearly defined artistic features that identify them as late branches of the great old tree.

In the first centuries after Christ, Maya art was already condensed and mature. From its architecture to its jade carvings, it speaks a language highly articulate, rich and often flamboyant, and compares favorably not only with products from the other four areas but with the high arts of other continents as well.

The Maya had an amazingly accurate calendar, a triumph of mathematical genius, and had developed a system for recording time by hieroglyphics that was so perfected at the beginning of the Christian era that its origin must be sought in a much earlier period. They even had a sign for zero—a device which appeared in Europe only with the adoption of the Arabian numerical system and not before the 10th century.

The numerical and calendrical symbols of the Maya have, to a great extent, been deciphered, although the correlation of their dates to those of our calendar is still a matter of discussion. In this survey, the Goodman-Thompson-Martínez system will be used, which places the dates about 260 years later than that advocated by Herbert J. Spinden. The calendrical glyphs, however, should not be confused with the ideographical which constitute about two-thirds of the body of Maya writing and are as yet unsolved.[92]

The earliest dated object known is a jade plaque unearthed in Guatemala, whose glyphs would correspond to A.D. 320. The Maya had the custom of erecting inscribed monolithic stone monuments, or stelae, at the end of various time cycles. The oldest yet found is at Uaxactún in the state of Petén, Guatemala, and bears a date equivalent to A.D. 328. This does not necessarily mean that Uaxactún is the earliest Maya city—other sites in the same region appear as old —for other methods of recording dates were doubtless used before stelae. Maya architecture frequently employed wood for beams and lintels, elaborately carved, and the possibility that earlier dates were recorded on wood should be held in mind. There are also indications of records painted on stucco. Such media would naturally disintegrate much more rapidly than stone slabs.

Although the glyphs are often of great service in dating the ruins, it must also be taken into consideration that some monuments may have been commemorative in character and marked with a year already past. A case in point is Stela 16 at Tikal, which, though bearing the earliest date in the city, is in style among the latest and most mature. Furthermore, it often happened that a date on a monument was effaced and another added.[112]

The principal Early Maya cities are scattered over several present-day Middle American states; Copán in Honduras, Tikal and Piedras Negras in Guatemala, and Palenque in Chiapas, Mexico, have remnants of highest artistic importance. The early dates of all these fall between 436 and 534, our era. Within the next two centuries more settlements appeared, the best known of which is Quiriguá, Guatemala.

Then followed a period of unprecedented prosperity in this region, generally known as the "Old Empire." City after city arose, and the population must have been numerous. In agreement with J. Eric S. Thompson, we must regard these "cities" as religious centers, occupied chiefly by priests and ruling officials.[150] The common people were agriculturists and lived scattered over the surrounding country, coming to the centers for religious festivals, the administration of justice, and for trade at the market. Ordinary houses were of wood, thatch, and adobe, which crumbled under the assault of the jungle as soon as they were deserted, but the innumerable artificial mounds which were crowned with temples and palaces are impressive even today. Although in ruins and overgrown with trees, they testify to the remarkable talent and tremendous effort of a people who had at their disposal only primitive stone implements and no beasts of burden.

The end of the 9th century marks the close of the creative period in the region. The center of Maya activity then shifted north to the Yucatan Peninsula. Here deciphered dates that go back to the 6th century would indicate that this territory previously had formed part of the Old Empire, but only as a provincial district. The cause of this shift of culture can only be surmised. There may have been pressure from aggressive outside tribes. Economic breakdown and threatened or actual famine resulting from wasteful primitive agricultural methods may have contributed to the decline. Revolts against the existing hierarchy have been suggested in explanation, as well as the ravages of plague.

Dr. Ira B. Bartle, bacteriologist, recently tested material from a number of Maya sites of this period, taking samples from the seemingly undisturbed heart of various ruins. Bacterial cultures of these specimens have revealed a spirillum of an extraordinarily virulent nature, with symptoms similar to cholera. These findings present a new angle for study. However, there is much more work to be done in this line before conclusions can be drawn.[5]

Whatever the cause, the fact remains that after six hundred years of intense activity, culture flickered out in the Old Empire and came to new flowering else-where. This does not necessarily mean that all the ancient centers were abandoned. There may have been a transplantation of culture such as occurred in the Eastern Hemisphere, where artistic achievements of one area traveled and bore new fruit in another without a mass movement among the populace or any wholesale catastrophe. With the acceptance and spread of the Gospel, the early Christian Syrian and Armenian communities did not migrate nor were they driven forth by any cosmic or economic upheaval; yet their powerful artistic influence is traceable in the iconography of western Europe. The cultural wave moved onward and left the region of its origin stagnant and in decline. A further parallel can be observed in the decay of Greece and the rise of Rome with its strong derivative culture, although no single event or general movement of population produced the shift of artistic vitality.

As early as the beginning of the 8th century, when the Old Empire was at the height of its power, a Maya people occupied the site of Chichén Itzá in Yucatan, erecting there a number of imposing edifices. Then, for some reason, cultural activity waned. After almost a hundred years, in the latter part of the 10th century, the Itzá appear, and with their occupation a number of Toltec traits were introduced.

About this same time, Mayapán and Uxmal, two other powerful independent city-states, seem to have risen, revived by other migrant tribes, and the three are said to have formed the League of Mayapán. This marks the start of the so-called "New Empire." The Aztecs at this time had not even reached the marshy borders of Lake Texcoco.

Like most of Europe's medieval alliances, the League was not successful for any length of time. About two hundred years later, aided by Nahua mercenaries from the Mexican plateau, the city of Mayapán campaigned against her rivals. In 1204 Chichen Itzá fell, though it remained until the Conquest a much-frequented pilgrimage center. The tribe of Itzá wandered south to the shores of Lake Petén. Diminished in number but unbroken in spirit, they established themselves on an island in the lake, as the Aztecs did when they arrived in the high plateau of Mexico, taking advantage of the protection offered by the surrounding water. Here they held out against all comers until 1697, preserving their independence not only against hostile Indians but even against the Spanish invaders for a century and a half after all the other tribes had been vanquished.[150]

In the meantime, in Yucatan, renewed struggles against the domination of Mayapán finally brought about its downfall in 1451. The cities continued fighting each other, however, soliciting the help of foreign migrating tribesmen. Natural catastrophes hastened the destruction brought about by wars. A great hurricane is reported to have swept the country, destroying whole towns and the surrounding forests. Famine and plague depopulated the once dense settlements, and the Spaniards on their arrival found a weakened life, quite different from the glory of earlier epochs.

Under Spanish rule the area was divided into governmental districts, all parts of the vast dominion of New Spain. As its control of the region was still far from complete in the 17th century, the Spanish administration concentrated on making secure its land and water communications. The Indians were enslaved and had no voice in the administration of their land. They were converted by force, and all vestiges of a former religion ruthlessly destroyed. The Inquisition was alert to prevent backsliding. Over the ancient religious centers the jungle spread. In the 18th century, when the Spanish plantations prospered, many ruined Maya sites were stumbled upon, and toward the end of the century, the Spanish crown ordered reports on the most famous spots.

With the movement for independence, the area was divided. Chiapas, Tabasco, and the Yucatan sector became border states of Mexico. Guatemala and Honduras formed independent republics. A small strip of the eastern coast, for centuries an outpost famous for its logwood and mahogany and once the stronghold of the English pirate, Wallace (whose name survives in the native version "Belize"), became an English crown colony under the name of British Honduras.

The remoteness of most of this area has delayed scientific investigation. Until the closing years of the last century, only a few undaunted travelers had brought back reliable descriptions. In the interior of Yucatan, Honduras, and Guatemala, the Spanish administration did not change completely the way of life. The vitality and traditions of the once great people persist to a certain degree. Pottery and textile techniques are similar to the old, and some pattern and color arrangements survive. In the vicinity of Nebaj in the Guatemala highlands, a calendar is still in use with the 260-day count, with many date names that have come down from medieval Maya practice. Ethnologists are seeking the key to ancient riddles among the customs of inaccessible highland villages, hoping that the relatively few internal upheavals may have left more of the past. Perhaps the remoteness of the regions where the old Maya civilization experienced its first flowering has helped to conserve its traditions, for here, where it was less tinged with Nahua culture, it also happened to escape the most ruthless pursuit of the Spaniards.

INTERLYING AREA

In the Interlying Area, between the Maya and the Andean, were several cultures with rich remains in pottery, stone, and, in most of them, metal-work. The crafts show a mixture of original traits with influence from both north and south, forming a bridge for investigators in other areas. No ruins of great architectural beauty have been found, but mounds and certain carved stone fragments hint that here, too, the people had substantial buildings. Besides the systematic destruction of the conquerors, the tropical climate is responsible for this lack of evidence, and the same circumstance can be blamed for the complete disappearance of woven materials that must have existed. The metal-work of this area, even if not of highest artistic standing, shows fine craftsmanship and in many cases amazing stylistic and technical combinations. The excellence of the pottery is not surprising, as all pre-Columbian cultures were highly advanced in the potter's art. In this survey specimens are included from the work of the Chorotegan culture in Honduras and farther south, the Guetar of Costa Rica, the Chiriquí and Coclé peoples of Panama, and the Quimbaya and Chibcha of Colombia.

The Isthmus around Panama was strongly policed by the Spaniards from the first. It was here that Balboa first sighted the Pacific in 1513. The Spaniards took great pains to explore these regions, believing that a sea passage between North and South America must exist. Stimulated by the dazzling material success in Mexico, they established a naval base in the Gulf of San Miguel on the Pacific in southern Panama, and from here, between 1525 and 1529, Pizarro and his reconnoitering flotillas set sail. Prescott's *Conquest of Peru* brings out the tremendous fighting courage and the infinite endurance of these doughty warriors. After the hazardous voyage across the Atlantic—which had been navigated for only a few years—the adventurers had still to cross the mountains of the Isthmus and, there in the wilderness, hastily construct crude ships for their advance into uncharted waters and undiscovered lands. It is hard to say which accomplishment is the more noteworthy, that of Cortés who opened the door to the New World or that of Pizarro who had greater distances and greater difficulties to overcome.

For the passage of Inca treasures across the Isthmus, terminal cities were founded, Nombre de Dios and Colón on the Atlantic and Panama on the Pacific. Here through the 16th and 17th centuries plodded mule trains laden with gold and silver. Tempted by the loot of this famous and perilous trail, Sir Francis

Drake and his successors, a whole coterie of privateers, pirates, and desperadoes, dared to land to attack and plunder the transports.

ANDEAN AREA

Among the five areas presented in this survey, archaeology is most fortunate in the Andean. The panorama of life and the arts here is the easiest to reconstruct because so much has been preserved by the arid climate.

About the middle of the great range of the Andes there is a high plateau averaging 12,000 feet in elevation, from one to two hundred miles wide, and more than two thousand miles long. West of this, bordering on the Pacific, lies a narrow sandy coastal zone, less than a hundred miles in width, with tropical vegetation appearing toward the mountains. One section is isolated from another by stretches of desert—a terrain theoretically unfavorable for the diffusion of civilization.

Nevertheless, a number of high aboriginal cultures existed here, firmly established at the beginning of the Middle Ages, for the most part in what is now Peru. Migrations, probably from the north, had brought a primitive agriculture to the coast, superseding an earlier existence of hunting and fishing. Several individual cultures arose in the region based on elaborate systems of irrigation: on the North Coast, the Mochica and later the Chimú; in the southern coastal sector, the Nazca, named after the river valley where it flourished. Between them lay the cultures of the Central Coast—Ancón, Chancay, Rímac, and Pachacámac. At the same time other regional cultures prevailed in the mountains, the most noteworthy of these being the Tiahuanaco, which prospered in Bolivia along the shores of Lake Titicaca, and to the north, in Peru, the Chavín.

Between the 5th and 6th centuries after Christ, the Tiahuanaco culture was spread, apparently by conquest, throughout the high plateau, absorbing the earlier cultures. It continued in power for about three hundred years, exerting a noticeable influence even in the coastal regions. At its decline, the highlands seem to have been under the changing sway of petty chiefs until the rise of the Incas. A certain shifting and unstable character is apparent in the art of this period. In the meantime, about the middle of the 12th century, a revival in the Nazca and Chimú cultures set in.

It is generally accepted that the Incas were not outsiders as were the Aztecs in the Valley of Mexico; they descended from one of the highland tribes that probably inhabited the valleys along the tributaries of the Urubamba River, having their principal seat near Cuzco, over 11,000 feet above sea level. Here at the beginning of the 12th century their chieftain established hegemony over a small group of tribes, laying the foundation of the later empire. His successors consolidated their position and advanced southward until a large region, including Lake Titicaca, was under their control. By the end of the 14th century the Inca Empire contained 155,000 square miles, or as much territory as Italy, Switzerland, and Bavaria taken together.[84] At the close of the 15th century, the tenth Inca governed not only what is today Peru, but also Ecuador, parts of Chile and Bolivia, and even a fraction of the Argentine, holding the various regional cultures together under a highly organized and ingenious administration.

The pre-Inca division of most of these separate peoples into groups with communal possessions was the basis of the feudalistic system of Inca administration. These groups formed the units in a bureaucratic network whose highest official was the ruling Inca, a benevolent but absolute monarch. With increasing power, the rulers became highly dynastic, and intermarriage of blood relatives was frequent among them. The chiefs of annexed territories were generally allowed to retain their aristocratic position, and their children received careful education at the Inca capital. Here, while practically hostages, they were taught the power and value of the existing system and proved, on the average, useful converts.

Owing to the vast extent of the Empire, a second capital was established at Quito, in northern Ecuador, for administrative purposes, and it was here that the last happy Inca ruler, Huayna Cápac, died in 1525. His two sons, Huáscar and Atahualpa, were engaged in a fratricidal war while the Spaniards were exploring along the coast of the Pacific.

The march of Pizarro into the capital of Cuzco in 1533 marked the beginning of the end of Inca grandeur. The following centuries were not without violence. As in other areas, the Indians were not subdued immediately and staged many revolts. As late as 1781, when the Revolutionary War in the United States was working toward its climax, there was a widespread rebellion. The leader of the insurrection, in the presence of his family, had his tongue cut out and was torn to pieces by horses; subsequently his body was burned and his head and limbs were exposed on poles.

When Napoleon put his own brother, Joseph Bonaparte, on the throne of Spain, the New World colonies began the movement which resulted in their independence. Not only were the colonials no longer bound to the mother country by loyalty to the dynasty, but they were embittered by the action of the new administration which set its seal of approval on the highly unsatisfactory colonial government. The American-born Spaniards, that is, the Creoles, and still more the *mestizos* of Spanish and Indian blood, were thoroughly disgusted and angered with their administrators, for the highest officials in Peru were still sent over from the mother country, appointed by the Council of the Indies from its seat in the lavish Renaissance palace at Seville, more than five thousand miles away from the life and problems of the colonies.

As early as 1810, the Venezuelan, Simón Bolívar, headed a revolutionary movement which forced out the viceregal administration and formed the first locally chosen government in Spanish America. Another uprising was led by the Argentine, José de San Martín, who did more than any other man for the liberation of his country as well as of Chile and Peru. In 1824 victory was won, breaking forever Spanish domination in the New World.

The standard of living for the aborigines, enslaved during the colonial regime, long remained in many respects below that of the pre-Conquest period. Lately the various governments have shown a growing understanding of the Indian and pride in his medieval past. Archaeological excavations and the preservation of collections in museums are promoted. Splendidly baroque buildings of colonial times and remnants from the pagan Indian centuries together color the background of modern Latin America.

III

Architecture

WHEN primitive man came out of his cave and constructed for him-self a shelter, architecture—the most enduring art of mankind—had its beginning. In man's building, his powers of creation, talent for monumental expression, and quest after variety are displayed at their best.

Pre-Columbian civilization traveled a long road from its first obscure stages to the impressive structures to be discussed here. Lofty buildings characterize the architecture of most of the areas which show outstanding artistic achieve-ment in other fields. Side by side, however, with the magnificent palace and sumptuous temple stood the primitive hut, just as in the European Middle Ages the shadow of imposing castles fell upon mud hovels.

The rise of civilization in the various regions under discussion was roughly parallel in time, so that contrasts are evident not only within one area but also in the comparison of that area with others. For instance, some architecture of a high standard, like the Maya, employed only doors in its massive façades, while the less splendid culture of the Pueblos availed itself occasionally of the window as well. The Pueblo Indian used a ladder to reach the upper stories of his house, while the oldest structures of the Maya, Mexicans, and Peruvians, in some cases as early as the 3rd century, show grandiose stairways.

THE SOUTHWEST

FRIJOLES CANYON

At a remote period in their existence, the people of the Southwest made use of hollows in the cliffs for temporary shelter and storage. Later, more complex buildings were pasted fast to the vertical rocks on the sloping talus at the foot of the cliff. *Pl. 1, fig. a* shows both the cave chambers and the remains of the talus-houses in Frijoles Canyon, New Mexico. The bored holes for securing the beam ends can be seen in the rock, indicating the height of the structures.[46] In the fore-ground lie the ruins of a semicircular community house of later date.

Seeking security from predatory tribes, the Cliff-dwellers fitted their compact group dwellings into natural alcoves far above their fields (*fig. b*). In many cases the caverns could be reached only by means of perilous hand and foot holds cut into the precipitous canyon walls. For building material they quarried a buff sandstone in pieces rather thinner but wider than an ordinary brick and considerably harder than the cliffs themselves.

The first simple system of chambers developed into a honeycomb conglomerate of community dwellings in a style that occurs nowhere else. As the population multiplied, second, third, and even fourth stories were superimposed in receding terraces upon the roofs of the old. The dark inner rooms, reached by hatchways, were used for food storage, and the high crevices, difficult of access, were built out into granaries. Round buildings—a technical problem for architects of all the ages—were erected with the same facility as square ones. Towers jutting up from the stone terraces or placed at strategic points on the table-land made excellent lookouts. The culture of the Cliff-dwellers reached its height between the 12th and 13th centuries.

MESA VERDE

The best known and perhaps the most beautiful examples of Cliff-dweller technique are found at Mesa Verde in Colorado. The Green Mesa, verdant with juniper and piñon trees, rises to a height of 8575 feet above the sea. On one side there is a sheer drop of a thousand feet and a view on a clear day for one hundred fifty miles; on the other, narrow gorges spread like the fingers of an open hand, dotted with shallow eroded caves, nearly all of which bear evidence of human habitation. Occasionally a site is fortunate enough to have a spring near by.

Cliff Palace (*Pl. 2, fig. a*), built into a cavern 425 feet long, 80 feet in depth, and 70 to 80 feet at its greatest height, is the largest of the cliff-dwellings in this group. The floor of the cave is uneven and the level of the ground structure varies to conform with it. There are square as well as round towers, and the doors and windows are placed asymmetrically, seemingly at individual convenience. The T-door occurs frequently. For the roofs or upper floors, as the case might be, staunch timbers were set, with smaller branches laid at right angles across them; brush and twigs filled the chinks, and a final cover of packed clay was added. Slots can be seen in the standing walls into which the beams were laid.

Cliff Palace contains one hundred seventeen rooms, ninety-four of which have fireplaces and the marks of fire. Out-of-door hearths are also common.[38] This great apartment house, which its tree rings place in the 12th century, shows evidence not only of additions in an improved technique but also of rebuilding. New partitions were erected, walls changed, new levels established; the first-story ceilings were braced for the additional weight of rooms to be added above. The different hatchings that appear on the plan (*fig. b*) show the various heights of the buildings. On some interiors are traces of designs, similar to those used on the pottery of the period, painted in red and brown on a white ground of smooth gypsum.[46]

Besides the square rooms where the inhabitants slept and stored their food, the circular subterranean chambers, called "kivas," so striking in the photograph, were an integral part of every cliff-dwelling. Indeed, the kiva still plays an essential rôle in the life of the modern Indians of the Southwest as the meeting place and ritual chamber of the various clans and societies in the involved tribal life. It has been suggested that they are associated in tradition with the sunken pit-houses of the earliest tribal ancestors.[61] They are usually circular and are sunk into the courtyard or open plaza, varying in size from 10 to 30 feet or more in diameter. Entrance is generally through hatchways in the timber roofs. Within there is usually a fire pit near the center of the floor, with a low wall or slab of masonry near it, serving as an air deflector, and a flue of some size extending up one wall. This vent is supposed to provide the means of access to the spirit people of the other world, whose coöperation is necessary to the successful conduct of life.

Square Tower Ruin (*fig. c*), also at Mesa Verde, creates a most artistic atmosphere, with its buildings on the narrow ledge leaned against the canyon wall.

BETATAKIN

Another site with spectacular Pueblo ruins of the Cliff-dweller type is situated in the northeast corner of Arizona surrounded today by the Navaho Indian Reservation. Its more famous groups are Betatakin, Keet-Seel, and Inscription House, the whole complex now named Navaho National Monument.

Fig. d shows the ruins of Betatakin, Navaho for "hillside house." They stand in the depths of a colossal cave, 400 feet high, 300 long, and 150 deep, carved by stream meander and wind erosion out of the side of a red sandstone cliff that forms the sheer north wall of the picturesque canyon. Tree-ring dates reveal that the cluster of almost one hundred fifty rooms within was built and occupied in the second half of the 13th century. While in most ruins the kivas are similar to those at Mesa Verde, there is no evidence here of sunken chambers and they must have been constructed at ground level. Other interesting architectural characteristics of the site are wattle and daub walls, small doorways closed with inset stone slabs, and loom-ties found in some of the chambers. Rectangular rooms are typical, as are the poles which form the roofs and extend beyond the walls. This latter feature has survived and can be seen today in the living Pueblo villages (see *Pl. 6*).[73]

CANYON DE CHELLY

Highly romantic are the ruins at Canyon de Chelly (*Pl. 3*), a name distorted from the Navaho *Tse-yee,* meaning "within the rocks." They lie in northeastern Arizona in a canyon full of quicksand, the light-colored stone of the White House standing in brilliant contrast to the red wall of the overtowering cliff.

The great drought of 1276–1299 hastened the abandonment of the cliff-dwellings, and when the Spaniards came, they found the Indians living in communal structures of stone and adobe, or sun-dried brick, built in the open around one or more ceremonial chambers. To such a settlement the conquerors gave the name *pueblo,* meaning "village." This type of architecture still prevails in the Southwest.

Castañeda, chronicler of Coronado's expedition, wrote of one such pueblo: "It is square, situated on a rock with a large court in the middle containing kivas. The houses are all alike, four stories high. One can go over the top of the whole village without . . . a street to hinder. There are terraces going all around it at the first stories. . . . These are like outside balconies and they are able to protect themselves under these. The houses do not have doors below, but they use ladders which can be lifted up like a drawbridge and so go up to the terraces which are on the inside of the village. As the doors of the houses open on the terraces of that story, the terrace serves as a street. The village is inclosed by a low wall of stone."[4]

PUEBLO BONITO

Pueblo Bonito, "beautiful village" (*Pl. 4, fig. a*), is one of twelve ruined community houses in the narrow valley of Chaco Canyon, New Mexico, and an excellent example of Pueblo architecture. The structure resembles a capital D;

some of the other settlements, apparently all striving for major security, are quadrangular or E-shaped.

Pueblo Bonito is 667 feet in length and 315 at its greatest width. It contained more than six hundred chambers and could have sheltered twelve hundred inhabitants within its walls (*fig. b*). The illustration shows clearly its amphitheater form, with its tiers of rooms, originally four or five stories high, built around a court that held about twenty kivas. Across the straight front was a double row of single-story rooms that opened on the inclosure. There was only one narrow entrance, behind which a barrier of masonry was placed in such a way that only one person at a time could enter the village.

The high wall in the rear, unbroken on the outside by any opening and still rising to more than 40 feet in places, testifies to the fortress-like character of the building. The tallest section shown in the picture was recently crushed by a fall of rock from the canyon wall, a catastrophe that must have been impending for centuries, for the ancient inhabitants had buttressed the cliff.

The masonry varies in character from the medium-sized hewn stones that compose the first story to the small flat ones in the upper walls, dressed to form a smooth outer surface.[38] Timber is used to strengthen the walls, and some of the floors have been found in place. Due to the extremely dry atmosphere, the wood remains dry and hard and so does not constitute a major weakness as in the tropical regions of Central America. The tree-ring calendar dates this structure as existing between A.D. 919 and 1130.

CHETRO KETL AND AZTEC RUIN

Some of the kivas in Pueblo settlements were very large, reaching 60 feet in diameter at Chetro Ketl, Chaco (*Pl. 5, fig. a*), and 50 at Aztec Ruin, New Mexico (*fig. b*). In both cases, the entrance was from the side, not through the roof, and there were two large fire pits and a raised masonry bench or dais around the wall, visible in the illustrations. The same type of roof was probably used at Chetro Ketl as is shown reconstructed in Aztec Ruin, the set-back in the upper section of the wall providing space for the roof beams, which were apparently supported by wooden or masonry pillars. The inner walls contain a number of recesses, in which ceremonial caches of shell, onyx, and turquoise beads were found. The name Aztec Ruin is unfortunate, since this settlement had nothing to do with the Aztec people.

Although the Spanish chronicler writes that the Pueblos boasted of never having been conquered, the danger of attack by nomadic tribes from the north and east must have been constant. Their careful accumulation of agricultural products was certainly a great attraction to those roving hunters in times of scarcity. For causes unknown a period of decline and depopulation occurred in the 14th century, doubtless connected with failing food and water supply, as well as depredations from outside.[47] Many of the large Pueblo ruins of the Southwest were already forsaken at the time of the Conquest.

There are, however, living settlements today which date back into medieval times. The Hopi town of Walpi (*Pl. 6, fig. a*) in Arizona is one of these, with its square one-family houses of chipped stone perched on a jutting rock high above the plain. The villages of Acoma and Zuñi are as ancient and represent somewhat the same type, while Taos (*fig. b*) is more like Pueblo Bonito, with two large tiered community houses of adobe standing in a broad valley.

The villages everywhere used the material most conveniently at hand for their building. Casa Grande in Arizona is constructed entirely of a mixture of adobe and gravel, which has dried to incredible hardness. Gila and Salt River settlements, having no quarries near, used water-ground boulders with a mud binder.[38]

Southwest architecture, with its living quarters arranged around the nucleus of the circular kivas, suggests the crystalline structure of a mineral. The tiered or set-back stories of the great houses, like huge massed terraces, varying in size and height, are very striking, and have at least optically something in common with the terraced substructures of the Mexican and Maya areas. The method of constructing flat roofs was probably similar in all our areas.

Pueblo architecture is the only pre-Columbian style which still survives. Pueblo customs and the crafts of pottery making and weaving also remain remarkably virile. This is perhaps because the art here, for the most part, served a more secular purpose and not a hieratic pagan religion as in the other areas. All the manifestations of ancient architecture elsewhere were extinguished during Spanish colonial occupation, so that all that is left for study there is in a state of ruin.

MEXICAN AREA

TEOTIHUACÁN

In the Mexican Area the imposing remnants of Toltec temple structures stand only twenty-eight miles from the Mexican capital in the middle of a central valley. Generally called the Pyramids of Teotihuacán, they retain in their modern name the Nahua word meaning "where the gods reside." The site (*Pl. 7, fig. a*) covers a great area, but our main objectives lie along a straight avenue bordered by ruins, all accurately oriented. A great temple-base, a truncated pyramid, the highest in the entire Mexican region, rises at the right of one side. It was the custom of the pre-Columbian peoples from very early times to elevate their temples or altars on an artificial mound, a practice taken by some as an indication that the rites were first performed on hilltops.

It is unfortunate that the word "pyramid" persists in connection with this type of temple-base, because of the term's inevitable association with the pyramids of Egypt. The huge monuments on the lower Nile were built of great stone blocks to house the burial pomp of kings—gigantic tombstones, memorials to the dead. The pyramidal structures of pre-Columbian America were made sometimes of adobe or of smaller pieces of stone on a core of rubble and stood at the living center of religious activity. They served as an extraordinary and dramatic base for the temple proper, the holy of holies, which was erected on the top. It must be remembered that these ruins have changed much since the time they were in use. The temples themselves have disappeared, the masonry about them has collapsed, the facing crumbled. After such vicissitudes, with their original lines destroyed or blurred, it was only on superficial resemblance that these substructures were called pyramids.

Apparently, it was the inclination of science in the 16th to 18th centuries to explain away all the phenomena of pre-Columbian civilization with Old World parallels. It was impossible for that age to conceive of the cultures of the American continent except as transplantations from the world already known. Much that was written and sketched of these ruins in the early days was distorted by the mirage of this theory, and we still carry over, even into our scientific literature, ambiguous terms which give impetus to fantastic theories and sensational statements.

The Pyramid of the Sun (*fig. b*) is then the immense base for a temple of which nothing now remains. Built of selected or roughly dressed basaltic lava on an adobe hearting,[49] it rises 216 feet and covers about $10\frac{1}{4}$ acres of ground with its base, 720 by 760 feet. At the summit is the rectangular platform upon which stood the temple, the nerve center of the ritual. The conservation work, undertaken several decades ago, is now considered to have forced the contours of the temple-base somewhat along preconceived lines. However, nothing can detract from its imposing proportions.

The structure as it stands is divided into five sections. On the west, the one great stairway, varying in outline as it ascends each division, mounts to the summit. At its foot is a tiered dais. This, together with the esplanades around the temple-base built at different levels, furnished the setting for the elaborate pageantry of the Toltec religious rites, for the great mass of the people could see very little of what was taking place in the temple itself. Prescott (1843) describes the building as "splendidly barbaric," and quotes the chronicler Boturini (1746) as stating that within, facing the east, stood "a colossal statue of its presiding deity, the Sun, made of one entire block of stone. . . . Its breast was protected by a plate of burnished gold and silver, on which the first rays of the rising luminary rested." Whether the description from this late date is accurate or not, there is no doubt that such an immense monument, eclipsing in size everything else in the Mexican Area, must once have been of utmost importance.

The Toltecs were the first people of the region to leave legendary accounts behind them and the first Nahua-speaking residents of the district. Their culture in the high Valley of Mexico is believed to date from about A.D. 700, and the ruins now visible are placed in the 9th century. However, from pottery finds and other remnants discovered on the site, it can be surmised that the spot had already been a pilgrim center for earlier inhabitants.

It was the custom of most pre-Columbian tribes of Mexico and Central America to rebuild and enlarge their temples periodically. In the former area this generally occurred at the end of a cycle of 52 years, a time which marked the coincidence of the sacred almanac of 260 days with the solar calendar of 365 days that ran concurrently.[151] Examination of the huge Pyramid of the Sun has shown that this structure also was superimposed upon other buildings, and the remnants of several series of stairways have been uncovered, buried under the fill of later additions.[76]

Left of the Pyramid of the Sun, on the same plate, can be seen the Pyramid of the Moon, which shows a similar division into four sections. Approximately half the size of the other, it stands some 140 feet high with a base that measures 426 by 511 feet. To date, it has been left unrestored.

About a mile south of these buildings along the same imposing avenue, rises the Temple of Quetzalcóatl (*Pl. 8*). Quetzalcóatl was the Mexican Wind-god, the Great Feathered Serpent. His symbol, the conch shell, runs through Mexican mythology and is also conventionalized into a fret with its many variations. In this pre-Columbian ruin we can best visualize the splendor and brilliance of a sunken culture, for nowhere else in the Mexican Area is such a large and well preserved section of substructure to be seen. Its good condition is due to the custom just mentioned of burying one temple under a new and larger one. The excavated façade (*fig. a*), measuring about 110 feet in width and 55 in height, was found at the heart of another edifice. A large portion of one side was intact, and its reconstruction was carried out by enlightened, modern, archaeological methods.

This base, faced with smooth stone blocks, has six receding terraces, with unusually deep offsets, uniform in height and ornamented in identical fashion. On the face of each is a long vertical panel, framed top and bottom with projecting cornices and featuring fierce sculptured heads of the Feathered Serpent (*fig. b*). His fangs are whitened, his eyes glittering with an inlay of obsidian. He wears a radiating leafy collar, and the body is indicated by the rattles and feathers in relief at either side, all the more admirably executed when we consider how often and how painstakingly the repetition is carried out. The other creature, somewhat less intelligible to us, is generally interpreted as a conventionalized mask of the Rain-god, Tlaloc.[151] Various shells are scattered throughout the rhythmically recurrent pattern. Below the panel, on the oblique base of the terrace, is a relief of stone showing the undulating body of the plumed snake and a series of shells.

Remnants of color were clearly visible on our first visit to the site a short time after its excavation but have faded considerably now from exposure. Especially noteworthy were the brilliant green of the serpent body and Tlaloc mask, the clear red rings in the headdress of the latter, and the enameled pink and white of the shells. The ramp of the wide steep stairway, ornamented with similar serpent heads, was stuccoed and also painted.

This magnificent façade and the ruin which has covered it stand in the center of a quadrangular inclosure, called the Citadel, the outer walls of which have been restored and show a continuous rampart. (See *Pl. 302, fig. a.*) The structure may have had military importance, but this aspect must be given secondary consideration in view of its obvious ceremonial character. Stairways give access to the top from both inside and outside. A number of small terraced platforms, each with its flight of steps, are placed symmetrically at intervals, clearly visible in *fig. a* of the preceding plate, especially the inset. They are similar in outline to the terraces of the Temple of Quetzalcóatl but have no ornamentation. Remnants of stucco in the empty panels and along the balustrades indicate that the complex was embellished with fresco decorations.

Because of the variety in Teotihuacán and the long period over which it flourished, this city holds a special place in the history of the Mexican Area. Its contribution to the arts other than architecture is also great, and the site must have been among the most grandiose of the Mexican high plateau. After the arrival of more aggressive tribes and the southward shift of Toltec influence in the 11th century, the center may have declined. Moreover, the Aztec Tenochtitlán soon rose to overshadow all other sites. At any rate, neither Cortés nor Bernal Díaz makes any mention of it, although they must have passed close to the place. Perhaps it was by that time completely abandoned and the astonishing "pyramids" looked to the *conquistadores* like natural mounds.

XOCHICALCO

The temple at Xochicalco (*Pl. 9, fig. a*), near Cuernavaca, in the state of Morelos, also belongs to the period of Toltec dominance of the Mexican high plateau. It is said to have been built about the middle of the 10th or in the early 11th century by a Nahua-speaking people.[99] The structure stands on a fortified height nearly two miles in circumference overlooking deep valleys. The entire hill is artificially graded and laid out in five terraces with ramparts. There are a number of other ruins, now only heaps of rectangular stones. A sugar factory in the vicinity drew on the site for its construction material. Such vandalism was frequently perpetrated on pre-Columbian buildings. The first generation after the Conquest, led by the priests, destroyed everything of the ancient world upon which they could lay their hands, and much has been lost because of the jealous bigotry which ran wild in those times.

The Nahua name *Xochicalco* means "in the place of flowers." We know that the pre-Columbian peoples held flowers in great esteem, assigning a special god to them. The ancient cult still survives in picturesque Xochimilco, "place where the flowers are," near the Mexican capital. An extraordinary tenderness and felicity characterize the Indian's handling of them, whether it be the gesture of a little boy making an offering of calla lilies in a church, or an old woman sprinkling her wild carnations as she proffers them for sale by the roadside. Their presence among the wares even of the most remote native markets shows that they are not gathered merely to attract the tourist's eye.

The temple structure illustrated is the only one at Xochicalco that has been reconstructed to a certain degree. The ruin shows the great feeling of the builders for linear variety and is outstanding, not only for its magnificently decorated substructure but for the evidences of a masonry temple on top—the only one besides Teopanzolco known in the Mexican Area today.[146]

The substructure, measuring 60 by 69 feet, is a single unit, unbroken by terraces, and the slanting base, which was kept as narrow as possible below the rectangular panels of Teotihuacán's Citadel, here constitutes a major element. It is nearly 9 feet high with a batter of about 15 degrees. This slant lends the impression that the building is implanted deep in the soil, giving the structure, incomplete as it is, more weight and stability than would a perpendicular line.

The foundation is crowned by a vertical frieze about 3½ feet high, overhanging it somewhat, which in turn is topped by a sharply protruding cornice, clearly visible in the photograph. Here we have a fine feature not occurring in earlier architecture. The play with architectural line, the counterbalancing of receding and jutting angles, and the contrasting of various constructional elements for the sake of variety are signs of development not only in technique but in creative imagination. The deliberate divergence from the perpendicular appears in European architecture also, but quite late; provincial rococo made considerable use of it in mid-18th century.

The low relief of stone which covers the slanting base is dominated by eight elaborate plumed serpents, ingeniously conceived and skillfully executed. A fluent unbroken line marks the upper outline of the snake bodies, forming an unobtrusive but consistent coupling of the main decorative motif. The smaller broken elements, representing the luxurious plumage, give weight and vibration to the figure. The rattles end in quetzal plumes, and the head of the snake shows fangs and a forked tongue which invite comparison with the three-dimensional serpent head on the Temple of Quetzalcóatl on the preceding plate. Contrast also the vigorous movement and rippling feathers of the undulating bodies here with the more even and static rendition in the older work.

In the spaces created by the curves of the serpents, human figures and glyphs are applied alternately in the same relief technique (*fig. b*). The glyphs remind us of those classed as Zapotec. In this case, they have been identified as referring to the ceremony of "kindling the new fire," held at the beginning of each 52-year cycle.[99] The eight plumed serpents are also associated with this occasion.

The human figures deserve special attention, since, used as they are here as sculptural ornament, they are unique in the Valley of Mexico. The nearest parallel will be found at Tajín, but stylistically they are still more suggestive of the Maya. The chief or god is seen from the front, with the head turned in profile, in a pose that will become familiar later in stone and jade carvings. In

Egyptian art this always seems a neck-breaking attitude, but here it is made to appear elastic and natural. The figure is poised and sinuous. The headdress, representing the upper jaw of a monster decorated with long feathers, is well posed despite its obvious weight. There are ornaments on the ankles, the wrists, around the neck, and in the ears. Though carved with primitive tools and composed into the space allowed by the curving serpent body, the figure is neither crowded nor distorted. Certain contours are emphasized with an extra incised line well within the edge, which slenderizes the mass and even gives a suggestion of three dimensions. The most expressive detail from a purely artistic point of view is his raised left hand, placed in front of the body and showing only four fingers. Beauty, grace, and dignity are in the gesture. Not merely an element in the tangled decoration of the temple-base, the figure is commanding. On the narrow frieze above the great snake, there was once also a relief of seated priestly figures with flowers and glyphs.

A stairway of fourteen steps leads up the west side. Its balustrade was decorated with a carved pattern suggesting serpent scales or rattles, but only a fragmentary reconstruction of this was possible. Of the temple proper, a low section of the wall remains, which, however, helps us little in picturing its original form. It also was carved with reliefs of both seated and standing figures interspersed with glyphs.

The entire edifice is faced with trachyte, a light-colored volcanic stone, in large uniform slabs laid without mortar. The carving was apparently done before the stones were set and was touched up afterwards.[99] Like most of the architecture of the Mexican and Maya areas, the structure was brightly painted; the chief colors remaining are red and green.

Artificial caverns honeycomb the limestone hill and some of the connecting underground chambers contain stuccoed painted walls. The style of decoration at Xochicalco, as well as the practice of subterranean building, would bring this site nearer the Zapotec-Mixtec region in idea than anything else on the high plateau of Mexico.

MALINALCO

In the southwest corner of the state of Mexico, separated by a mountain range from the town of Tenancingo, stand the ruins of Malinalco, looking down from a mountain ledge on the sleepy village from which the site takes its name, "the place of the dry grass." The approach lies along the rocky bed of a mountain stream and over the steep shoulder of one of the wild and barren hills which characterize the landscape, an even more spectacular location than that of Xochicalco.

Malinalco is of outstanding importance as one of the very few pre-Columbian sites discovered so far where buildings were hewn from living rock. The most notable temple (*Pl. 10, fig. a*) meets the visitor's eye at once, as it stands on a small plaza facing a deep gorge to the south. The main stairway of fourteen steep steps, the same number as at Xochicalco, and the wide balustrade are carved out of the ledge itself, an integral part of the hillside. The rock has weathered to a golden brown. Traces of paint are still visible and the ramps also show remnants of decoration on plaster.

The walls are cut to resemble the façade of a substructure with two terraces. On either side of the stairway, a large feline animal keeps guard, of one piece with the building and the low platform upon which it is seated. The upper parts of the bodies have been destroyed, probably on the occasion of later alteration, when this edifice was covered by another of the usual Aztec stone-and-mortar construction. The center of the lowest stair juts out to form a sort of podium, perhaps to accommodate some stone or pottery object, above which stood a large carving, now only a fragment, which must have represented a seated figure.

The single doorway leading into the temple proper is carved to form a round arch (*fig. b*). Hewn out of solid rock, it does not constitute a keystone arch. In this case there was no problem of construction for the support of a mass of masonry; the roof was light and perishable, probably wooden beams with a covering of grass or thatch. The top part of the arch is broken, perhaps by an earthquake or by the later transformations. Two immense serpent profiles ornament the entrance, deeply incised and so placed that together they present the front view of a single snake, the arched door representing its yawning mouth and the forked tongue forming a very low dais that extends nearly to the first step of the landing. On a protruding serpent head at the right of the door stands a squat defaced figure, interpreted as an eagle-clan warrior, while on the opposite side a similar one surmounts a war drum.

Upon passing through the distended jaws of the great serpent, one enters a circular chamber about 16 feet in diameter and over 11 feet high (*fig. c*).[63] A broad low bench of living rock, some 4 feet wide, extends around the inner wall of the inclosure. In the center lies a large sculptured eagle altar, the wings half-spread and the head raised off the floor, its fierce curving beak facing the entrance. The smooth line of the bench is broken by three animal figures, cut somewhat flatter than the altar. Two of these represent eagles; between them, and directly opposite the door, is the figure of a jaguar or ocelot, flattened out like a rug, with furry head and bulky paws carved in the round and the tail extending up the wall. The sculpturing shows competence, avoiding the conventionalization of elements difficult to represent. All the eyes are cut in such a manner as to suggest inlay. Small cists occur at intervals in the wall, perhaps for the personal and ritualistic objects of those who participated in the ceremonies.

On one side, the temple structure blends into the natural rock, where there are marks of a waterfall. On the right, a series of three stairways mounts beyond it to the upper levels of the hillside. Here is furrowed an elaborate system of gutters, cut in the solid stone. A deep channel also follows the outline of the circular wall from above. These may have been designed to protect the buildings from the gushing tropical rains, but the rush of life-giving water from the mountain ledge into the fertile valley may well have been used for symbolical effect.

Two other buildings on the site make use of the living rock. One is a large rectangular chamber, with three walls as well as the floor carved out of the hillside. The other, constructed of stone and mortar in an unusual semicircular form, has a rectangular antechamber, with fire pits and pillar foundations cut from the solid floor. This building boasts a fluelike vent on one side reminiscent of the air shafts of Southwestern kivas.

Near here is a wall, once buried by later construction, with a fresco of warriors. A large pyramidal base of more common type holds a predominant position on the edge of the cliff, and beside it, overlooking the gorge, is the outline of a circular masonry structure, the shape and position of which seem to indicate some sort of observatory.

Other monolithic structures are found at the site of Texcotzingo nearer the Mexican capital, where there are basins, or baths, carved in the rock of the hill, as well as an elaborate system of channels.

The pottery remains at Malinalco have been identified as Matlatzincan and Aztec, and the site is believed to date from the 14th or 15th century.[63] It would seem a pre-Aztec creation which was taken over and rebuilt—an assumption that would account for the mutilation of the carvings and the different types of construction to be found there.

There are on this site certain resemblances in idea that lead us far afield. The eagle and jaguar motifs seen in the monolithic temple occur on carved panels in Chichén Itzá devouring human hearts. (See *Pl. 63.*) The entrance into the temple through the yawning jaws of a serpent is found more than once in the ancient Maya city of Copán. And the position of the ruins, perched daringly on a rocky ledge, recalls somewhat the balcony houses of the Cliff-dwellers of the Southwest. The four carved animals in the interior do not have the complex and conventionalized expression of Aztec monumental carving, but display a greater realism, though stylized, a lighter and more simplified manner, much more closely related to the modeling and carving of the Indians north of the Mexican border. The snake to the right of the outer doorway is reminiscent of the reptiles from Tenayuca, to be discussed on the next page, and of Chichén Itzá, except that it has flint blades bristling from its body instead of undulating plumage.

There is a large round structure at the Ocmulgee National Monument near Macon, Georgia, called the Ceremonial Earth Lodge. It is 42 feet in diameter with benches and seats around the inner wall. Opposite the main entrance stands a raised effigy platform in the shape of an eagle made of stone and mortar and represented with outspread wings. It is by no means stated that identical tribes produced both of these works, but a relation or influence of idea can be felt. Many pre-Columbian peoples claim in their legends to have "come from the north." Linguistic kin of the Nahua, as we have seen, extend even today as far as Oregon and Montana, and we meet repeatedly with the tradition of eagle-warrior clans in pre-Columbian cultures of both Middle and North America. The similarity of the Earth Lodge in Georgia and the carved rock temple at Malinalco is another evidence of the distance that influence, perhaps even peoples, may have traveled in medieval America.

CALIXTLAHUACA

The infrequent round shape occurs at Malinalco in what might be called "negative" and "positive" forms—the circular chamber carved from the ledge, and the round building constructed opposite it on the small plaza. The latter realization is met also at Calixtlahuaca (*fig. d*), a Matlatzincan site in the valley of Toluca.[76] Among the numerous ruins, two deserve special mention here: the remnants of a barracks-like settlement at the base of the hill, thought to have been a "seminary" for priests or living quarters for young warriors, and the round Temple of Quetzalcóatl shown in the illustration. The different angles of the sloping wall sections visible in the photograph are the result of the second and third rebuilding of the temple-base. The latest enlargement seems to have been made during the 15th century. Each terrace was edged with pro-jecting stone serpent heads placed at intervals. A few of these still stare out of the wall, giving an idea of the original impressive effect.[57] Here too, as in Malinalco, pottery of Matlatzincan and Aztec types was found. With its conquest by the Aztecs, however, the site seems to have been abandoned, and the Aztec town was laid on the plain.

TENAYUCA

One more ruin should be presented before we leave that high plateau, the Valley of Mexico. Six miles north of Mexico, D.F., are the remnants of an Aztec temple at San Bartolo Tenayuca. Cortés and Díaz both mention this town. It lay directly in the path of the Conquest and had strategic importance in the siege of Tenochtitlán, for the pipeline of clay culverts which furnished part of the drinking water for the Aztec capital was situated on the northern shore of Lake Texcoco, not far from Tenayuca. Fighting occurred around the place in 1520, and the Spaniards destroyed the water-supply system. Díaz speaks of it as Puebla de las Sierpes, "the town of the serpents"; and Torquemada, the Franciscan historian of the early colonial empire, complains that the destruction of this and other pagan temples after the Conquest was so superficial that they could all too easily be reconditioned.

Nevertheless, this edifice seems to have fallen into disrepair and oblivion.[146] Before 1925, when the ruins were excavated and partly reconstructed, it had been the popular belief that the mound was of natural origin, overgrown as it was with vegetation upon which the village cattle and poultry fed.

The temple-base (*Pl. 11, fig. a*) is 58 feet high and measures 162 wide and 201 long, exclusive of the great double stairway which, extending beyond the base, adds another 45 feet to the general length. It is faced with cut stone laid with mortar and then covered with plaster. Brilliantly painted designs studded with projecting serpent heads of carved stone break the rigid character of the broad surfaces. The two temples on the summit were probably of more perishable material, with wooden roofs, plastered and painted. Atop the solid proportions of the base, they must have looked like gaudy lids.

The twin stairway (*fig. b*), nearly 150 feet long, belongs to an earlier structure unearthed in excavation and rises behind the mass of masonry at the left in the picture. It has the usual very steep grade. Wide ramps at the side of the stairs and a double one in the center, which divides the imposing flight, are crowned with large masonry blocks, visible at the top center of the general view. They show clever masonry work, with keystones set between the large flat slabs and at right angles to them, firmly integrating them with the body of the structure. All the corners or edges are bonded in the same manner. It is assumed that the edifice was dedicated conjointly to the gods of war and rain. This would indicate two buildings, one beside the other, on the vast platform (117 by 140 feet). Here the hieratic conception triumphed, probably to the detriment of architectural beauty.

The most characteristic feature of the temple-base at Tenayuca is the long row of serpent bodies stretched along a low platform at the foot of this structure, as if guarding its three unbroken sides. There are one hundred fifty-six coiled snakes, their carved heads, some gigantic, projecting beyond the edge of the terrace on which they lie. Here we are confronted with evidence of mass production, for only the heads of the reptiles are carved of solid stone. The bodies are composed of smaller stones and mortar and appear rather shapeless now, although a definite outline was doubtless achieved by their original covering of painted stucco. Traces of blue, red, black, ochre, and white are still visible on some of the figures. The hues were applied according to orientation: blue predominates in those on the south and southeast, and black on the north and northeast. The bright flowing colors, applied very liquid on fresh plaster, must have once made the coiled serpents seem shimmering and alive.

Two great "fire serpents" crowned with symbolic headdresses lie apart from the others on the north and south sides of the temple, some 10 feet from the base (*fig. c*). These are connected with altars and oriented toward the sunsets of May 16 and July 26, special days in the ceremonies of the cult.[146] The characteristic rendering of the head is noteworthy, with the tongue hanging sideward as at Malinalco and Xochicalco.

The archaeological importance of Tenayuca is greatly augmented by the fact that investigations have revealed buildings of seven different epochs within the largest and last temple-base, together with intermediary changes and additions. All of these were edifices with double stairways and two temples. The first building measures 104 feet by 58 by 26 feet high and carries back to the earliest migration of the Nahua-speaking Chichimecan people into the Valley of Mexico at the end of the 12th century in our era. Thus the time-span involved is around three hundred years.

The digging at Tenayuca revealed pottery, jade beads, obsidian, stone and copper objects, indicative of at least three different stages of civilization super-imposed on each other. As it is so near the capital and, in its last phase, of such a late date, we can be sure that many of the buildings wrecked by the Spaniards were similar in type.

Other important excavations near the capital were made at Copilco and Cuicuilco at the foot of an extinct volcano, Pedregal, where at some undetermi-nable prehistoric time settlements were buried by lava flow. Until recently this site was believed to be extremely ancient, but the artifacts found here can be connected with other known sites. Possibly it was in existence when the first base of the Sun Temple at Teotihuacán was laid down.[151] The *metates,* or maize grinders, discovered are almost indistinguishable from those in use today.[76]

TAJÍN

The Totonac people, who flourished between the 11th and 13th centuries, inhabited the semitropical regions between the coastal lands and the high plateau in what is now the state of Vera Cruz. Although characteristic figurines and other small objects fashioned by them are found widely scattered throughout the district, eloquent evidence of high civilization is concentrated in only a few places.[136] Six miles from the town of Papantla, northeast of the Valley of Mexico, lies the Totonac temple, El Tajín, "the thunderbolt" (*Pl. 12, fig. c*).

The temple-base is one of four artificial mounds grouped around a plaza; other ruins are spread over quite a distance. This striking substructure (*fig. a*) is 82 feet square, has an approximate height of 70 feet, and rises in seven receding terraces, the last of which served as the sanctuary floor. The clean-cut, accu-rately fitted stone slabs of the edifice show even in decay the excellent quality of workmanship, a strong contrast to the rougher masonry in the Mexican Valley.[151] In its profile, the building is actually akin to the Temple of Quetzalcóatl at Teotihuacán, as each section has a low battered base supporting a rectangular panel. At Tajín, however, each terrace is completed with a cornice, projecting obliquely, and instead of the extravagant richness of sculptured decoration, seven tiers of niches—apparently ninety on a side which would make three hun-dred sixty in all—are arranged with amazing rhythm and symmetry.

This number, corresponding as it does to the days in a regular calendar year, reflects knowledge of an accurate day count and its application in the religious and social life of the people. Each panel of niches is accentuated by its position between the slanting base and angled cornice, suggesting that the recesses might have been used as day-shrines. They do not lead into the edifice but serve only as stone frames, perhaps for idols, incense burners, or offerings. At the corners of the building they are open at the sides, giving greater lightness to the whole structure. There are indications that they were plastered inside and painted.

A broad stairway (*fig. b*) leads to the top on the east side, inclined toward the building like a ladder so that its base extends well beyond the substructure. This method of construction is common among the Maya also. The wide balustrade, typical of all later Mexican and Maya buildings, is present, and may have had at least two recesses built in at the foot. The center lane of the stairs is broken by several niche stations, standing in groups of three, with vertical walls and heavy oblique cornices. Although they are not so large or so complex as the others, the detail is thus kept in uniform style with the rest of the construction.

Ceremonial daises or built-in altars at the bottom of the stairway occur in the Early Maya sites. Even today at Chichicastenango, Guatemala, where the Maya-Quiché Indians still practice many of their medieval customs, we find an analogy. At the foot of the semicircular stairway leading to the door of the church, there is an open construction, like a fireplace, with two shelves and a stone slab laid on top. Here the Indians commence their ritual, lighting and swinging their *incensarios* filled with copal, which are not permitted within the building. Whoever has witnessed the tense and agitated ceremony there, with the façade of the church shrouded in clouds of copal smoke, can imagine the impressiveness of a pre-Columbian ceremony.

Scattered about the ruins of the ancient plaza were found a number of carved stones, two of which are shown in the chapter on sculpture. (See *Pl. 63, fig. a* and *Pl. 83, fig. c.*) Here, however, attention should be called to the manner in which the smooth stone surfaces are alternated with stucco, the flat sections stressing by contrast the application of stone relief where it occurs.

The ruins around Tajin are not the only typical Totonac settlements. There is another Totonac site with characteristics similar to Tajín's at Yohualichan, thirty-six miles south of Papantla, as well as later buildings in other places in the state of Vera Cruz.[136] It is interesting that part of this region now lies outside the Totonac language belt and that Nahua is spoken there.

Although the work of the Totonac builders was doubtless influenced by the greater neighboring cultures, they achieved nevertheless their own individual architectural expression. The region where this type of architecture is found formed perhaps a pocket in which the style was best preserved. The Totonac structures demonstrate best that the pre-Columbian temple-bases, aside from the accident of geometric form, have nothing in common with the pyramids of Egypt.

MONTE ALBÁN

One of the most extensive ruins in the Mexican Area is a hilltop settlement in the southern part of Mexico (*Pl. 13, fig. a*), seven miles to the southwest of the thriving state capital, Oaxaca, "place covered with trees." Called by the Spaniards Monte Albán, or "white mountain," it rises 6331 feet above sea level. It is here that the discovery of a unique grave-treasure of gold, turquoise, pearl, jade, and bone was made, which awakened general interest in pre-Columbian civilization more than any other single revelation within the last century. These findings will be discussed in their respective chapters, but the site deserves consideration on its own merits.

This dead city of the Zapotec, and later the Mixtec, peoples has the most beautiful topographical situation of all the ruins in the Mexican Area. Situated on a promontory of immense size, it overlooks the convergence of three valleys, with the peaks of the Sierra Madre del Sur forming a dramatic backdrop for the scene. Hilltop sites are not uncommon in the Oaxaca region, though other peoples in Mexico and Central America seem to have preferred valleys and plains. The dominating position of the ancient city, some thousand feet higher than the fertile fields that provided it with its food supply, and the ruggedness of the steep slopes minimized the danger of attack.

The mountain has seven summits, all of them covered with grass-topped mounds, concealed temples, palaces, baths, and tombs. The settlement is said to extend over twenty square miles, and indeed, when one looks over the surrounding slopes on a clear morning, the whole region appears shaped by the hand of man. It might be said in passing that so bountiful is the Valley of Oaxaca that of all Mexico Cortés chose it for his marquisate, although politics and intrigues at home prevented him from ever enjoying his realm.

According to the opinion of Dr. Caso, who conducted the excavations, Monte Albán was rather a ceremonial center than a military fortress.[24] Its history falls into five periods, the first four covering the time when the Zapotecs or their immediate predecessors ruled here, and the fifth and last connected with the activities of the Mixtecs on the same spot. Altogether a time-span of some two thousand years of civilization elapsed before the coming of the white man.

There is a Mexican opinion that Monte Albán, as a settlement, is even older than the famous and much acclaimed sites of the Maya Area, some of the most important ruins of which are located in Chiapas, a neighboring state to Oaxaca. The beginnings of all these cultures are shrouded in obscurity. Nevertheless, the cluster of structures as it now stands shows acquaintance with the architectural accomplishments of the Maya.

In contrast to the other sites of the Mexican Area, in which one pyramidal base or a small group seems to command the spot, we find here a number of monticles, averaging about 30 feet in height, giving a very different but in no way less grand impression.

The city apparently centered about a vast plaza, 1000 by 650 feet, accurately oriented and dominated on the north and south by two immense artificial mounds, each of which supported a number of buildings. On the long sides it was flanked by a row of lesser elevations, varying in size and height, their rear walls erected on the brink of the mountain. Roughly down the center and parallel to these lies another group of monticles, and there are many more beyond the plaza, still untouched by the excavator. To have need of and maintain so many structures would indicate a flourishing civic and religious life, one that required numerous ceremonies, participants, and dignitaries.

The practice of superimposing one building upon another was prevalent also here; in one case five separate floor levels have been uncovered. The earlier periods seem to be characterized by more durable structures, erected of larger slabs and set on lower platforms, and occasionally worked slabs are found used again in later buildings. All the edifices were greatly enhanced by the bland coating of stucco, sections of which were painted in bright colors.

Judging from the architectural material now visible at the site, great stylistic differences are not apparent, but each building has, nevertheless, individuality and variety of detail. The stairway may be a massive, almost separate structure, beginning at a distance from the base of the temple mound with smooth unbroken balustrades like buttresses on either side; or it may be incorporated into the edifice, nestling, as it were, between the shoulders of the terraced podium. Or again, flanked by wide ramps, it may occupy a full side of the substructure with several abrupt vertical breaks. In one case, Monticle J (*fig. b*), a narrow vaulted passageway cuts into the structure behind the stair. Note the glyphs on the walls.

The great stairway of thirty-three steps at the north end of the plaza (*fig. a, upper right*) is believed the widest in all pre-Columbian America. It is nearly 125 feet broad and 40 high. The ramp here becomes a primary feature. It is 39 feet wide on either side, and with its static extended surface counterbalances the mounting line of the stairs.[22] The double meander that decorates the structure is an ornament characteristic of the site and is most clearly seen in *fig. c,* showing Monticle M.

Pl. 14, fig. a gives the view looking south from the top of the stairs. A number of square sections of masonry, presumably the foundations of pillars, are visible. In the foreground is a sunken court, somewhat reminiscent of the Citadel at Teotihuacán. This complex continues in a group of platform mounds, many yet not investigated, rising in an irregular mass of terraced walls and sloping steps, in itself a mountain of masonry. *Pl. 15, fig. a* shows the north end.

As in numerous other pre-Columbian sites from both the Mexican and Maya areas, a ball court was found, here in the northwest corner of the plaza (*Pl. 14, fig. b*). As a whole, it does not compare artistically with those of the Maya, but has, nevertheless, a beautifully flowing broad line of stairs and is well proportioned with daises cleverly applied. Here particularly, the complete disappearance of all embellishment prevents us from receiving an adequate impression.

But even without the ruins of religious and civic buildings, the overwhelming number of carefully built and decorated tombs would secure for Monte Albán a particular place in medieval American history. It seems that the Zapotecs especially developed the tradition of housing their dead in masonry tombs. The subterranean chambers at Mitla, also within the Zapotec realm, are more imposing in size and show greater skill in decoration, but both types testify convincingly to the importance of an after-life in the beliefs of these people.

Beyond the main cluster of buildings, where a few burials have been discovered, the sloping hillsides constitute an extensive cemetery. Jagged stones from ancient tombs lie scattered far and wide across the tilled fields of the region. The burial chambers all have a somewhat similar construction, rectangular in shape and roofed with stone slabs, laid flat from wall to wall or placed together to form an inverted V. They are not comfortable places for the living, as they are generally too low for one to stand erect in and are suffocatingly hot, but they provided ample space for several dead with their personal paraphernalia, for incense burners and funerary urns, in which the cremated bones of disinterred bodies were placed for a second burial.

Pl. 15, fig. b shows the reconstructed entrance of the fabulous Tomb 7, discovered in the relaying of the road which leads to the great plaza. Of Zapotec origin, it had been appropriated by the Mixtecs, but since their time had lain undisturbed. It can be seen that the grave chamber was covered by a building with a chapel-like room at the end. In some tombs this edifice amounts to a veritable little temple with podium and stairway of considerable size and generally a patio in the center. A narrow flight of stone steps, once concealed, leads down to the entrance, where two large stone jambs support the heavy lintel.

The entrances to the tombs of Monte Albán are frequently decorated. A serpent (*fig. c*), probably represented with a painted body, guarded the door of Tomb 125, and a pottery figure (*fig. d*) was discovered cemented firmly above the doorway of Tomb 104. The headdress here is unusually detailed and the large jade mask depicted on the breast should also be noted.

The interiors were made of stone, with one niche always built into the wall opposite the doorway and one, or sometimes two, in each of the long side walls. These are often empty, even in an unviolated tomb, but in certain cases have been found to contain pottery and jewelry. It is a matter of speculation whether these recesses indicate the degeneration of a former cruciform construction, as is held by some Mexican archaeologists. One structure in the form of a cross has been found at Monte Albán, but the type is more frequent in the Mitla region. The walls were often stuccoed and sometimes painted, an example of which, the most remarkable discovered to date—the interior of Tomb 104 mentioned above—is reproduced in *Pl. 264*. This practice of interring the dead in decorated chambers, built with impressive portals and vaulted roofs in a manner to suggest houses, brings to mind the Etruscan graves of Tuscany and Umbria, which also had their subterranean halls with frescoes and pottery sarcophagi.

The region of Monte Albán has been riddled by treasure hunters ever since the Conquest. Most of the temple-bases have been ruthlessly tunneled, doubtless with the mistaken idea that they were pyramids built over the tombs of kings, and many of the recently excavated graves show signs of age-old plundering. It is fortunate that some were spared for 20th-century archaeology.

One of the outstanding pioneer archaeologists of the Maya Area, Alfred Percival Maudslay, showed his brilliant intuition when, after finishing his repeated and thorough surveys of the Maya country, he became interested in Monte Albán. At that time he was working a small gold mine, which he had inherited, at Zavaleta near Oaxaca City, but his chief ambition was to excavate and study the near-by Zapotec site. Around the turn of the century, however, an archaeologist was still looked upon as somewhat moonstruck. The motives of research were regarded with suspicion and reluctance, despite the fact that adventurers came and went almost at will, camping for a few days on the site and moving on unchallenged. In vain Maudslay lobbied and wrote to the authorities for permission to carry on his work. Even the fact that he held an honorary title from the University of Mexico was of little avail. After his years of success and fame in the Maya jungle, he became restless and disheartened over the failure of this new project, and, unwilling to wait longer, he sold his property and sailed for England. Some of the older residents of Oaxaca still speak of this great personality with real attachment, invariably mentioning the beautiful garden on which he spent so many hours during the years he lived there.

Governments and attitudes have changed since then, and in 1931 a more enlightened administration gave authority to Dr. Caso to begin work at Monte Albán. No one can estimate the loss that occurred during that lapse of thirty or forty years before scientific methods were applied in the excavations, but the great number of so-called "Oaxaca" type specimens of jewelry, jade, and pottery that are current on the market or have found their way into museums and private collections can give us a faint idea of the riches once buried in the Zapotec and Mixtec graves.

MITLA

Our last stop on the way to the Maya Area is at Mitla. The town is situated some twenty miles southeast of Monte Albán, and in contrast to that hilltop settlement, lies in the lap of a fertile valley. It is on the route which once connected several important pre-Columbian centers and its culture profited from this. The district has retained its importance, and now the Pan-American Highway passes near Mitla. According to one chronicler, in 1494 the place fell into the hands of the Aztecs, interested in controlling the road by which cocoa was sent from the Isthmus of Tehuantepec to the Mexican highlands, but if there was an Aztec occupation of the town, it seems to have left little impression on the arts of the place.

The Aztec word *Mictlán* signifies "underworld" or "realm of the dead," while the Zapotec name means rather "house of beatitudes." [129] Tradition has it that here dwelt the Great High Priest of the nation, who was consulted by dignitaries from far and wide.

As Mitla had never been buried or overgrown with vegetation, it was among the first of the ruined cities to be described. Speculation ran rife as to the age of the buildings, and fantastic uses were contrived for them, which subsequent examination has failed to corroborate. In view of the devastation of the Conquest and the ruthless methods of early "explorers," it is a miracle that the ruins of Mitla exist at all. Indeed, enough stones were carried away to build haciendas and churches, one of which rises from the flank of an ancient quadrangle, and farming goes on in the midst of crumbling plazas.

Interest at this site centers in three large quadrangular groups, which show great originality in style and ornament. Happily, enough remains of these to give an idea of their architecture. Although they do not seem to have been carefully related to one another, each in itself is accurately oriented.[49]

The building called the Palace of the Six Columns (Palace II) is the best preserved (*Pl. 16, fig. a*). It stands at the north end of a complex of two quadrangular courts, each about 150 feet at the greatest width and placed obliquely, corner to corner. The courts are inclosed by nearly vertical ramparts, 6 or 7 feet high, which served as bases. In the center stood a square altar or shrine, the outlines of which are visible in this photograph. The plaza was paved with thick cement and, according to a custom prevalent in Mexico and Central America, it as well as the stuccoed surface of the podiums and the floors of the buildings was stained red.

As it stands, the façade of the palace measures 133 feet long by about 14 high. A broad steep stairway leads up to the imposing triple entrance. Its walls, sometimes 4 feet thick, are constructed on the usual core of irregular stone and adobe mortar, with an amazingly intricate facing of smooth, well-cut trachyte in various sizes, tenòned into the cement core (*Pl. 17, fig. a*). The slanting base-line is present, and above it are rectangular panels of fretwork set within the turns of a double-coursed meander, such as was used on the ramps and terraces of Monte Albán. This is topped with a course of stone slanted outward in opposition to the incline of the base. Large slabs mark the corners. The four round holes visible above the paneled sections at the entrance were doubtless for poles supporting an awning. The lintel, more clearly seen from within, consists of three immense stone blocks, each some 10 feet long, 2 to 4 feet thick, and 5 broad. On the outside it is ingeniously carved to harmonize with the composite fretwork panels on the walls.

The photographs illustrate more clearly than any text not only the great architectural imagination necessary for the conception of such a grandiose plan, but also the technical knowledge required for the execution of a design involving so many front levels and such counterpoint of decoration. Stucco and paint must be added in imagination to all the plain surfaces of the buildings as they stand.

At the end of the last century the enthusiasm for all that was classic laid much emphasis on the Greek-type frets used in the ornamental panels at Mitla. But while classical Europe used the grecque in a narrow line as edging to an undecorated surface, in Mitla the fretted panels with smooth stone bands as frame made up the wall itself.

The fretwork is composed of small pieces of stone, cut and arranged in a mosaic-like manner into not less than fourteen separate designs (*Pl. 16, fig. b*). The grecque and the simple square combine in rhythmic sequence or fantastic zigzag into patterns, including the cross, the diamond, the step-fret, interlocking T's, and many other variations which alternate upon the walls in splendid harmony. It is noteworthy that the component pieces are not uniform, as is usual with the blocks or tiles which we combine to form a varied geometric design, but that each piece was obviously cut for the spot which it occupies. The stones have tenons at the back and thus are imbedded into the mass of mortar behind the panel with the same technique, as Thompson points out, as that used in fabricating the turquoise plaques and shell mosaics, but on a larger scale.[151] Eighty thousand pieces are said to have been needed for the wall of the inner court alone.

The patterns in their strict geometric build-up seem to be derived from textile designs. The complete absence of human, animal, and plant motifs is noteworthy. As the fret, and particularly the step-fret, or "winged fret" as it might be called, is a sign of the Great Plumed Serpent, there is doubtless also symbolical significance in the decoration here.

By this time all confused comparison to Greek and Roman art should have been dismissed from the mind of the reader. The restless polyphonic decoration of the palaces at Mitla has nothing in common with the suave homogeneous structures of the classical world, however serene and balanced its effect may be at a distance.

The triple doorway opens upon the Hall of the Columns, 23 feet wide by 125 long, which runs the full width of the building and seems to have been stuccoed. The six huge tapering stone columns down the middle of the floor are 11 feet high as they stand and probably are sunken some 4 or 5 feet below the cement floor. Their diameter is over 30 inches and their weight approximates six to eight tons each. They served as supports for the roof, which was built apparently in the traditional manner with poles laid across heavier beams and sealed with mortar or plaster.

From this inner hall a small door leads through an anteroom into an open patio, 31 feet square, flanked on all sides by long narrow inclosed chambers (*Pl. 17, fig. b*). Decorations similar to the outside of the building embellish the court, while the walls of the narrow rooms carry free-flowing bands of the composite reliefs, separated from one another by only a single narrow course of smooth stone (*fig. c*). The mosaics were painted white on a red ground,[129] and the interplay of light and shadow on them even today multiplies their amazing variety. Just as the recurrence of a rich and ingenious melody in a symphony does not dull our ears, so these fretwork variations please the eye on every wall and in every position they are found, however often repeated.

It may be assumed that the other buildings facing the open plazas were similar in execution but had generally a single long narrow hall. These impressive edifices are called "palaces" because their structure was definitely different from the type known to be temples throughout Middle America. The room arrangement would have lent itself well for audiences and consultations, if not too congenial as household quarters. None of the buildings seems to have other access than by way of the great courts of the quadrangles.

In the west quadrangle of the same complex are found the two subterranean chambers that give special importance to the site. The entrances (*Pl. 18, fig. a*), constructed with stone lintels and jambs, as is the case in the buildings, lie in the plaza near the center and were probably closed with a slab or sealed. At the foot of the descending stairs an uneven passage runs in each case directly under the building, so that the great cruciform vaults may be said to lie rather within the artificial base of the edifice than actually underground. They were doubtless constructed from above, then sealed with the floor. The photograph shows part of the upper floor of the palace, as well as the construction of the passage beneath.

The impressive subterranean galleries are about 5 feet wide by 6½ to 8 feet high. The cross arms extend some 42 feet, or, in the case of the shorter ones, 12 to 15 feet. Large stone slabs, evenly cut and fitted, form the ceiling. The tomb below the north building has composite mosaic-like panels such as are used in the outside walls, while in the east vault the fretwork decorations are carved in the stone (*fig. b*). Other cruciform vaults are known within the environs of Mitla. All these underground chambers were robbed of their contents so long ago that no clue remains of what they may have contained.

The two other palace complexes at Mitla have no substructures but stand on the ground level so that the buildings inclosing the various quadrangles have continuous walls. Nevertheless they all show such uniformity of plan and decoration that they must have been erected within a time-span not too remote from the Group of the Columns just described. Remnants of murals in negative painting have been found on some of the inner lintels (see *Pl. 265, fig. a*), where figures resembling those of the codices are drawn with fine red lines on a grayish plaster and the background filled in with brilliant red.[49]

The Zapotecs are thought to have taken possession of the Mitla region about the 11th century, and how many centuries of pre-Columbian life the site witnessed prior to that is not known. The ruins shown here are placed between 1200 and 1300. We may assume that there was some antecedent architecture before this splendid and perfected style, for that which we see today must have been not only late chronologically, but the highest achievement of their talent.

The variety of buildings in the Mexican Area is manifested in the eight architectural sites here presented. Beyond the fundamental homogeneity of idea, not one can be called a copy or a reproduction of another. Relatively low podiums follow mountain-high temple-bases. Predominantly flat surfaces, smoothed over with a bland covering of stucco and paint, stand not far from terraces decorated with sculptural ornaments in barbaric pomp. In one case animal representations, in another purely geometrical bands and patterns show the divergence in imagination. Wide panels of low relief contrast with sculpture in the round, and huge blocks, with carefully fitted smaller stones. What is common is the disposition to rise above the natural level, to make the place of ceremony or worship dominate its vicinity. Another mutual feature is the gregarious character of the buildings; in every case that we know, adjacent mounds prove that numerous structures added their weight to the general effect. Ritual had a primary part in the life of the medieval Americans. Their religious ceremonies were likewise their theatrical show and required a number of settings.

These sites radiate a spirit alien to us. Some may belittle it, but none can deny that majesty lies in the structures. Whether crude in workmanship or sophisticated in execution, all their variants remain consistently within the same framework of thought.

MAYA AREA

In Mexico we saw within a comparatively short radius the diverse architectural achievement of various peoples. The Maya Area, on the other hand, we find populated by a single race throughout the Middle Ages, who, though stimulated by outside influence and later even dominated by another nation, retained its striking talents and special characteristics in art and civilization. The language map even today shows remarkable solidarity in this region extending from Tabasco throughout Yucatan and covering most of Guatemala and a section of Honduras, roughly the territory occupied by the ancient Maya.[52]

Each Maya city presents great originality of conception in its architecture and variation in detail, but a distinct continuity of character is nevertheless traceable from the first sites, which date from about the beginning of our era, to the powerful Toltec-influenced cities of Yucatan that prospered until shortly before the Conquest.

The great civilization that once flourished here was based on the development of agriculture. Life was dependent upon and religion was closely allied to the crops, and rain or drought was a vital factor in the existence of these people. The custom of burning off and replanting a succession of fields was ingenious enough, considering the primitive quality of the tools at hand and the terrific vitality of the jungle, but the method tended to exhaust the soil, which produced less and less after the first season, even if allowed for a time to lie fallow.[66] The fluctuations of population, whether sudden or gradual, which led finally to the abandonment of the great sites is attributable in part to these facts.

One of the conditioning factors of Maya building was the presence of limestone practically throughout the area. Lime was extracted and excellent stucco, cement, and lime mortar were produced at a very early date.

Out of this knowledge these people found their own ingenious solution to the roofing problem by inventing a type of corbeled arch. The Maya builders are sometimes spoken of disparagingly for not having discovered the principle of the keystone arch. Ignorance of this architectural device, however, is not considered a disgrace elsewhere in archaeology, and there is no need for the Americanist to apologize for it. The famous structures of Mesopotamia, China, Egypt, and Greece—to mention only the best known of the ancient civilizations— are not belittled because of a lack of it. Their architecture is acknowledged as great and splendid, although they all used horizontally laid stone slabs and wooden beams in roofing. With them even the corbeled vault was rare. The subsequent illustrations should convince any one that medieval America also achieved great building without the knowledge of the Roman arch.

The Maya corbeled vault made use of a series of stones firmly held at one end and so placed that each course overlapped the one below it; thus the sides gradually approached each other. Usually a slab capped the arch. The earliest vault so far discovered appears at Uaxactún in Structure A-V, tentatively dated toward the end of the 4th century.[131] The excellent cement of the limestone regions served to make the arch essentially monolithic. The use of wooden cross-beams was common, though their purpose is still a matter of discussion.

A number of variations were developed, all using the same principle, from the spectacular trefoil arch at Palenque to the bottle shapes at Tulum and other Yucatecan east-coast sites and the rounded constructions at Labná and Chichén Itzá. The great height of the vaults from the spring-line necessarily conditioned the appearance of the outside of the building, giving an extensive upper zone, or "entablature section," characteristic of the Maya and well adapted to lavish decoration.

The chronology of the Old Empire falls roughly into three periods: the Early, beginning in the first centuries after the birth of Christ and closing in the 7th century; the Middle, which lasted only about a hundred years, and the Late, which extended from the early 8th century to 889, the last date recorded on stelae. These periods make themselves apparent in the art production, and were first differentiated by Dr. Spinden on the basis of the evolution of the carving on stelae uninfluenced by the dates they bore.[137] The Late Period is sometimes called the Great, since most of the famous Old Empire cities came to their flowering within this time-span, reaching the zenith of their creative genius in mid-8th century. The date 790 marks the peak of time-recording and is found on stelae, altars, or lintels of nineteen Maya sites.[150] The term "Transition" is sometimes applied to that period between the decline of the Old Empire and the emergence of the New.

The great cities of the Old Empire are difficult of access, with many of them situated in the depths of what is today an almost impenetrable jungle. Chicle hunters, tapping the forest for raw material for chewing gum, have rendered pioneer service in locating and reporting many a ruin, and their trails are used even today by archaeologists when a site does not afford a landing for an airplane.

UAXACTÚN

The earliest structure known to date was excavated at Uaxactún, which lies north of Lake Flores, Petén, Guatemala, and about ninety miles west of Belize, port of British Honduras. This site appears to have been occupied for one of the longest spans of time in the Old Empire, although not in unbroken continuity, with date sequences ranging from 327 to 889. It is large, with a number of

ARCHITECTURE

beautifully laid-out groups of buildings. As in Mexico, there is evidence of frequent alteration and rebuilding.

In one case (Structure A-I) five antecedent substructures were uncovered beneath the ruins of the sixth and last. All, down to the earliest, revealed the characteristic fundamentals of Maya construction. They were built over a loose core of fill and rubble covered with a backing of concrete, upon which a facing of cut stone was applied. In the substructures of this complex can be traced the entire progression of the technique in applying the facing, from the tenoned-in type of stone locked into the cement behind, through a rough veneering, to a final and perfected facing only superficially bound to the hearting.[135]

The temple-bases investigated consisted of receding terraces, generally three, each with slightly battered profile and one stairway. All bore a smooth stucco surface, but there had been apparently no attempt at decoration. The temples on top seem to have been of poles and thatch, some with a low masonry foundation wall and post holes suggesting roof construction. There is no conclusive evidence here of the famous vault which was to flower in so many rich variations at a later period. The excavations of this group yielded a large number of painted pottery vessels, extraordinarily fine.

In the great plaza of the city were unearthed stone monuments, the dates of which correspond to A.D. 328. At the same time an edifice was uncovered (*Pl. 19, fig. a*) that apparently had already been buried at the time the stelae were erected. It was in remarkably fine condition, having been preserved by the building superimposed upon it.

This early structure, E-VII, is of a different style from that of the later edifices in the city, and might be called pre-Maya. It consists of a well-proportioned temple-base (*fig. b*), 85 feet square and 25 high, of rough undressed stone, covered thickly with brilliant white stucco. A series of low receding platforms with heavy projecting cornices makes up the lower portion of the base, and wide stairways with balustrades lead up all four sides. The last section consists of a considerably higher terrace block. Large grotesque masks decorate the abutments. The subtle handling of the stairways gives suavity to the whole building. Indeed, the stairway as decorative factor is as fully utilized as in the much later buildings of this and the Mexican Area. Astonishing ripeness is revealed in the sure command over contour and mass and the excellent feeling for light and shade. The dramatic sense, so often present in the architecture of the pre-Columbian cultures, is strongly evident here.

Whether or not a building once stood on top of this structure is a matter of conjecture. No evidence was found at the time of excavation. There was probably some kind of altar, even perhaps a roof, which could not have been of very solid construction.

Certain features already present in this early example forecast those that characterize Maya building. The gigantic stucco masks are the forerunners of the stone masks and the stucco reliefs that constitute the crowning glory of Maya architecture. These masks, which here might already be considered rigid and conventionalized in their idea, hold their own throughout the course of Maya building, although techniques became more mobile and the field for delineation more varied. The striving for imposing elevation, always a factor in the architecture of the Maya, was exaggerated and consciously applied with great effect, especially in the cities Tikal, Guatemala, and Palenque, Mexico. The altar sheds on the early bases grew into temples of more solid structure, with inner divisions into sanctuaries and antechambers, and the decorative motifs, first applied to the substructure, were transplanted later to the temple itself and lavished chiefly upon the upper zones.

COPÁN

The earliest description of the ruins of Copán, Honduras, is to be found in a letter dated March, 1576, from Diego García de Palacio, an officer of the *Audiencia de Guatemala,* to his king, Philip II of Spain. It is, however, as Maudslay writes, "not to Palacio's letter, which was only comparatively recently unearthed from Spanish archives, but to the charming pages of Stephens and the beautiful drawings of Catherwood that the world in general is indebted for a knowledge of the wonders of Copan." [81]

This intrepid gentleman, John L. Stephens, was commissioned in 1839 by Martin Van Buren, President of the United States, to make a general survey of the possibilities of a canal across Nicaragua connecting the Atlantic and Pacific, but was balked in this task by civil and guerrilla warfare then prevalent in Central America. He nevertheless succeeded in journeying nearly three thousand miles through the strife-torn interiors, visiting eight ruined cities, which he discusses with truly brilliant perception and accuracy in his famous book, *Incidents of Travel in Central America, Chiapas and Yucatan,* illustrated by the English artist, Frederick Catherwood.

So enthusiastic was Stephens about Copán that he bought the ruined city for fifty dollars in cash, with the idea of moving as much of it as possible to greater safety. Difficulties of transportation, however, prevented him from carrying out his enterprise.[58]

In this great religious center may be seen one of the finest examples in the Old Empire of the elaborate city-planning of the Maya. Many of their early cities do not appear to have been so carefully oriented as those of the Mexican Area and their position was seemingly influenced by the character of the landscape.[49] There was apparently little concern over the matter of defense; within the cities there are no remnants of fences or walled inclosures. The buildings were generally linked with one another by staircases or broad mounting terraces, with that kind of community spirit that blended all into one body of architecture.

The general view of the site as reconstructed by Maudslay will give a clearer idea of the complicated grouping than any lengthy description could (*Pl. 20, fig. b*). Ruins belonging to the city extend for many miles but the area here shown along the river bank doubtless constituted the heart of the community.

In the foreground is visible an immense mound, roughly rectangular in shape, with additions and outcroppings, upon the top of which, over one hundred feet above the natural level, several buildings of various sizes are grouped about two sunken courts. That the Great Mound is for the most part artificial has been revealed by the river, which, in the shift of its bed during the centuries, has cut deeply into one side, disclosing in the cross-section not only the hard-packed rubble of the core but also several pavement levels of concrete and a number of drains leading from the upper courts. It is noteworthy that the sides of the Great Mound and of the various courts are faced with an almost unbroken series of steps, extremely gracious in their effect and indicative of superior building.

To the north of this structure is situated a vast open plaza on the natural level (*fig. a*), surrounded on three sides by grass-grown ramparts and low platforms, the foundations for smaller buildings. Its position on the site is designated by *a* on the model. Carved altars and fragments of monuments stand in the field, stelae of rulers and priests, some set over small cruciform vaults containing caches. There are a number of mounds, apparently ruined substructures, near by, some arranged to form quadrangles. The chief evidences of human habitation lie at the left in the picture of the model.

The visitor's first great impression of Copán is of the two imposing stairways that stand at right angles to each other, forming the southeast corner of the plaza. The broader of the two extends across the entire side of the Great Mound. Giant gray ceiba trees have gained a firm foothold on the very summit of the buildings, planted there by nature after the city was abandoned, so that now the monumental weather-beaten statue at the foot of the stairs is nearly always in deep shadow.

The stairway to the east (*b* in the model) is not so broad as the first and belongs to a separate substructure which, however, is contiguous to the Great Mound. This steep narrow temple-base was greatly damaged by a recent landslide, and of the temple which once stood on top, only traces of the cement pavement remain. The stairway (*Pl. 21, fig. a*), under reconstruction at the time of our visit, ascends at a characteristically steep angle and is 26 feet broad. The risers of the steps, calculated to have numbered eighty to ninety, each about a foot high, carry carved hieroglyphic computations, the longest Maya inscription yet discovered. The glyphs are executed with beauty and precise detail and so arranged as to be read in lines across each step, not, as was usual, in columns. The many figures representing the elements of Maya time-count—human, animal, and monster heads in various positions within their shieldlike frames, and the dots and bars which stand for numbers—constitute a gigantic open scroll, a frozen page of a strange medieval book at which we gaze in fascination, even though conscious of our own mental limitations in fathoming its meaning.

About every twelve steps, in the center, a carved seated figure is placed, priest or dignitary magnificently arrayed, each with his head framed in a monster's jaws. One of these statues is missing (see *Pl. 87*); the rest are heavily damaged, yet each is arresting for its individuality. A giant stela stands at the foot of the stairs facing a carved altar, and behind it another altar-like platform is built into the body of the staircase.

The stairway is flanked on either side by a balustrade, 3½ feet wide, with curved, almost crescent-shaped masks (*fig. b*). Although only a few of these are left in place, they seem at one and the same time to bind the stair to the substructure and, with their winglike effect, to disencumber the whole mass of its weight. All the carving was apparently only roughed in before the stones were set in place and finished afterward.[39] The inscription dates the stair in 770, placing it among the latest structures at Copán; stylistically also it shows some of the most mature work.

Copán too has its Ball Court (*Pl. 20, fig. d*), which lies at right angles to the Hieroglyphic Stairway in the position indicated by *c* on the model, although reconstruction has proved it to be of very different design than Maudslay shows.

It was a comparatively narrow open court and smoothly paved. The low slanting ramps on either side present a feature different from the ball courts in the New Empire in Yucatan, where the walls are high and vertical. Apparently the game was not identical in all regions. The top of the ramp is decorated by a number of gigantic parrot heads. To the right and left behind these, rise buildings that were perhaps used by the chiefs and high priests, while the dilapidated stair at the north end may have served as the stand for the common people. In the axis the tall stela "points up" the linear composition. The whole construction forms an ideal arena in which from any point one has a feeling of proximity to the players.

In the West Court on top of the Great Mound is an unusual building (d in the model), reconstructed by the Carnegie Institution of Washington and named Structure 11, or the Reviewing Stand (fig. c). The substructure is severe, with plain walls and a series of doorlike niches. Doubtless paint on a plastered ground furnished added decoration. Six steps lead up from the level of the court, the top riser of which carries finely carved glyphs. The only other ornamentation is two kneeling figures, one at either end of the top stair. The legs, in profile, and the squared shoulders, as well as the fantastic appendage attached to the creature's back are executed in relief, while the demon head and the torch in his left hand are worked in the round. There is animation in the malevolent face, and the writhing snake held in tusklike teeth is realistically carved.

The structure on the summit is decorated with beautifully executed glyphs, and fragmentary sculpture about the entrance indicates that it represented a yawning serpent jaw.[39] Were it not for the foliage, this height would command a splendid view of the great plaza.

On the East Court of the Great Mound stands the Temple of the Sculptured Doorway, or Structure 22 (e in the model). The building remained in a state of partial preservation until 1934, when it was razed by an earthquake. Maudslay's careful notes and photographs were of great assistance when its excavation and restoration were undertaken shortly afterward.[159]

The edifice (Pl. 22, fig. a), originally about 80 by 40 feet, is built of the soft greenish tufa abundant in the region and is accurately oriented. It stands on its own E-shaped podium on top of the 20-foot terrace that frames the entire court. It is dated in mid-8th century and was not erected over an older structure. Close by runs the slash cut by the river which has now been diverted from its destructive course. A stair of seven steps (fig. b) laid with unusually massive stones mounts to the entrance. The top one is carved to represent the jaw and lower lip of a scaly monster, and two curving stone tusks are inset at the sides. Large composite masks were found in place at the corners, and finely carved figures in the round, of the type known as Maize-god and illustrated on *Pl. 90,* decorated the façade. It contains four rooms, vaulted apparently in the typical Maya manner and separated by what appear to us as disproportionately thick walls, some of which are nearly 9 feet through.

The north chamber may have been the inner sanctuary. It is raised over two feet above the general floor level, and its only access is by way of the superb sculptured doorway (*Pl. 23, fig. c*) that gives the structure its name.

This doorway stands unique in all the architecture of medieval America that has been preserved or reconstructed. It occupies two-thirds of the wall space of the narrow anteroom which one must enter first, but, set back and shielded by the outside walls, it is invisible from the outside. A sculptured human figure, larger than life size, sits hunched at either side (*figs. a* and *b*), crouching above an enormous death's-head carved from a single piece of stone. The men support on their backs the twisted mass of a fantastic two-headed monster, whose shoulder and bent limb are visible directly above the human head. The face of the beast rests upon the upraised hands, while the writhing body forms the lintel, held in place by a thick wooden beam. In and out of the S-shaped convolutions of the creature weave small grotesque human figures with elaborate headdresses and jewels, their arms and legs interwoven as if in struggle with the elements. The high sill is also carved with death's-heads and glyphs, so that the entire entrance to the inner room is framed with sculpture.

The carving was covered with a thin layer of plaster and once brightly painted, refurbished so often that some of the exquisite detail of feathers, incised decorations, tassels, individual hands and feet were lost in the thickening coating. From the sockets that are still visible in the walls, it appears that the doors to the adjacent rooms were closed with screens or curtains, doubtless of brilliant hues.

A ceremony witnessed here must have been immensely awe-inspiring. But whether we go to the trouble of imagining a scene from the sunken world or examine the doorway only as a piece of architectural sculpture, the highly decorative management of mass and line, the pulsing rhythm in the various motifs are arresting for every one.

The word "baroque" still carries with it a tinge of disparagement in the United States, although in Europe and Latin America the style is highly appreciated. It is intended here only as praise when we venture to describe this sculptured doorway as the best Maya "baroque." Baroque it is—in feeling, in its complication of design and ebullience of detail, in the dramatic dynamics of its whole conception, in the untrammeled freedom of its execution.

There can be no doubt that this elaborate portal had involved mythological significance for the Maya. The heavy mysterious creature has been interpreted as the sky monster and the two crushed human figures upholding the monstrous garland as two of the four "Bacabs" who support the four corners of the firmament.[153]

In it we have a document in stone, voicing the supernatural occult elements behind Maya religion. This is not one sculptor's arbitrary interpretation of some religious or mystic thought, but the articulation of a complex collective imagination expressed with such clarity that even the Christian of the 20th century is struck, not only by its physical power but by the vision of this alien and vigorous fantasy-world.

TIKAL

Tikal, "place where spirit voices are heard" (*Pl. 24*), is one of the larger sites in the Maya Area, the ruins occupying roughly one square mile. Situated on a plain in the district that includes the northeastern part of Guatemala, with the Usumacinta River and Lake Petén, it belongs to the region where Maya civilization reached its greatest height. Its dates extend from the Early Period to the 9th century.

Like other ancient Maya cities of importance, its plan is characterized by a large court or plaza, stretching in this case over 300 feet from east to west, within which a great number of stelae and altars were grouped.

Owing to its comparative isolation, Tikal has been less visited than most of the larger Maya sites. The first written report appeared in 1848, extremely late in comparison with other descriptions that were made shortly after the Conquest or during the viceregal period. Unlike Copán, Quiriguá, Chichén Itzá, where various institutions, chiefly American, held government contracts over a period of years for the thorough study and preservation of the site, Tikal has never been systematically excavated. The clearing of the dense jungle growth was always a major problem to the investigators, who had only a limited time to spend among the ruins. All existing photographs show a tangle of vegetation and felled trees, restricting a grasp of the city's grandeur. Less sculptured material has been found here so far than one would expect in a city of its cultural height, but many revelations may be expected when exhaustive excavation is undertaken. The Government of Guatemala has a road now under construction which will shortly open up this important region.

Two types of buildings are, in general, distinguishable in Maya sites: the "temples," usually single structures with an inner room or sanctuary, placed on a separate lofty pyramidal base; and the residential type or "palaces" of more rambling proportions usually built on lower, broader platforms. In the latter the high priests and leading nobility are believed to have dwelt or functioned, while the simple populace erected thatch-roofed huts of wood and withes, such as are pictured on the façades of certain buildings and in the murals of a later period (see *Pl. 32, fig. a*).

Besides five major temples, Tikal contains an unusual number and variety of palaces, no two alike in outer appearance or arrangement of apartments. There are also several truncated pyramidal bases with no trace of a building on top but with stairways leading up all four sides, in the manner, though apparently without the ornamentation, of the structure described at near-by Uaxactún. The Castillo at Chichén Itzá with its nine terraces and four stairways from four directions, erected some four hundred years later, is an interesting hark-back to this ancient type (see *Pl. 41*).

The buildings of Tikal are, relatively speaking, the best preserved of the Old Empire. This is due partly to the very thick walls and few doors, in contrast to the thinner walls and wider portals at Palenque, for instance. Besides, the palaces were frequently constructed with an upper tier of rooms, which, in collapsing, served to preserve the lower story.

The use of wood is a characteristic of the site. Beams of the extremely hard *chico-sapote* were employed at the spring-line of the narrow Maya vaults and also as lintels, where several were placed side by side to cover the span between the massive walls. The fact that it has rotted or been torn away has caused the collapse of many of the entrances and surmounting masonry. Surviving fragments, one of which will be discussed later (see *Pl. 274*), show that much of this wood was elaborately carved in low relief and painted.

Superimposed stories are unusual in Maya architecture, evidently because of the great weight of masonry involved, and whenever a two-story effect was desired, it was generally achieved by the "stepping-back" of the second tier and placing it over a solid core. In Tikal, however, two and even three stories are found, actually built one above the other.[156]

The Palace of Five Stories (Structure 10), called by Teobert Maler the

Sacerdotal Palace, is an example of this. It rises at the edge of a wide ravine with one of the terraced hills directly behind it. A retaining wall from the bottom of the gorge supports the first two stories, forming a wide esplanade in front of them, as shown in the plan (*Pl. 25, fig. b*). These actually back against the hillside, but the three upper stories, receding some 30 feet from the façade of the lower section, stand free.

Each story is marked by a projecting entablature section, beginning at the spring-line of the inner vault and extending beyond its peak, which is decorated with carving or stucco work (*fig. a*). There are no signs of stairways either within or without the palaces, and it is surmised that the upper levels were reached by wooden stairs or ladders.

Inside, the first four stories each contained two rows of rooms, one behind the other—fourteen in all, not counting the rambling wings. The width and height of the chambers were conditioned by the inverted-V-shaped vault, averaging about 5 and 13 feet respectively, while in length they varied from 8 to 25 feet. Maler calculates the height from the lowest esplanade to the topmost edge of the frieze of the fifth story as nearly 90 feet.[75]

The other residential buildings show great variety in the arrangement of chambers—some opening on courts, some on galleries—which are often connected by narrow passages. Small round or square apertures were constructed in the walls, probably for ventilation. Inside, around the sides of the rooms, are a number of low benches, built of stone or of rubble plastered over. The walls are also smoothly plastered, and several incised drawings have been found both in palaces and temples, though there are few traces of color. In a chamber of the third story of the palace just described a stone carving in relief was discovered, picturing a woman of rank presenting a high priest with a fattened turkey as sacrificial gift. Cupboard-like niches are frequent in the palaces, and there are indications that hangings may have covered them as well as the doorways.

In contrast to the diverse palace buildings, the five major temples show an unusual uniformity of plan. All stand on truncated pyramidal bases, considerably steeper than those in other Maya sites. All of them are divided into nine terraces with the exception of Temple II, which has four. The profile is slanting and the ground plan often shows inset corners and offset panels. A broad flight of stairs leads up one side. In each case there is only one entrance to the temple building. The vaulted chambers usually number three, one behind the other, connected by a series of beamed passageways or corridors that are often more spacious than the rooms themselves.

The extremely limited space of the interiors in comparison with the great thickness of the walls has frequently been pointed out in descriptions of the temples of Tikal, but this mass was evidently deemed necessary to support the enormous weight of the high decorative roof-comb, one of the most individual features of the site. This structure—a veritable headdress of masonry, weighted with ornament—seems to have no other purpose than the further embellishment of the edifice and extension of its height, an effect so sought after by the Maya builders.

Often the back of the roof-comb seems to descend in a line with the rear wall of the building and in some cases the substructure beneath it falls away at a steeper angle than in front. In Temple II, Maler, taking into consideration the fact that the top of the roof-comb had crumbled, estimated the total height of temple and roof-comb at about 73 feet, while its base measured only 68.

As imposing as it appears, this is the smallest of the five temples. Temple IV, in the western section of the city, is the tallest. The substructure here stands 147 feet high and carries on the top a temple building and roof-comb which together approximate another 80 feet. Its stairway is 58 feet broad at the base. In the photograph on *Pl. 24,* taken from across the great plaza, reading from left to right Temples III, II, and IV can be seen. The stunning effect of the staggered heights is evident.

At this site the evolution of the roof-comb can be traced from what might be considered the earliest type attempted—that of massive walls on more or less solid foundations—through a series of experiments aimed to lighten the weight and thus enlarge the interiors of the temples. The crumbling of some of these constructions reveals that hollow spaces were introduced, until, in Temple V, the roof-comb approximates two leaning walls which gradually converge. From this, it is only a step to the lattice-work and the lighter roof-combs in the buildings of Yaxchilán, Piedras Negras, and Palenque.[157]

PALENQUE

The variety and high artistry manifest in its buildings elevate Palenque to an extraordinary position among the ruined cities of pre-Columbian civilization, though it is quite small when compared with the religious centers just considered. It is situated in Chiapas, the southernmost state in Mexico, some hundred and fifty miles from Tikal, and lies at the mouth of a deep gorge, flanked on three sides by steep wooded hills and on the north by a broad sloping plain. The region is heavily forested, damp, and truly tropical. At all times can be heard the music of falling water.[49]

Although difficult of approach, this city has been the object of numerous visits and investigations in the last century and a half. In 1787, on the order of the King of Spain, Captain Antonio del Río "explored" it under protection of several companies of Spanish soldiers. Two hundred Indians with axes and bill-hooks were set to work clearing the ruins of the jungle vegetation. The house-keeping of the 18th-century colonial soldiers here in the wilderness can be imagined. Stones were removed at convenience to make fireplaces, hooks were driven through the fragile stucco on the walls for the hanging of armament and hammocks; the horses were stabled under roofs which remained. The Indians were illiterate, suspicious, and full of superstition.

"I am convinced," writes del Río, "that in order to form some idea of the first inhabitants and of the antiquities connected with their establishment, it would be indispensably necessary to make several excavations. . . . By dint of perseverance I affected all that was necessary to be done, so that ultimately there remained neither a window nor a doorway blocked up, a partition that was not thrown down, nor a room, corridor, court, tower, nor a subterranean passage in which excavations were not affected from two to three yards in depth." [18] It is to the true glory of the builders at Palenque that after such "investigations," anything at all remains today. Since then, the ruins have thrilled many visitors. However, like Tikal, the place was never thoroughly explored.

Of all the sites, Palenque demonstrates most clearly that the Maya had a broad and elastic architectural conception which they adapted to local conditions and topography, never allowing it to become crystallized into stereotyped patterns that limited their artistic activity.

The entire terrain is graded and terraced. The mountain stream, which runs out of the gorge and through the narrow valley where the city stands, is directed into a vaulted culvert four feet high, apparently large enough to accommodate the swollen waters of the rainy season. Farther below, masonry construction of somewhat different type serves as a bridge or viaduct. Thus in an area which must have been a much frequented part of the city, the unruly stream was brought under control. Today, however, the upper end of the channel has become clogged with débris and, unrestrained, the water pours over the ground, damaging the foundations of the buildings.

Palenque's damp and rainy climate may have influenced its distinctive type of architecture. In all the buildings the entablature section has even a more marked inward slant than at Tikal, running roughly parallel to the angle of the inner vault. The roof surface, consequently small, is also sloping, giving the general effect of a mansard.

The chief buildings here consist of a palace complex and five temples, three of which are grouped around a quadrangular court. Open courts, terraces, and stairways connect in a logical system. Doorways are many, three or five in a row, and are placed with a sense of balance—extending in some cases across the entire façade of the building, with the wall spaces between them so reduced that they seem like squarish pillars. Within, the chambers are always arranged in groups of two vaulted galleries, one behind the other.

The stone of the region is brittle and consequently difficult to work, and the buildings are covered either with stucco, modeled into life-size figures and painted, or with facings of large thin slabs carved in relief. Examples of these are shown on *Pl. 79* and *Pl. 91, fig. a.* Holmes notes the lavish use of color both inside and out. Black, white, blue, two shades of red, yellow, and green are visible, with traces of repainting. The plain surfaces of inner walls also show signs of having been tinted or decorated in colored geometric designs.

An especially involved plan can be observed in the Palace Group (*Pl. 26, fig. a*). It stands on a platform mound, measuring 30 feet at its greatest height and about 200 by 225 feet across the top.[49] The buildings inclose four sunken courts, and the whole complex seems to have been surrounded, except on the south, by a double gallery, divided into a number of chambers. Frequent doorways give access to these rooms on both the inner and outer sides, and occasional connecting doors are cut through the central partition. This is also pierced by a series of trefoil openings through the vault section, an unusual construction, best visible in the next plate. All the lintels were of wood, and their collapse has greatly damaged the façades.

Fig. b shows the west face of House A. On the relatively broad ramp, as well as on the pierlike sections of the substructure, large human figures are carved in relief. Panels of incised glyphs alternate with the carvings and appear also on the risers of a few of the steps.

More or less in the center of the group, on a base about 30 feet square, stands the remarkable three-story tower, one of the most unusual constructions in pre-Columbian architecture (*fig. a,* right center). A massive central pier contains a stone stairway only about 20 inches wide. Each story consists of a narrow gallery around this center block.

Towers, both square and round, occur, though infrequently, in other regions.

ARCHITECTURE

The Caracol at Chichén Itzá has an ascending ramp around a circular inner column, and, in the Andean Area, the grave towers, or *chulpas,* are somewhat similar in shape. In the Southwest, some of the Cliff-dwellers built tower-like constructions which were supported on one side by the cave wall.

The temples of the Sun, the Cross, and the Foliated Cross are all small gems of Maya architecture. They stand together but each on its own base, facing a quadrangular court across the ravine from the Palace. Their substructures are spreading and relatively low.

In *Pl. 27, fig. a,* the ruined Temple of the Cross is seen, the outer façade of which has collapsed, leaving only the stumps of stuccoed piers and revealing the inner wall and entrance to the sanctuary. Débris is piled almost to the spring-line of the vaults, and it should be remembered that the vertical lower walls rise about as high as the arch, that is, a little over 10 feet.

The model shown in *fig. b* gives a clearer idea of the structures. All three appear to have had triple doorways in the front with the remaining wall surface devoted to decorative stucco reliefs. The sloping frieze sections offered an excellent opportunity for bold flowing design, and elaborate roof-combs fittingly crowned the edifices. This feature here consists of two walls slanting toward each other, as at Tikal, but the mass was so lightened as to form only a trellis, a background for figures and other ornaments molded from stucco. Stones have been discovered projecting from the building which may have served as steps to the summit. Other jutting pieces were fixed in the masonry as support for the larger masses of stucco, much as wood or wire forms are used by a sculptor today. The height of temple and roof-comb is about 35 feet.

The inner corridor of each of the three temples is divided by transverse walls into three rooms. The middle one contains the "sanctuary" or tablet chamber, constructed against the back wall like a small building, with outer frieze, projecting cornices, wooden lintel, and vaulted inner space. Here were found, set into the walls, the magnificent tablets of limestone, from which the temples derived their names. Upon each is carved a different central symbol, officiating priests, and columns of glyphs. They will be discussed in greater detail under sculpture. (See *Pl. 75.*)

The thick outside walls are pierced with small T-shaped apertures, one or two to each chamber, doubtless for ventilation. The V-shaped concrete mass which forms the sides of the vaults is also cut through, above the partition walls, with large windows shaped like keyholes. All these features have great decorative value, serving not only to lighten the weight of the building but to increase and diffuse the illumination of the interior. Their function as ventilators will be appreciated especially by those who have experienced the suffocating humidity of inclosed quarters in the tropics.

Although the temples at Palenque are quite similar to one another in their construction and artistic conception, individuality and variety are apparent in each, and the effect, though homogeneous, is far from monotonous. Nowhere in Palenque has one the impression of mass production.

Louis J. Halle, Jr., explorer and naturalist, gives a just summing-up in his recent book. "The temples of Palenque . . . are exquisite rather than imposing; refined, rather than massive. They are quite content with the earth they stand on, and do not, like their predecessors, reach for the sky. Like precious jewels, they are beautiful and complete in themselves. . . . The earlier gods (if they are gods) in the sculptures of Tikal, Copan, Quiriguá seem to represent great natural forces, the forces that caused the maize to grow and the rain to fall; these gods, here at Palenque, are the members of an elegant aristocracy that rules gracefully over the destinies of man. There is a touch of courtliness about them that you do not find in their more barbaric forerunners." [42]

PIEDRAS NEGRAS

A day's ride by mule up the Usumacinta River, which separates Mexico and Guatemala, brings one deeper into the country of precipitous gorges to Piedras Negras, a site discovered much later than Palenque and one of primary importance. Some of the finest stone carving of the Old Empire, discussed under sculpture, comes from this city. The buildings are generally in a very bad state of preservation, but the excavations of the University of Pennsylvania have revealed interesting architectural details.

The site shows much rebuilding, as well as frequent minor changes in the substructures, entrances, and stairways. Sometimes as many as five separate layers were superimposed. Very heavy rear walls suggest the use of roof-combs, although the lack of débris indicates that these may have been dismantled later. One building (J-29) shows a narrow entrance hall and raised sanctuary reminiscent of Temple 22 at Copán. The vault seems not to have made its appearance here until quite late, roughly in the 7th century.

The terraced substructures at Piedras Negras are elaborate in plan with rounded and inset corners, raised panels, projecting buttresses, and coffered sections. Remnants of gigantic masks, one 4½ feet high and 9 wide, testify to the type of ornamentation.

The series of built-in platforms and carved "thrones" within the palaces indicate that these edifices served ceremonial purposes. There are no signs of fire or domesticity in them, while masonry platforms on the edge of the city suggest foundations there for the living quarters of the hierarchy.[120]

RÍO BEC

In the region of the New Empire, between the 7th and 10th centuries, an architectural style very different from that of the most splendid period of the Old Empire is evident. Changed environments and contact with other nations left their imprint on the Maya; besides, any artistic activity that lasts for centuries undergoes a natural evolution. Certain organic elements which had in the beginning functional importance became purely decorative. Technical difficulties which at first limited the expansion of architecture were eliminated, and the inclination and talent of the builder turned toward new possibilities and new problems.

Until recently the southeastern section of the Yucatan Peninsula was very little known. Maps published at the beginning of the present century still defined as "Territory of Independent Indians" the region which today covers parts of Yucatan and Campeche. In 1908 Maurice de Périgny found on the border between the states of Campeche and Quintana Roo an ancient city which he named Río Beque, after the stream that ran near by. In 1912 the Peabody Museum of Harvard University sent an expedition into the same territory under Dr. R. E. Merwin, seconded by Clarence L. Hay. Another group of ruins was found a quarter mile distant from that of Périgny and the two were distinguished from each other by calling them Río Bec A and B in the order of their discovery.

The newer site achieved considerable importance. *Pl. 28* shows the building of Río Bec B and a model of its theoretical reconstruction. The material is here rubble, faced with a veneer of precisely cut limestone, as is usual in Maya building, and the walls were covered with plaster, now present only in sparse fragments. But the difference in style when compared with that of the Early Period is seen at a glance. It does not stand on a monumental base. On three sides it rises directly from the ground and only in front of the entrance, which faces east, is there a terrace, in this case about 5 feet high and 35 long.

The structure is actually of the palace type, but the eye is deceived by its most outstanding feature, the two towers 55 feet high at the corners of the façade. In contrast to the tower in Palenque, these contain no rooms and their only function apparently is to serve monumentality. Huge masks of stone covered with stucco are applied on the frieze sections and above them rises a small roof-comb. A steep flight of stairs leads from the terrace straight up the face of each. The door at the top is blind, and the angle of the stairs (only eight degrees from the perpendicular) so sharp that even the Maya Indian with his wild-cat tread would have been unable to ascend them; only a bird could have hopped upon them.

Thus the imagination of the builders incorporated the old tradition of a steep substructure and a temple on top, complete with sculptured frieze and roof-comb, into their new style, transforming the former complex edifice into a purely decorative feature with little reduction of scale. Structure II at Horni-guero shows a similar artistic scheme. Such a monumental presentation as here pictured is rare, though we shall later see miniature replicas of dwelling houses used to embellish the façades of larger buildings, as at Labná and Uxmal.

To the side of and a little behind the towers, stone trellises, single vertical walls, stand side by side on the roof (*fig. b*). Unlike the roof-combs at Palenque, they do not run the entire length of the building; they comprise a decorative screen rather than the heavy double-walled "headdress" of the Old Empire. The human figures, over life size, applied in stucco, are effectively brought out against the perforated background. By comparing the roof-combs on the towers, which reproduced the earlier type, it will be seen that the screenlike constructions in the center of the building are deliberate modifications for a new effect.

The difference in length between the east and west sides, which are more than 84 feet long, amounts to only an inch. This accuracy may be taken as evidence of the technical skill of the Maya builder, and when a structure shows greater asymmetry, we may assume that the divergence was intentional.

There is an entrance on each of three sides, the back being a solid wall. Río Bec B contains six rooms. All are vaulted with the corbeled arch and are about 16 feet high, relatively spacious. The grille-work panels on either side of the doors, the high foundation incorporated as an integral part of the building, the absence of stone steps before the doorways are features which recur in other sites in Yucatan.

Since no stelae and little pottery have been found at Río Bec B, it is difficult to assign a date to it. Nevertheless, it can be roughly dated between the 8th and 10th centuries.

The site was characterized by enough individuality to attract further investigation. The next expedition relocated Río Bec A and added other important ruins to its survey, but the quarter mile which was given as the distance from one site to the other proved a vast one in the jungle, for Río Bec B has never been found again. The jungle is indeed a jealous guardian of its mysteries.[45]

On the threshold of the 11th century—and here it is impossible not to recall by contrast contemporary Europe with its barren gloomy buildings and its attenuated sculptures—the Maya civilization entered its final flowering, centered at this time in the northernmost part of the Yucatan Peninsula. Towns, hitherto provincial, attained importance and grew into artistic centers. The Toltecs, pressed by invasions in the north, were moving from the high plateau of Mexico, and their influence, both good and bad, becomes increasingly evident in the culture of Yucatan.

There can be no doubt that the era, which came into being with the League of Mayapán, brought new and noteworthy elements into Maya architecture. The flamboyant spirit that dominated the architecture of the Old Empire changes and, in many cases, the stylistic effects of the New seem, in comparison, calculated. New plastic figures are introduced into the decoration and there is a change in the general proportions of the buildings. We see rambling edifices replacing the tightly woven structures of the older regions and incidental ornament instead of systematic elaboration. These new building influences are apparent throughout Yucatan, as well as on the East Coast. The fact that they are often puzzlingly diverse and do not always seem to fit the general scheme of Toltec attributes may be ascribed to the presence of scattered tribes from southern Mexico, dislocated in the general out-surge.[154]

From a constructional point of view, many technical difficulties of the Old Empire were overcome, resulting finally in thinner walls and more spacious interiors. Probably the greatest innovation for the Maya Area was the introduction of the column, and its use as functional as well as decorative element should be noted. It was a relatively late achievement in pre-Columbian architecture. In the Mexican Area we have seen the great monolithic shafts at Mitla; the Huaxtec and Totonac regions also had columns, but put together from small chipped stones imbedded in mortar. Its use in the New Empire, however, was never universal, and it did not appear in Yucatan until long after the Maya had settled there. While nearly all the seacoast sites have this feature, only about ten of the very many investigated in other regions of Yucatan boast it.[67]

Had it been known to the builders of the Early Period, Maya architecture would have produced very different manifestations. But the time from its appearance to the arrival of the Spaniards was too short for a culture to revolutionize and transform the basic principles of its architecture. Besides solving the problem of space inside the building, it made wider entrances possible and was sometimes employed to support corners. Engaged, it furnished a new decorative motif for slenderizing the massive piers and breaking the wall surfaces.

The buildings of the New Empire were often very large, with many rooms arranged on several levels. Stairs were dramatically placed; from first to last, the imposing effect of the broad stairway remained one of the most characteristic features of Maya building. Portal arches came into use, and stone lintels sometimes replaced wooden ones, especially on the outside.

On the façades, geometric patterns appear, often the result of the conventionalization of symbolic animal shapes, and monster-masks, chiefly of the Rain-god with his projecting hooked snout, rise in tiers on walls or corners or decorate the panels above the entrances. The old and the newly acquired style elements were condensed, compressed into an ornamental system. The free-flowing curve of the old Maya is occasionally seen, but in general the designs are angular in line. Human figures appear as elements of decoration in the friezes, as atlantes holding cornices or altar tables (see *Pl. 93, fig. a*).

The general custom of erecting stelae at the termination of a definite time period had been abandoned in the Old Empire after 889, giving way, perhaps, to records in the form of manuscripts and codices. For this reason, the dating of the sites in the New Empire is at present often more precarious than in the older regions.

TULUM

Tulum, the principal settlement on the East Coast of Yucatan, was first described by Stephens, who tells in his lively yet exact manner how he and his companions battled there with impossible conditions, not the least of which was a plague of mosquitoes. The Temple of the Frescoes, discussed later, was stumbled upon by Mr. Catherwood and Dr. Cabot just as the party was packed and ready to turn its back on the infected spot. Unwilling to leave the new find unrecorded, they prolonged their stay until good drawings and a precise description could be made.

The first striking feature of the city is its situation. It lies at the edge of the sea on a precipitous cliff about 40 feet high that forms a natural wall 1300 feet long on one side (*Pl. 29, fig. a*). From the water, the site is imposing, and we may well suppose that Tulum was that "city as big as Seville" mentioned in the first reports of the *conquistadores*. Many important cities in Yucatan were fortified—an innovation in Maya city-planning, the result of the general conflict of the times.[67] Here we find not only the natural bulwark utilized for defense but a long stone wall about 20 feet thick and from 15 to 20 high built to inclose the city on the other three sides. (See also *Pl. 301, fig. b.*)

Archaeological evidence points to the colonization of the coast of Yucatan between the 5th and 7th centuries, and it would appear that by 560 Tulum was settled. Then comes a hiatus with no identifiable remains. The greatest period of Tulum seems to fall during the 13th and 14th centuries, and the great wall is dated early in that epoch.

The largest edifice, called the Castillo, is illustrated in *fig. b*. Including the two wings, it measures 100 feet across the base. Originally it appears to have been a rectangular structure of the palace type built on a low platform, the ends of which now form the two side wings. The ceiling is flat, laid on cross-beams in the manner used at Mitla, and composite round stone columns, capped with square abacuses, support the entrance. Later the center of this building was filled in to carry the weight of the upper edifice, and a grand stairway, 30 feet wide, was superimposed up the center of the still broader original steps. The heavy buttress at the back of the structure is also impressive.

The upper section is interesting for its bottle-shaped inner vaulting, common in Tulum and in some other East Coast sites, and for the entrance columns that represent a rattlesnake, with head recumbent and tail supporting the lintel and cornice. This is a new feature in Maya architecture, but as Chichén Itzá has the finest of the type, it will be illustrated there. (See *Pl. 40, fig. a* and *Pl. 42, fig. b.*) In the recesses above the doorway separate ornaments were placed. Two corridors, each 26 feet long, make up the interior of the building.

The other structure of special importance at Tulum is the Temple of the Frescoes that was discovered by Stephens's party. *Pl. 30, fig. a* shows the west, or main, façade, and *fig. b*, a model of the same, a little more from the side so as to include the hypothetical wooden stairway arrangement. This temple also went through several architectural transformations. The original contained one chamber only, about 7 feet by 11, three sides of which were later inclosed by a colonnaded passage so that now the façade measures 27 feet. Between the columns can be seen the remnants of frescoes on the main wall (once the outside), better preserved than most because of their protected position (see *Pl. 265, fig. b*). The upper room was a later addition.

Study of the profile, beginning with the low step on which the whole sturdy structure rests, reveals a remarkable difference in verticalities. This outline is governed in part by the bottle-shaped inner vault, the spring-line of which comes much lower than that of the usual corbeled arch of the earlier period. The outward slope of the exterior wall is actually an element of strength as it tends to balance the interior projection.

The sunken stucco panel over the doorway, with its figure of the Diving-god executed on a framework of stone, is a frequent feature in Tulum and other East Coast sites. Abundant mural painting also seems to have been common. Dr. Lothrop finds general similarities in the frescoes to the rendition of certain Maya codices. Another point of affiliation might be found in the recessed panels with broken or modified cornices, such as those at Monte Albán in which pottery figurines were set (see *Pl. 15, fig. d*). The plastic human features of the huge faces on the corners are as yet unrecorded elsewhere. Neatness of finish and the lavish use of color add up to a picturesque impression, in spite of the somewhat peripheral character of the decoration.

Fifty-four ruins have been counted within the walled inclosure of Tulum, as well as two small buildings, like watchtowers, on the walls. Beyond the barrier lie many more which have as yet never been approached or described.

These walls have been the scene of many battles. After the unrecorded fights of pre-Columbian days, the site was occupied three times by the troops of the Mexican Government in an attempt to subdue the independent Indians of the region. In this case the wall kept the invaders in, beleaguered from the side of the jungle by their intended quarry. Peace was made in 1913 and the rights of the natives were acknowledged. Since 1920 several chicle concessions have been granted in the district, one of which has established headquarters near the site of Tulum.

SAYIL

Approximately in the same geographical latitude as Tulum but across the peninsula in the western part of Yucatan lie the ruins of the great Palace of Sayil. According to tradition, the city was already a powerful center at the time of the founding of the League of Mayapán.

The edifice (*Pl. 31, fig. a*), one of the most spreading in Yucatan, measures 275 feet across the front and about 130 deep. It is made up of three tiers, each in turn set back and resting on a solid core well within the outer shell of vaulted chambers. A broad stairway at the front of the building leads to the top of the third story, and at the rear is another, a later addition. More than eighty rooms were counted in the one building, some over 30 feet in length and nearly 16 wide —an unusual span for the Maya corbeled arch.

The ground floor, now completely in ruins, may have been elaborately decorated (Stephens says so), while the top story apparently was left quite plain. This, however, serves to throw the finely proportioned second story into even sharper relief. Here the column, as decorative as well as functional element, is repeated and modulated, bringing to the essentially massive façade of Maya architecture an open, almost airy touch. The single shafts in the unusually wide openings are 6½ feet high, bulging at the center, and crowned with a square abacus. Compact rows of slender engaged columns make up what wall space there is. We have just seen the use of columns as entrance supports in smaller buildings at Tulum. Rather a technical solution there, here this architectural element is applied with greater freedom and subtlety and becomes the striking feature of the building.

Composite stone masks and other carvings are applied on the frieze in the center and over the two doorways. A lively serpent with gaping jaws and diminutive body can be identified, as well as a diving figure in the same posture as that at Tulum, here terminating in a square grotesque mask. The column motif is repeated between the carvings and separates the horizontal lines in the moldings.

It is possible that this suave motif, used here so effectively, was derived from the wood construction of the primitive houses of the common folk. These houses were usually built with a thatched roof and rounded ends and had only two doors, one on each long side, which furnished good ventilation.

Fig. b shows a present-day house, the wall of which, formed of small logs, harks back to ancient tradition. A number of suggestions for the graceful façade of the Palace of Sayil might have been derived from the forerunner of this type.

LABNÁ

Not far from Sayil are situated the ruins of Labná, a contemporary city. The Great Palace, the west section of which is illustrated in *Pl. 32, fig. b,* shows a certain similarity to Sayil, with its columnettes and masks, but even more to

Uxmal that will follow. It consisted of several stories and stands on a podium almost 20 feet high, about 400 long, and 250 deep, facing a vast plaza.

Groups of neatly tied columns in relief set off the doorways and are put to effective use at the corners. The serpent motif appears in a new interpretation in the vertical panels on the left. At the angle of the frieze (right center of picture) projects a serpent's head with gaping jaws from which a human head emerges. This is another favorite motif in northern Yucatan, notably in the much photographed fragment from Uxmal.

The stones of the composite frieze section are combined with much surface decoration, such as incised rosettes and frets in relief, which makes the work still more elaborate. At the base of the building appear short cylindrical elements, an endless spindle row.

The Labná Gateway (*fig. a*) furnishes an excellent example of the independent portal arch as used by the Maya in northern Yucatan. This photograph presents the side that faces the Palace court. The spring-line of the vault, on a level with the lower edge of the frieze, can be readily seen, and the eye follows the curving line of the rising stones to the top, where a broad but relatively thin slab bridges the gap. The span is about 13 feet. The lattice-work, scalloped zigzag motif, and stepped elements in the upper molding will be met frequently at other sites.

Above the two doorways, each of which leads to a small chamber, are replicas of the huts in which the populace lived. Shaped stones represent the peaked thatched roofs, even showing the ridgepole and the tuft above it. These niches, together with the doors and the tall arch, assist in producing a vertical effect rare in Maya building.

On the back, the Gateway is plainer and has no doorways. Two great composite frets decorate each side of the frieze with a pattern that is also used impressively on the Governor's Palace at Uxmal. (See *Pl. 36, fig. a.*)

Another view of Labná (*Pl. 33, fig. a*) shows the west façade of Structure XI of the Portal Group in the foreground, with a wall decoration of columnettes related to that shown on the preceding plate. The panels that appear on first glance to be masks are purely geometrical and are characterized by delicate tracery.

Beyond and above this structure, the sharp profile of another building demonstrates more clearly than any description the meaning of "flying façade." Here this highly decorative, unsupported construction rises on a line with the front wall to a height of 30 feet, and, according to Stephens, was covered with colossal figures and designs in stucco. At the neighboring site of Sabacche, a small temple (*fig. b*) has as its only ornament a flying façade with graceful lattice-work.

Fig. c takes us to Chichén Itzá, where the Red House (Casa Colorada) shows a more sturdy example, with mask panels flanked by frets as decoration. As in the preceding structure, the entire building is otherwise plain. A model (*fig. d*) offers a cross-section of the same edifice. It can be seen that in this case besides a flying façade there was a roof-comb, which was placed over the massive inner wall. The structure of the corbeled vaults is also well illustrated.

On cathedrals of the Late Romanesque in Europe a purely decorative screen-like wall serves similarly to enrich the building with sculptural and architectural embellishments.

KABAH

Kabah is a neighboring site which flourished at the same time as Labná and Sayil. The place is interesting, not so much for any structural differences it may present but on account of the splendid application of the mask as decorative feature.

Palace I at Kabah, a most unusual building, even among the great variety in Yucatan, stands on a low platform measuring over 150 feet across the front (*Pl. 34, fig. a*). It is in very bad condition and at one end has entirely collapsed, revealing a section of the inner structure, with smoothly dressed stone surfaces and a second narrower row of chambers behind the first. Remnants of a roof-comb, which Stephens describes as 15 feet high and 4 thick, are still visible, composed of well polished and evenly laid stone blocks that form an openwork step-fret.

A portion of the north wall about 25 feet long is in the best state of preservation (*fig. b*). Here we are confronted with an original idea. Six tiers of masks —one in the foundation, three in the middle wall, and two in the frieze—cover the surface of the building.

As a result of their serialization, the uniformity of the masks is more than usually apparent. Each shares ears and earplugs with its neighbor except in the bottom row, where each figure with its own two ears forms a broader unit than above, giving the illusion of greater weight at the base of the building and, incidentally, preventing a too rigid effect in the repetition.

Monotony is also avoided by the plastic contours of the individual masks. The curling snouts jut far beyond the façade. Each half of the face is composed on a semicylindrical unit, while the earplugs and lateral ornaments provide a flat vertical surface. The mouths are hollow, as are the eye sockets, and outlined by jagged teeth sharpened by the shadows behind them. The conical stones set into the cavities for eyeballs give the faces animation.

As there are no lines of demarcation between the rows of masks, the moldings produce the only horizontal trend in the façade. The medial molding especially is bold and elaborate, its scalloped and zigzag band ingeniously put together of smaller pieces of stone with space enough between to allow for the added play of light and shade on the pattern. This design impressed Stephens and Catherwood to such an extent that they used it on the binding of their *Incidents of Travel in Yucatan,* and in homage to these pioneer explorers it was also chosen to border the jacket of my first edition. As Stephens writes: "The cornice running over the doorways . . . , tried by the severest rules of art recognized among us, would embellish the architecture of any known era, and, amid a mass of barbarism, of rude and uncouth conceptions, it stands as an offering by American builders worthy of the acceptance of a polished people." [140]

MAYAPÁN

Mayapán, which was the religious and administrative center of the League of Mayapán, shows evidence of lengthy occupation, but most of its architecture seems to date from the early 13th century. An uncommon feature for Maya cities is the great wall, five and a half miles in length, which surrounded it.[150] Practically destroyed in the course of the devastating wars that ended its period of domination in 1461, the city fell into such complete ruin that even Stephens found little to be recorded. One circular building is reported to have stood until the early part of the 19th century, when it was struck by lightning and demolished.[109]

UXMAL

Certain legends place the beginnings of Uxmal in the 5th or 6th centuries and make it a center of the first Toltec immigrants to the region.

Pl. 35, fig. a pictures the highest structure on the site, called the House of the Dwarf, or Adivino, meaning "the soothsayer." The name is legendary and the same edifice is also known as the Temple of Kukulcán, the Maya name for the Great Feathered Serpent. The substructure measures some 240 feet long by 160 wide and rises at a very sharp angle to over 80 feet. Besides its height, the unusual elliptical form is immediately striking. Some of the even slabs are still in place, attesting to the skill with which the rounded corners were faced.

Two splendid stairways ascend on opposite sides. The broader one, said to have more than two hundred steps (see *Pl. 305, fig. a*), leads up the east face to the topmost platform, upon which stands a rectangular building with three chambers. It is interesting that the central room does not face the stair, as one might expect, but opens on the opposite side toward the west. From this vantage point the panorama of the Uxmal region opens up, a vast level expanse of jungle bush. The rounded contours of artificial mounds, overgrown and bristling with green, roughly mark the extent of the city. Depressions toward the northwest indicate the sites of former wells, now clogged with vegetation and dangerously infested with malaria.

Just in front of the doorway, another building, about 22 feet square, juts from the side, as if grafted onto the temple-base, its roof on a level with the upper esplanade. A narrower and perhaps even more precipitous stairway leads about two-thirds up the substructure to its entrance. In the interior, two chambers are set one behind the other, in the manner of Tikal. The façade of this temple, as well as the supporting walls, is a mass of elaborate composite stone ornamentation, showing an enormous mask above the doorway, flanked by tiers of smaller ones.[49] The broken surfaces of the decoration must have formed a stunning contrast to the smooth facing of the base and the austerity of the building above it.

The loftiness of the structure has led to the opinion that it was a sacrificial temple. Intact, in the full brilliance of its barbaric colors, with the splendid figures of its high priests moving on the stairways and along the narrow platform, it doubtless presented an impressive spectacle for the people gathered below.

Across a small court from this great pile lie four separate buildings of the palace type, grouped to form a square (left in *fig. a*). These were called by the Spaniards the House of the Nuns, a name derived, according to one version, from the cell-like chambers of the complex—ninety in all—and, to another, from the elaborate stone lattices of the friezes and the delicate carvings which reminded the conquerors of the lace work of their nuns. The entire complex stands on a large artificial platform, about 15 feet high, and the irregular inner court measures about 258 feet long by 214 wide.

After the visit of Fray Antonio de Ciudad Real to the "very renowned edifices of Uxmal" in 1588, he wrote the following description of the Nunnery.

"The jambs were of stone carved with great delicacy. On the façades of the building, both on those which face the plaza or courtyard, as well as on those which face outward, there are many figures of serpents, idols and shields, many screens or latticework and many other carvings which are beautiful and fine, especially if one look at them from a distance like a painting of Flanders, and they are all carved from the same kind of stone. In the middle of this building a great arch is made so that it takes in all the depth of this building and therefore it is the entrance to the courtyard or the above-mentioned plaza. It would appear that this entrance had been plastered and that on the plaster painting had been made in blue, red and yellow color, since even now some of them remain and can be seen." [124]

Each of the four buildings is quite different in ornamentation. Notable are the small models of houses set into the friezes of the north and south structures and, on the west building, the great serpents carved in the round that wind in and out of the pattern for the entire length of the façade, bringing animation to the geometric design of the frieze (*Pl. 36, fig. c*). The east building (*Pl. 37, fig. b*) is unusual in that the stone lattice-work runs around all four sides. The large V-shaped motifs, representing double-headed serpents, are subtly spaced in relation to the doors. A tier of Rain-god masks crowns the center entrance, and the corners bear superb masks of the same deity, so placed that the profile with the great hooked nose projects at the angle (*Pl. 36, fig. b*).

Each building is raised on its own podium, so that the towering flying façade of the north structure seems at a distance to merge with the comparatively low building opposite and to form a single colossal and magnificent façade (*Pl. 37, fig. a*).

South of the House of the Nuns, two crumbling parallel mounds indicate the site of a ball court. Beyond this lies an immense rectangular platform, about 600 feet long and 5 high. A second and smaller terrace with practically the same contours rises from this, like a gigantic tray, upon which is set, on the third and smallest podium, the House of the Governor (left, *Pl. 35, fig. b*). The name, like all the others at Uxmal, is a creation of the Spaniards, based rather on imagination than fact and inspired no doubt by its grandeur.

The plan of the structure falls into three parts: a central section and two wings, separated by two transverse arches, 20 feet high by 25 deep, now walled up (*Pl. 36, fig. a*). Eleven doorways break the façade. All the lintels were of *sapote* beams, 8 feet long, 18 to 20 inches wide, and 12 to 14 inches thick.

Stephens writes that at the time of his visit in 1839 nearly all the wood was in place, successfully supporting the great weight of stone above it,[140] but when we saw the site nearly a century later, many of the beams had fallen to decay, carrying part of the composite sculptured frieze with them and giving the building a dilapidated appearance. Since then, the Mexican Government has undertaken extensive conservation. In the opinion of many, the House of the Governor was the best preserved structure in the region even before the recent work began.

The lower part of the walls is faced with masterly cut stones, uniform in size and so skillfully shaped and joined that no mortar can be seen between them. The elaborate composite frieze, 10 feet high, runs all the way around the building, a distance of 720 feet.[49] Here the sculptured motifs are arranged into a gigantic counterpoint. Coffered frets on a lattice ground follow one pattern, and a line of masks in an immense meander crosses and recrosses them. The serpent bars appear, supporting rows of glyphs—rare in Uxmal—and small human figures crown the doorways.

At the right and somewhat behind the Governor's Palace, on a sort of spur of the second terrace, stands a very dilapidated building called the House of the Turtles, from the realistic carvings of this reptile worked into the upper cornice (center foreground, *Pl. 35, fig. b*). The sole decoration of the frieze consists of a row of engaged columns in corduroy effect, also seen at Sayil and Labná.

Roughly west of this group an impressive serrated roof-comb with nine gables looms over the thick vegetation (right background). This belongs to the north building of another quadrangle group, now practically demolished. The edifice bears the name of the House of the Doves, as the perforations suggest a dovecote. The manner of construction, however, and the stones projecting at various points indicate that it was a backing for an elaborate stucco relief, remnants of which were noted by Stephens. A transverse arch divides the structure, forming an entrance to the inner court, as in the Nunnery. The entire north wall has collapsed, revealing an interesting cross-section of Maya vault construction.

This patrician city, Uxmal, is characterized by its homogeneity. Although not ranged in streets, the buildings are well placed in relation to each other. The whole city was set on artificial platforms, and the courts and connecting ways were paved with finely polished cement. A native limestone of soft yellow or pinkish-gray tone was used throughout. The masonry is of uniformly fine finish, and excellent craftsmanship is also shown in the careful treatment of the foundations and in the delicate fillet-moldings. Although familiar elements are used in the composite carved decorations, the effect is varied and individual. The broad entablature sections generally cover almost half the wall space and, with their boldly projecting cornices, dominate the façade like splendid feather headdresses.

CHICHÉN ITZÁ

The name, Chichén Itzá, meaning "the mouth of the wells of the Itzá," has reference to the two natural pools, or *cenotes,* within the confines of the settlement, a factor which made the site invaluable in a region where there is no surface water.

The buildings of Chichén are the most understandable for the European-trained eye. They have about them a certain lightness that has not been met before. The architectural line is less complicated; the ornament, considerably simplified and more sparingly used. It would be difficult to define how much of this was due to outside influence and how much to the natural evolutionary development through the thousand or more years which are covered by Maya architecture. The divergence and variety of ornamental detail are proof of the constantly moving spirit which urged the Maya builders onward during the centuries.

Chichén Itzá shows great diversity in building types. Some features, familiar from the Old Empire, reappear here used with assurance, while other early characteristics are found diluted in concept. On the other hand, vigorous new elements make their appearance to take their place beside the old. The Nunnery (*Pl. 38*), the Red House (*Pl. 33*), and the House of the Three Lintels (*Pl. 39*) are identified as belonging to that early era when the great cities of the Old Empire were still thriving. From the late 10th to the 13th centuries many new edifices were erected. By then new technical achievements had greatly reduced the time necessary to complete a single building.

During and after this period, Chichén Itzá was a great pilgrim center. One of its *cenotes* was deemed sacred to the Rain-god, and on certain days of the year, particularly in a time of drought, tribes from far and near came to petition favor for their crops. As a part of the ceremony, young girls and boys, festively attired and adorned with jewels, were sacrificed as messengers to the deity. Diving activities instituted by the late E. H. Thompson brought up jade, turquoise mosaics, gold and copper bells, copal incense, and fragments of unidentified objects which had been flung into the pool as offerings.[149]

As Chichén Itzá has been the most thoroughly investigated of all Maya sites within recent years, we shall confine ourselves, because of limited space, to the main features of architecture interesting from our point of view—that of the art-historian. For further information, we direct the reader to the various publications on the excavations.

Among the structures to be discussed here, the Nunnery (*Pl. 38, fig. a*) is generally classified as the oldest. It is, perhaps, the most massive of them all, not only in the actual stone involved but in its compact appearance. The substructure consists of a huge solid block, 228 feet across the front, 115 deep, and 32 high. Its chief grandeur is the monumental stairway, 56 feet wide, which, at the time of subsequent alteration, was continued across the face of the original structure to a new edifice on top. Maudslay shows that the balustrades were once embellished by a line of projecting sculptured shapes, like conventionalized tongues, curling at the lower ends.[81] The original building, which is of the palace type, has a slanting entablature section, reminiscent of Palenque, but here left unornamented, while the walls below it carry the decoration. The enlargement was effected by filling in the central hall of this building so as to support the weight of the second smaller structure above it.

On the ground level, to the east of the substructure (left in the illustration), are a wing and two separate annexes, which, from their decoration, are judged to be from about the same period as the main block. *Fig. b* shows the façade of this L-shaped wing, some 35 feet wide and covered with elaborate masks. The ornate moldings, the upper quite different from the lower, are so heavy that the entablature section seems to overhang the lower walls. Even the flaring coping stones are carved.

The treatment of the doorway, which suggests a serpent's head, is strikingly original. In the center of the frieze and within a sort of aureole is a seated statue with flowing feather headdress. Two serpents form a frame about him. Colors originally enhanced the effect. In this entrance with all its details, we feel a liveliness akin to that of Romanesque stone work in Europe.

Of the two unattached annexes which complete the complex, the one visible at the right in *fig. b,* called the *Iglesia,* or "church," is the smaller but by far the more lavishly decorated. It is about 38 feet by 14 and 20 feet high. With its walls leaning slightly outward and the lower surface a band of plain masonry, the structure seems top-heavy with carving.

About three miles from the Nunnery, in Chichén Viejo, or Old Chichén, stands the House of the Three Lintels, surrounded now by jungle bush (*Pl. 39, fig. b*). This serene little palace is built without platform on a low foundation ornamented with lattice-work. As the level of the floor is about three feet from the ground, it has been suggested that wooden steps or a short ladder was used for the ascent to the doors. The three entrances, two of which have stone lintels inscribed with carving, lead into separate vaulted chambers. The middle wall section is plain, as is usual in the later period, and an engaged column is set at each corner. A snake motif, the same zigzag that delighted Stephens at Kabah, runs all the way around the house, bringing a welcome contrast in the otherwise restrained ornamentation.

The structure has variety in its horizontal and vertical lines and must be visualized as strongly colored. The Maya architect took the effects of *plein-air* into full consideration, reckoning with the brilliant lighting of the tropics to show off his building to advantage.

The Caracol (*Pl. 39, fig. a*), one of the rare round buildings of the Maya Area, dates from the Mexican period of the city. It was probably connected with the rites of the Wind-god, Kukulcán, just as the round structures of Mexico are associated with his Mexican counterpart, Quetzalcóatl.[109] At the same time, it is possible that the building may have served as an observatory. Inside, two vaulted circular galleries inclose a masonry core, within which lies the spiral ascent that gives the building its name—"snail shell" or "winding stairway." There is a small chamber on top, now almost in shambles, with a stone-lined passage facing due west. Carefully checked investigations have shown that a diagonal drawn from the right jamb of the inner door to the left one of an outside aperture marks the line along which the sun sets on March 21st and September 23rd, or the vernal and autumnal equinoxes.[117]

The tower itself measures 36 feet in diameter and about 43 in height. Skillfully posed on its two irregular platforms, it reveals an architectural maturity that recalls the famous round structures of Rome and Ravenna. Visually its most arresting feature aside from its form is a five-part molding, the double flaring bands of which seem to be tied in by the fillet, as if by a ribbon. A fringe of serpents and figures in panels constituted other ornamentation on the walls. Around the edge of the upper terrace, incense burners in the form of human heads with hollow eyes and mouths were set along the coping. We can visualize the tower as it stood intact in the velvety tropical night, its curving walls illumined by the glow of burning copal.

The sacred ball game played an important part in the life of this religious center. Chosen from among the physically outstanding youths, the ball players were accorded special privileges, and, when victorious, were overwhelmed with gifts from the ruler and nobility. The great Ball Court (*Pl. 40, fig. b*), 120 feet wide and flanked by two massive walls, 274 feet long by 28 high, formed an impressive stadium. Compare the different types of ball-court construction at Monte Albán (*Pl. 14*), Copán (*Pl. 20*), and Chichén Itzá to see how the game varied.

On one end of the east wall, which forms a narrow esplanade in front of it, and overlooking the Court, stands the Temple of the Tigers (*fig. a*)—the only one of this complex to be reconstructed. A corner is visible at the extreme right of the lower illustration. The name derives from the confused Spanish term *tigre;* the "Temple of the Jaguars" would be more exact, as there were no tigers in America. The only opening of the temple is toward the arena, and the approach is by way of an insignificant stair at one side. In front there is very little space, and we may surmise that the building was used only in ceremonies connected with the game—perhaps a box for the hierarchy.

The profile of the building is quite different from that which we have grown accustomed to regard as typically Maya. Carved serpent bodies cling to the edge of the podium and their gaping heads project from the balustrade. The large stone blocks that strengthen the corners and the high battered base of the temple building extending almost halfway up the sides of the doorway are rather suggestive of Mitla. Two massive serpent columns divide the entrance, their heads resting on the floor, while the bodies rise vertically beneath the lintel and the tails curve first forward and then upward across the façade, terminating in a fantasy design of conventionalized rattles and plumes. They were once brightly painted and their deep-set eyes inlaid with obsidian or some colored substance. The plumes of the tail hide part of the carved frieze, which was, nevertheless, completely worked out.

The entablature section is not so sharply differentiated here as in most Maya buildings. A fine carved frieze of jaguars, approaching a circular shield in groups of two, extends clear around the building. Although the same motif is continuously repeated, the movement of the beasts is not stereotyped but fluent and differentiated enough to give a realistic impression. A similar motif, but executed with less distinction, was unearthed among the débris at Monte Albán.[24]

The jaguar frieze is framed by bands, upon which plumed serpent bodies intertwine about a row of symbolic disks. Above this, the entire upper portion is set back, a crest adorned with conventional snake designs, panels of disks, and small "spindle" columnettes. Maudslay speaks of an open fretwork, no longer extant, around the top of the building and a central ornament of three crossed arrows bound with a ribbon—a Mexican symbol.

Within there is a vaulted antechamber and an inner room, the stuccoed walls of which were covered with frescoes in lively yellow, red, brown, and blue, today almost obliterated (see *Pl. 263*). The jambs of the doorways consist of square engaged pillars, intricately carved in relief with figures in ceremonial dress.

The Temple of the Tigers is a shining example of the deliberation and assurance with which the Maya builders even of a late period used the decorative motifs handed down to them.

El Castillo (*Pl. 41*), sometimes called the Temple of Kukulcán, faces the straight lane that leads to the Sacred Well. The nine receding terraces that make up the substructure, some 75 feet high, successively diminish in height and the coffered design on each—suggestive of Monte Albán—is reduced proportionately. This subtle method of handling the terraces gives the whole structure an effect of lightness as well as exaggerated height. The stairways, extending beyond the base in typical Maya fashion, serve to emphasize the remarkable feeling that the building is rooted in the ground and stands poised like a tree. Two feet wider at the top than at the bottom, they appear even steeper than they are. (See *Pl. 304, fig. a*.)

A system of numbers is involved in the architecture. On each side of the temple-base, using the stairway as a dividing line, are two sets of nine terraces; this adds to eighteen, the number of months in the Maya calendar. There are four flights of ninety steps each, or three hundred and sixty in all, the number of days in the Maya year, as the short "month" of five days, used to balance the time-count, was considered unlucky and not "recognized."

The temple building itself is constructed with a heavy battered base. The entablature section no longer receives major attention and is adorned only by masks above each door. There are four entrances, oriented approximately to the four directions, with the broadest on the north divided by two gigantic serpent columns such as were seen in the Temple of the Tigers. Here, as well as in a number of other buildings at Chichén, a sort of fretwork rises out of the edge of the coping. The lintels were of *sapote* wood, all visible parts decorated with a delicate tracery of figures.

The pre-Maya temple-base at Uaxactún and the Toltec-Maya El Castillo both apply four stairways mounting the sides of a pyramidal construction. They

ARCHITECTURE

are among the first and last creations of a continuously developing style which fed nevertheless from the same deep roots.

The interior arrangement of the temple of El Castillo offers a departure from the old. It is obvious that new conditions demanded greater interior space; the ritual was expanding, the cast becoming more numerous. The inner sanctuary, flanked by narrow galleries, is made more spacious by the use of three vaults supported on heavy *sapote* beams, which in turn were held by two massive carved pillars on a line with the door jambs.

Within the substructure of the Castillo were found almost intact a smaller base with only one stairway and a temple which had been filled in with rubble and covered when the new building was erected over it. The floor of the present structure is only three feet above the roof of the old. At the heart of the buried building, the jaguar throne illustrated on *Pl. 92* was discovered.

With its four similar sides the Castillo is the most dramatic building in Chichén Itzá. Its effect, however, is far beyond the theatrical; it was erected not for a passing night's entertainment, but for the eternal stage of Nature.

East of the Castillo lies a vast irregular quadrangle called the Court of the Thousand Columns. It was encompassed by a covered colonnade, roofed, like the inner sanctuary of the Castillo, by a series of vaults resting on beams. The square pillars which supported these were carved and brightly painted with life-size figures of armed warriors. The single profiles are individual, the movements varied, the costumes diverse, showing that even in a period of heightened activity no stencil was used for the designs. Enough color remains to give not only an idea of the dress and weapons of those days but also of the magnificence of this great open hall.

Standing on a spur of the colonnade, the Temple of the Warriors (*Pl. 42, fig. a*) represents the last high architectural period in Chichén Itzá. The resources of the Carnegie Institution of Washington and the ingenuity of its staff have made it possible to reconstruct this building out of a heap of débris.

Its stairway leads in an unbroken line through a cleverly constructed well in the colonnade vaulting to the top, where again, before a wide entrance, colossal serpent columns rise. Snake bodies are suggested on the ramps and terminate in fierce projecting heads. On each side of the stair at the top, small warrior statues stand with outstretched hands, the standard-bearers of ancient times, and before the portal reclines a sculptured figure of the type called Chacmool (see *Pl. 93, fig. b*).

As a result of the transformation in building technique, the temple, which has been reconstructed without the entablature zone and roof, is larger and more nearly square than earlier ones. Its walls are less massive than those of older buildings. Rain-god masks figure in the façade (*fig. b*), and serpents' heads in the round project from the plain wall surfaces with their spreading feather collars carved in relief.

The two chambers of the interior are about the same size, 61 feet by 29. In the first, the roof was supported by three transverse vaults; in the inner one, by five, placed at right angles to the others. Both rooms seem to have been painted with bright dadoes or impressive scenes (see *Pl. 263, fig. a*). Built-in masonry benches were revealed and altar slabs supported by small atlantean sculptured figures. During reconstruction, an earlier smaller temple was discovered, which had been filled in when the Temple of the Warriors was built.[94]

Chichén Itzá presents many changes in traditional Maya construction. Although the buildings became less massive, and therefore less durable, the interior space was greatly enlarged. The general outline acquires a plainer, more austere character. Decoration becomes diluted and more incidental. The style reminds one now of the Old Empire, now of the Mexican high plateau, now of the Zapotec region.

All this is an indication rather of transition than of degeneration. Although at the time of the Conquest such imposing cities as Uxmal and Chichén seem to have been deserted and Maya genius appears to have been at a low point, this does not necessarily mean a complete extinguishing of their creative and artistic capabilities. Just as in the Old World long periods of artistic stagnation were relieved by upward trends, in the land of the Maya their glorious tradition might have recovered enough to produce somewhere a third empire, had it not been torn asunder by impact with European civilization.

INTERLYING AREA

The present political boundaries of the Central American countries do not coincide with the prehistoric confines of their native peoples. East and south of the Guatemala border are the republics of Honduras and El Salvador. There the influence of the Maya and of the later migrants from southern Mexico, generally called the Pipils, is strongly visible, not so much in their scant architectural remains as in pottery and jade. Farther down, in Nicaragua, Costa Rica, and Panama, this gives way. The proximity of these lands to the South American continent made them more susceptible to tendencies from the south.

Architectural remnants of high artistic quality have not been found in these Isthmian regions up to the present day. It is possible that ruins of considerable importance may be discovered after further excavation. However, the *conquistadores* make no mention of any monumental architecture here comparable to that in the other areas.

In the applied arts, these people achieved much of consequence. A very positive artistic trend is prevalent in the pottery of all these countries and in the excellent metal-work wherever it appears.

ANDEAN AREA

The ruins of the Andean Area are concentrated chiefly in what is today Peru. In the coastal regions where there was much sand and clay, great edifices were constructed of adobe brick and clay blocks. In the mountains, stone, dressed and laid with amazing precision, was generally used.

While terraced substructures are the rule on the coast, in the highlands the temples and palaces rise from the ground. Nor do the remnants indicate exclusively buildings of religious or hieratic character. There are, in addition, fortified community dwellings of a type more advanced than found in the Southwest, and outspoken citadels appear both in the highlands and the coastal regions. Defense walls, infrequently met in any of the other areas, are a familiar feature here. The architectural differences between the ruins of the coastal regions from Ecuador to Chile and those in the mountain valleys and promontories of the Andes show how many tribes were working their way simultaneously toward a higher civilization when the coördinating skill of the Incas finally brought the whole territory under one head.

Most of the illustrations for this section will show structures built of perfectly shaped stone blocks, fitted with inexplicable skill without the use of mortar. Adobe and clay were also used, as well as rough stone laid in clay.

Bonded and locked joints are the rule here. Even in early phases of Tiahuanaco, copper cramps were employed. In some places, a sort of interior lock was fashioned, by means of which a groove in one block fitted over a corresponding protuberance in the other. All of these methods are especially efficacious in an earthquake region—as is the lack of mortar—and may account for the astonishing state of preservation of many of the ruins today.

The Andean Area brings a perfected line in the construction of rounded walls and corners, producing in many cases semicircular inclosures and even complete circles, as in the burial towers. The window, virtually non-existent in the Mexican and Maya areas although used in the Southwest, is also rare here, but niches of many types are frequent.

The less pretentious buildings, the huts of the common people, were put together of wood, reed, or adobe in the coastal regions, and of adobe, chipped stone, or stone blocks with and without mortar in the mountains. The roofs seem generally to have been thatched. The simple one-family dwelling remained throughout pre-Columbian times a modest abode. The great achievements of architecture in the Andean Area are the temples, palaces, and fortresses, which were at the same time the quarters of the priesthood, the nobility, civil and military officials, and their attendants.

After having seen the masterpieces of architecture in the Mexican and Maya areas, with their sometimes graceful, sometimes grandiose, always eloquent structures, one cannot escape the impression that Andean architecture is comparatively uncommunicative. In construction of their buildings, the talent of these intensely organized people was earthbound; nor did they often aspire to lavish and flamboyant decoration.

CHAN-CHAN

The northernmost section of the coastal region formed in pre-Inca times a kingdom, very rich and far advanced in the arts. Spanish historians tell us that the sovereign of these people was called the Grand Chimú, and that they were subdued by the Incas about four generations before the Conquest.

The first illustration on *Pl. 43* shows the ruins of the Chimú city, Chan-Chan, probably settled during the period between 800 and 1000, where the rivers Chicama and Moche form a very arable plain. It adjoins the present city of Trujillo, founded by Francisco Pizarro and named for his own birthplace in Spain.

The great extent of the ruins is evidence of the importance of Chan-Chan, which authorities accept as the capital of the wealthy Chimú people. The city covers about eleven square miles with four clearly defined "suburbs," or outlying districts, all encompassed by a high wall (see also *Pl. 302, fig. b*). It is constructed of adobe, which in the arid climate attained an almost concrete-like hardness. Districts of low rectangular houses alternate with vast terraced temple mounds, several hundred feet long and sometimes as much as 150 high.[139]

Irrigation for the cultivation of the land was highly developed. High in the mountains, an aqueduct led off the water of the Moche River and carried it along the valley on a lofty embankment, some sixty feet high, whence it was distributed into reservoirs and through smaller stone-lined channels across the plains. There were extensive gardens within the city itself, each with its irrigating canal.[77]

It is lamentable that time and treasure hunters have so devastated the city that it is difficult now to form an adequate picture of it. The enormous terraces upon which the temples stood are crumbling away, haphazardly tunneled through by reckless despoilers. The stuccoed and painted walls are in ruins. The roofs are gone, the verandas, once supported by the twisted trunks of trees, have vanished.

Fig. b shows a detail of the ornamentation applied on an adobe wall here. It is noteworthy that the patterns were always of small format and similar to the decorative motifs of the pottery, weaving, and metal-work. A Chimu design has always so much individuality that seldom can it be mistaken for one of another culture. The arabesques are made up chiefly of geometric elements, often conventionalized forms of birds and fish. The continuous flowing quality of the decoration shows perfection of technique, and by a change of pattern and composition in the more involved schemes, a monotonous effect is avoided.

PARAMONGA

The ruins of Paramonga (*Pl. 44*) lie at the southern end of the Chimú Kingdom, a few miles in from the ocean, occupying strategically a key position. For this reason, the name La Fortaleza, "the fortress," is most fitting. The adobe complex crowns the summit of a hill, rising in terraces, each of which is surrounded by a wall of clay. Four bastions that take advantage of the natural contours of the hill guard the corners. The greatest exterior length is 900 feet, while the innermost wall measures 600. Within the fort there are the remains of rectangular houses separated by narrow passageways.[139] An outer wall—which would today be called the first line of defense—encircles the entire structure. Remnants of this are most clearly seen in the foreground and in the upper right of the photograph.

The renowned scholar of Andean cultures, Philip Ainsworth Means, caught the spirit of the place when he wrote: "Dead and abandoned though it is now, it fills the beholder with the realization of the defiant pride of its builders; bristling . . . with a well-armed garrison provided with spears and spear-throwers, with bows and arrows, with stones and slings, with maces, clubs, and knives of copper, bronze, silver and gold, arrogant with banners, a-shout with battle-cries, it must indeed have presented itself as a redoubtable obstacle to further progress northwards. . . ."[84]

The fortress was taken by the Inca, Pachacutec, under whose leadership the Empire attained its greatest extent, power, and wealth in the early 15th century. With the fall of Paramonga, the Chimú people came under the sway of the Incas.

Yet, when we look at La Fortaleza, we can well forget the details of its past. Its commanding position, its thick walls, and jutting bastions speak an intercontinental language. It is the romantic fortress without locality, race, or age. From its protruding angles a valiant fight could have been waged against superior numbers of medieval warriors anywhere.

LA CENTINELA

The territory of the Chimú Kingdom terminated on the south around the fortress of Paramonga. Beyond lie a number of fertile valleys watered by rivers that empty into the Pacific. There is evidence that these regions also were inhabited from a very remote period. Proof of the dense population lies in the remains of extensive irrigation works that in some cases exhausted the river water before it reached the sea.[84]

In the Central Coast regions, interesting cultures are found in the valleys of Ancón, Chancay, and Rímac, where there are numerous architectural remains. Especially noteworthy is the site Pachacámac, the ruined walls of which once carried splendid polychrome fresco designs.[160]

On the South Coast the chiefs banded together in what is known today as the Chincha Confederacy, but the organization was not so closely knit as that of the Chimú. Their pottery and other applied arts prove that commercial intercourse existed not only with their immediate neighbors but also with the north and the highlands.

Means believes the Chincha Valley to have been an urban center comparable to Chan-Chan in the north, and, together with the Ica Valley, to have been the seat of the culture known as Ica, or Late Nazca, between 900 and 1400. As the territory of the Chincha Confederacy lay nearer the original realm of the Incas, it was subjugated earlier than the Chimú Kingdom, and the remains at

ARCHITECTURE

La Centinela, the largest and most prominent of the adobe ruins here, are representative of both pre-Inca and Inca periods.

This ruin measures some 1060 feet by 500, and in places attains a height of 50 feet. In its midst rises an irregular terraced temple-base (center, *Pl. 45, fig. a*), entirely surrounded by spreading palaces on platforms of varying heights. The general outline of the original construction is difficult to ascertain because of the havoc wrought by rain, earthquakes, and treasure hunters. Besides, as the ancient adobe bricks are far harder than new ones, they bring a price ten times as high in the market. Another destructive factor lies in the large crosses hung with the votive offerings of pilgrims, which have been erected on commanding points among the ruins. As some are nearly thirty feet high, they require a solid foundation, for which the material close at hand has been utilized. Walls were destroyed and levels disturbed so that it is now often impossible to trace the original lines of a building.[161]

Although the adjoining palace (*fig. b*) is of adobe, it shows the influence of Inca architecture. The most interesting characteristic of the structure is the niches, which, used in a building identified as late, probably date from a time when Inca domination had penetrated to this point. The hole to the right is recent and fortunately superficial, the work of treasure-seeking excavators who apparently gave up on reaching the sand at the heart of the adobe construction.

Niches have been found elsewhere in medieval America, fashioned of chipped stone in the kivas of the Southwest and hewn from the solid rock at Malinalco. We have mentioned niche-like constructions at Tajín, Labná, Uxmal, Mitla, and shall see many in Inca buildings in the highlands constructed of stone blocks. The niches at La Centinela are found in interior as well as exterior walls and consist of several types: large ones rising immediately from the floor; medium ones, resembling windows; small ones, either vertical or horizontal. The sides and back walls were whitewashed and some are double-framed with painted decorations. Objects which may have served religious purposes were found in a few.

Inside, the palace is divided into systems of galleries and chambers, with open courts and broad stairs that point to ceremonious living. Traces of wall-paintings show geometric patterns in red, black, and green, producing a decorative effect similar to that of our many-colored papers or stenciled walls. The indications of canals and reservoirs inside the palaces help one to imagine the pompous scale of life as it was lived here before the Conquest, with plants and flowers embellishing the buildings.

Although powerful cultures flourished farther south on the coast, whatever ruins remain are buried under shifting sands and give no noteworthy impressions. The Nazca Valley was an ancient focal point of culture because of its unfailing water supply. But early Nazca architecture is virtually unknown; the name is most often mentioned in reference to its pottery and textiles. The artistic characteristics of the district extend to neighboring valleys.[84]

The Paracas Peninsula, situated about a hundred miles north of the Nazca region, should also be mentioned here, although it owes its greatest fame to its excavated textiles, which reveal great variety and technical superiority.

Southward along the shores of the Pacific is found a strip of coast extending as far as present-day Chile that apparently did not support a dense population even in pre-Columbian times. Its aboriginal inhabitants were fisher folk, who used *balsas,* or floats, of inflated sealskin.[77] Neither legendary history nor minor arts of greater interest are evident.

It would appear then that below the Nazca and Paracas centers, the wave of civilization slowed down, and for further significant Andean cultures we must turn inland to the mountains. Here, especially around the shores and islands of Lake Titicaca, which today marks the border of Peru and Bolivia, there are early architectural remains of great importance.

TIAHUANACO

Lake Titicaca is a large body of water, 120 miles long and 40 wide, lying high in the Andes at an altitude of over 12,500 feet. The ruins of Tiahuanaco, situated near its shores, are considered among the earliest in the highland region and constitute another important center of pre-Columbian culture which developed at an exceptional altitude. The name is apparently of no great antiquity. The story goes that an Inca visiting the site, ancient even in his day, received a message there brought by a runner. Pleased with the young man's speed, he called him to rest, saying, *Tia, huanaco,* "Be seated, guanaco," giving to him in compliment the name of the fleetest of the llama group.[77]

The site of Tiahuanaco reveals several periods besides the final Inca. Classic Tiahuanaco is associated with the use of lava pillars and blocks and copper cramps for bolting the masonry together. This was followed by the Decadent Tiahuanaco period, in which stones from earlier buildings were reused in a cruder style.[8]

The most conspicuous and artistically important of the ruins at Tiahuanaco is the great monolithic gateway, generally called the Gateway of the Sun (*Pl. 46, fig. a*). Cut from a single piece of extremely hard trachyte, rather dark in color, it stands 7 feet 2 inches high, 13 feet 2 inches wide, and 18 inches thick. The stone is dressed with precision, its lines are perfectly drawn, and the right angles turned with absolute geometric accuracy. An elaborate carving decorates the upper part, while the wall space below is plain, except for two carefully cut niches. How the prehistoric workmen of the site were able to quarry, transport, and carve a stone of such mass in such a finished manner is an unanswered question.

Applied like an ornate headband, the sculptured section shows one principal figure as center of the composition (*fig. b*). He is presented in an elaborate tunic with a girdle embellished with puma heads. Means identifies him as Viracocha, the Creator-god, supreme deity of the highland folk.[84] The large square face framed by a radiating headdress is the most sharply defined element. A number of symbols, which may be part of a mask, are incised on the face, and round tears course down the carved cheeks, apparently typifying rain. The two highly conventionalized objects held in the hands are balanced in composition, though different in detail. One seems to represent a spear-thrower, the other, in the left hand, a quiver containing two darts. Standing on a terraced platform, with snake heads curling at the foot, he is attended by forty-eight personages of smaller size. The low relief in which they are carved stresses their subordination. These minor figures consist, in the first and third rows, of winged men, bearing staffs or spears and wearing tufted headdresses; in the middle row, they are personified birds, wearing cloaks, with their crested heads held high, in a similar arrangement. The deep carving of the eyes, like those of Viracocha, suggests inlay. Below the group runs a horizontal band composed of sun medallions set in an interesting version of the fret.

The little figures are either running toward or kneeling before the Creator-god—their posture, with ambiguously spread feet, might be explained either way. In contrast to their active pose, Viracocha stands on his pedestal in static immobility. The objects which the attendants hold divide the flowing horizontal rows into squares, forming vertical divisions throughout the design—like vigorous beats in a musical composition. The rhythm, even if strange, must impress us with its virility.

We understand this carving better if we look at it as a symbolic expression of cosmic order. The fact must not be lost sight of that this art was created and kept within prescribed limits, spiritually and technically, by the formalism of a hierarchic and religious culture that apparently became crystallized at a very early period. From this time on, the iconography of these figures is so fixed that they are easily recognizable in the pottery, fabrics, and metal-work of a number of Andean cultures.

The west side of the Gateway has no sculptural embellishment, but a number of deep carved niches were chiseled into the walls, some of which seem to have been fitted with doors. The inset doorway with its suggestion of a lintel is interesting.

The Gateway of the Sun stands in the northeast corner of a large inclosure, called the Calasasaya, which measures 440 feet on its longest side and is constructed of upright pillars with smaller blocks set in between. On the opposite side of the same complex is a fine stairway of six monumental steps hewn from massive blocks of lava. An enormous natural mound lies to the south, nearly 700 feet on a side, and faced with cut stone. Other doorways, also carved from single pieces of stone, have been found in the vicinity.[84]

The Gateway is identified as Classic Tiahuanaco, which falls between A.D. 600 and 900. As stone is the chief medium of architecture in the highlands, the locations and influences of Tiahuanaco can be traced over a widespread area. After 900 this fountain of culture began to lose its vitality, and new trends emanating from the Incas later become noticeable.

TITICACA REGION

Before leaving this section, however, we must view another type of building, the *chulpa,* or burial tower, usually rectangular but occasionally round in shape. The material of some of these is adobe, of others, uncut stone laid in clay, or large stone blocks set without mortar. These structures occur in a wide range, extending from the region of La Paz to the outskirts of Lima.[84]

Figs. a and *b* on *Pl. 47* show *chulpas* situated near Lake Titicaca. The first are Inca in style, the second, Classic Tiahuanaco. The round tower on the left (*fig. b*) is 39 feet high and 16 in diameter, widening as it rises so that at the spring of the dome, the diameter is nearly 5 feet greater than at the base. The cornice, 3 feet wide and somewhat protruding, seems to bind in the flaring line. The material is hard compact basalt, admirably cut, laid in almost even courses, and beautifully fitted. The largest of the stones, near the ground, is 5 feet high. To lift blocks of such dimensions to position without pulleys somewhat the same method may have been used that is still seen in some Latin American countries—

a rampart of earth is piled up beside the building and the heavy stones are pushed to the desired place upon it.

The low narrow entrance opens upon a vaulted chamber, 12 feet high and 10 in diameter. The ceiling of corbeled construction was once stuccoed, and in the center of it is an opening which leads to a smaller upper room, also with circular vault. Here human remains and pottery sherds were found at the time of exploration in 1877. All the *chulpas,* however, had been ransacked for centuries, the floors dug up, and the walls pried into, so that there is no record of the type of burial they contained.[139] The building on the right in *fig. b* shows where stones have been carried away since the Conquest.

Besides the technical skill displayed in the construction of these towers, we feel a radiation of considerable dignity. Where the dead were so honored, their spiritual bequest must also have been venerated. The *chulpas* of Sillustani are said to have come down from pre-Inca times, perpetuated legends. At the same time, they might be called the forerunners of Inca architecture, which in later centuries rose to grandeur.

CUZCO

We now reach the confines of the domain of the Incas, later so powerful. These people seem to have descended from one of the mountain tribes in the region near Cuzco or Ollantaytambo, some thirty miles to the northwest. They cultivated maize and potatoes as their staple foods and tended herds of llamas. After the decline of the Tiahuanaco culture, they rose to power, gradually gaining new strength and experience for their future expansion.[84]

Historically and geographically, the region around Cuzco and the valley of the Urubamba River with its tributaries remained the heart of the Inca Empire even at its height. Geographical conditions made this country with its perennial water supply a cultural center—one of the most important from an architectural point of view in medieval America.

Cuzco itself, the capital of the Inca Empire at the time of the Conquest, lies a few miles west of the river, at an altitude of 11,380 feet, surrounded by gardens, orchards, and cultivated fields and hemmed in by mountain peaks. Although it is only fourteen degrees south of the equator, its climate is rather chilly. A living city today, it boasts numerous remnants of Inca times. *Pl. 48, fig. a* shows an ancient wall later used as foundation for Spanish colonial dwellings. Stones of similar texture and size were trimmed to fit closely together without mortar, a sharp contrast to the *mélange* of masonry from post-Columbian days.

In this picture characteristics of Inca building are evident which will appear on a much grander scale in following sites. The fitting of irregular blocks is amazingly perfect, as can be seen in *fig. b,* the ruins at Tampumachay, near Cuzco. Sometimes the stones are rather rounded, and sometimes, as in the foundation of the Monastery of St. Dominic in Cuzco, so smoothly dressed that the joint is scarcely felt with the hand.

The ancient capital, laid out on a geometric plan, would seem rather forbidding to us, with its narrow paved streets and solid dark walls. Probably few of the houses were, however, more than one story high. Running water coursed through certain sections.

The puritanically sober stone blocks of the palaces and temples were sometimes embellished by decorations of fine textiles and sheets of gold. It is said that a golden frieze ran all the way around the outside of the Temple of the Sun and the interior walls and ceiling were plated with the same precious metal. An enormous sun disk, also of gold and incrusted with emeralds, covered the west wall, so placed as to reflect the rays of the rising sun at the time of the equinoxes. Five fountains played from pipes of gold within the temple, and outside was a garden with birds, trees, flowers, and little animals, all of gold and silver.[30] Other temples, dedicated to the moon, the stars, thunder and lightning, and the rainbow must have been as ingeniously adorned.

At Kenko, in the environs of Cuzco, is a ruin with an admirably precise semicircular wall, which according to authorities was an amphitheater in Inca times. In the center stands a solitary animal-shaped rock, about which the rites may have centered.[164]

SACSAHUAMÁN

On the hill which dominates the city of Cuzco from the north are the impressive ruins of the fortress, Sacsahuamán (*Pl. 49, fig. a*). The name is said to denote "the highland whose attack meant human corpses for the hawks." [139] Sacsahuaman rises in three jagged terraces to a total height of almost 60 feet. The fortress is constructed of heavy stone blocks of irregular size, joined without mortar. The first wall is 1200 feet long and averages 27 feet high. One of the giant boulders used in the construction measures 38 feet long by 18 high and 6 thick.[84] The second terrace steps back 35 feet and is 18 feet high, while the third recedes about 18 feet and is 14 high. The stones were quarried at a distance, sometimes of several miles, and had to be transported over rivers and across ravines. Contemporary Europe, which had the advantage of iron tools, pulleys, and wheeled vehicles—all unknown to the pre-Columbian native—could not have fitted these great blocks with more masterly precision. The walls today remind one somewhat of the ruins of Moorish fortresses in Spain and Africa.

Beyond the ramparts there are signs of living quarters. Water was supplied the garrison by means of canals, in part subterranean. On the very summit of the hill are broad "steps," hewn from the living rock and cut with matchless skill (*fig. b*). This dais is called the Throne of the Inca, but its purpose is unknown.

There are certain differences in construction which may indicate that the fortress was started by a pre-Inca people and only strengthened and enlarged by the same dynasty that in the end fought the Spaniards here. The outstanding position that Sacsahuamán holds as a masterpiece of construction, however, remains unquestioned.

It continued as a stronghold until shortly after the Conquest. Juan Pizarro, half-brother of the *conquistador,* was mortally wounded here in one of the battles between Spaniards and Incas, and here was dealt one of the last blows to independent Inca power. When the Indians lost the battle, the commander of the fortress hurled himself to the ground from a high promontory.

OLLANTAYTAMBO

Ollantaytambo, "the plain of the spider," [139] lies about thirty miles northwest of Cuzco in the valley of the Yucay, a tributary of the Urubamba. One of the several key fortresses that protected the "Sacred Valley" from the incursions of wild tribes from the north, it is among the most interesting ruins of the Andean Area, either from a historical or legendary point of view. Constructed in pre-Inca times and used throughout the regime of the Incas, it witnessed a Spanish defeat when its walls repulsed the attack of the troops of Hernando Pizarro. Here also is laid the scene of a famous drama of Inca tradition—the tale of a young warrior, an obdurate ruler, and the youth's tribulations in winning the lovely maiden—which could not have been staged against a more romantic and picturesque background.

High mountains rise precipitously all around the site, and a river flows through the valley at the foot of the cliffs. From here a steep path leads upward to a small artificially broadened plateau, and on this level space six immense stone slabs, averaging over 12 feet high and 6 broad, stand upright against the mountain side. According to early sources, here rose the Great Hall of the fortified palace of Ollantaytambo.[77] If used as inside walls, the smooth stone slabs must have produced much the same effect as the wood panels in European medieval halls.

The slope of the mountain below the palace was later cut into deep terraces, the walls of which were faced with stone and used as the inner walls of buildings. The Hall of the Niches (*Pl. 50, fig. b*) shows one of these. The protrusions visible on a number of the stones are thought by some to have been left for convenience in handling. Each of the nine niches, which may have held household goods or equipment, is 26 inches high by 16 deep with sides made up of single blocks. At the far end of the narrow structure is a handsome doorway, characteristically wider at the base, with a lintel that is dressed on all four sides. E. George Squier notes sockets carved on several blocks for T-shaped copper cramps, such as were found also at the ruins of Tiahuanaco.[139]

Another narrow gallery of tall niches above a series of terraces is seen in *fig. a,* at nearby Tampumachay. Here the wall surfaces show varying techniques in stone work. The lower terraces are composed of polygonal masonry, built of small stones, crude and rough in appearance. The center section, which may be of earlier date, is also put together like a jigsaw puzzle, but here much larger stones are used, dressed with care though lacking uniformity in size and shape. The wall with the niches is laid in even courses with well-spaced joints. Each lintel is a large smooth slab, and the task of lifting such pieces in this restricted passageway can be imagined.

The fountain is the only sign of life remaining. A steady stream of water splashes from the stone mouth into a small basin, to issue again from the double opening a few feet below. Running through the time of the pre-Incas, the Incas, the Spanish rule, and into the present day, it is the only living link with the generations that once teemed here.

The ground around and above such centers is graded for agriculture. Ruins of dwellings have been found on the hillsides. Following the line upon line of walls, still unshaken, on these sites, one is awestruck with the consummate skill of these early builders. The structures seem an embodiment of the cyclopean power which was able to build an empire spreading 380,000 square miles, as intricate in its coördination as is this admirable masonry.

PISAC

Agricultural terraces with their undulating outline, cut from the sloping hillsides, form a significant and dramatic setting for the citadel of Pisac, some fifteen miles northeast of Cuzco in the Urubamba Valley. Situated on a mountain plateau and overlooking the river and three converging valleys, a position comparable to that of Monte Albán, it had great tactical advantages.

The major part of the citadel lies 1000 feet above the river bed. Double- and triple-walled forts were worked into the defense system, with the walls and towers so placed that the fortress was practically impregnable to attack with such weapons as slings, darts, stone axes, and clubs. The scattered buildings and minor fortifications which crowd the terraced slopes would indicate that Pisac was almost a province, supporting not only a large number of warriors in the garrison but a considerable general population.

Back of the settlement lies a vast system of terraced fields, which here, as at Ollantaytambo, reached perfection. Hundreds of miles of them, carefully constructed and irrigated, produced crops which could provide for a widespread population. It is probable that Pisac was one of the hill garrisons that not only guarded the passes but provided depots where the garnered food supply was stored for the Empire as a reserve in case of war or a failure in the harvest. Ruined granaries and remnants of other separate buildings about the site bear out this theory.[48]

A section of smaller rooms worked into a semicircular unit is seen in *Pl. 51, fig. a,* connected and separate inclosures without their roofs. The thatch has long since fallen in and moldered away, but there is every reason to believe that the covering of these buildings was as neatly and skillfully constructed as their walls. The structure stands on the brow of the hill, and far below can be seen the contours of the meandering river valley.

The so-called Temple Group (*fig. b*) represents the climax in stone cutting and fitting. Nowhere in the Inca domain, or even in the world, can a higher grade of megalithic architecture be found. In addition to the expert finishing, the stones are cut in uniform sizes and laid in absolutely even courses. Vertical joints are avoided and even today the walls are still remarkably plumb. The thick rounded blocks for the corners had to be prepared with special care. The three window sills in the center are perfectly level and their lintels could not have been more evenly laid with modern tools.

The building with the curving wall (*Pl. 52, fig. a*) was the Sundial, or *Inti-huatana,* "the place where the sun is tied up." For this the top of a ledge was leveled, except for a truncated cone carved from it projecting from the floor (*fig. b*). It was inclosed within walls but open to the sky. The projection, in tracing with its shadow the course of sun or moon, is believed to have served as a pointer on the flat table of living rock.

When Squier visited the place, before 1877, he was told by the governor of the province that a flat bronze ring had once encircled the projection. Perhaps this was marked for astronomical observations, for the early Spanish chroniclers mention devices by which the Incas were able to determine the solstices and compute eclipses.

The elliptical wall which incloses the sundial rock reaches 20 feet in height. Here again is a remarkable piece of construction, with every unit executed, one might say sculptured, for its own particular position. It has an amazingly finished aspect in comparison with the irregular cyclopean blocks of Sacsahuamán. Crumpling walls of various types attest to the long occupation of the site.

There are a number of sundials within such temple courts in Inca settlements. All records of the *intihuatanas* show them to be carved from living rock. Their immobility seems to have been a major consideration. Perhaps a device which was part of the earth itself, living and natural—not to be tampered with arbitrarily by the hand of man—was held desirable for the observation of nature's greatest wonder.

The beauty of Pisac is enhanced by the soft pinkish gray of the granite used throughout. The irregular height of the remaining walls, the huge finished stones scattered here and there do not give it the appearance of dilapidation but rather the charm of a child's unfinished game with blocks, colored always by its monumental scale.

MACHU PICCHU

Last in our sequence, although among the first in importance, are the ruins of Machu Picchu, situated less than fifty miles northwest of Cuzco on one of the numerous mountain "knees" carved out by the Urubamba. This mountain fortress lies on a long ridge between two lofty peaks, the higher of which (10,300 feet) bears the name, Machu Picchu, or "old peak," while the lower (9000 feet) is called Huayna Picchu, or "young peak" (*Pl. 53*). Machu Picchu, as a name, became familiar to the public with the discovery and exploration of the site by Dr. Hiram Bingham in 1911.

Until this date there were only rumors of ruins in this general region. Wiener in his "picturesque but unreliable" book, *Pérou et Bolivie,* mentions hearing of them while he was in Ollantaytambo around 1875, and friends of Dr. Bingham reported local tales of their existence. The Urubamba River, here 6400 feet above sea level, is unnavigable at this point even for canoes. It flows between such sheer walls that all passage along the shore line was impossible, and the produce brought from the region into Cuzco had, until recently, to be carried a roundabout way over snow-filled passes.[12] Late in the last century the Peruvian Government constructed—rather, blasted out—a mule trail following the gorge of the river, and this new means of communication opened a new sector also to the explorer. It fell to the lot of the American expedition to find the site, which, to their good fortune, had been little disturbed by treasure hunters and was damaged only by the overgrowing mountain vegetation.

Here in the saddle between the two peaks, 2000 feet higher than the river bed, stands the ruined citadel, laid out with constant regard for the terrain. While toward the west was located the ceremonial and religious center (*Pl. 54, fig. a*), the greater part of the inhabitants apparently lived in the eastern section (*Pl. 56, fig. a* and *Pl. 305, fig. b*). Water channels, baths, smoothly rounded walls, all of fine white granite, furnish typical details of Inca architecture. With the growth of the population, dwelling houses and artificial terraces for agriculture were laid out in all directions wherever the precipitous rocks left space for them. Inclined ramps, narrow streets, and long stairways connected the parts of the fortress. Buildings were wedged in among boulders and under overhanging ledges, so ingeniously fitted that they stand today as firm as the living rock (*Pl. 55, fig. a*).

In the different edifices of Machu Picchu, the full variety of stone construction in the Andean Area can be observed. Superlative craftsmanship is displayed in the sloping wall that continues the line of the steep ledge used as a foundation (*fig. c*). In contrast, the terrace walls in the background, more clearly visible in *Pl. 56, fig. b,* show such rough fabrication that one wonders if they could be the work of the same people. Both flat and gabled roofs were used (*Pl. 56, fig. b*). The characteristic niches and well-cut windows of mature Inca style can be seen everywhere (*Pl. 54, fig. b*). Some of the protuberances on the stones are now believed to have been used in lashing on the roofing.

The history of Machu Picchu is still a matter of dispute. Some authorities are led by the variations in the masonry to conjecture a long life and numerous changes. Dr. Bingham holds the site to have been the capital of the first Inca ruler, around the 9th century, and to have been abandoned in the 14th for Cuzco.[13] According to Dr. Luis E. Valcárcel, the two-story houses, the considerable number of greatly expanded stairways, the three-sided, walled-in temple, and the plug-projections on the great stone blocks present pre-Inca features.[6] It is true that at the beginning of an empire, such a citadel would have been of great importance; and later when the Inca power had expanded and become stabilized, the population could have afforded to move to a less intrenched position. All pottery and tools found here, however, clearly show Inca style, and excavations so far have failed to produce traces of separate or considerably earlier cultures. For this reason, Means dates its construction in the first years of the 15th century, during the reign of Pachacutec. There is also a tradition that Machu Picchu was the last refuge of the Incas after the Conquest. Thus legendary tradition and historical evidence vacillate between placing it among the first or the final strongholds.

In this book where the extant remains of medieval American art are under discussion, Machu Picchu needs no proof of venerability to insure its prestige. In the daring and majesty of its isolation, it is a perfect expression of the austere and orderly mountain folk who created and maintained it.

In viewing the architecture of medieval America from the cliff-dwellings of the Southwest down into the Andes with its *grand finale* of Machu Picchu, one is overwhelmed to see such diversity in the methods used by these peoples in solving their building problems. Houses built on the earth and temples rising from impressive substructures, sober granite walls and flamboyant sculptured façades existed on this continent as it lived its own life and went its own way of development.

"All European architecture," as John Ruskin wrote, "good and bad, old and new is derived from Greece through Rome, and colored and perfected from the East. The history of architecture is nothing but the tracing of the various modes and directions of this derivation. Understand this once and for all: if you hold fast to this great connecting clue, you may string all the types of successive architectural invention upon it like so many beads. . . . Those old Greeks gave the shaft; Rome gave the arch; the Arabs pointed and foliated the arch." [118]

But pre-Columbian America knew nothing of this development in the Eastern Hemisphere, connected and cross-fertilized from many sources during the last five thousand years. For this reason, medieval American architecture would be of unique importance even had its achievements been less great than they are.

IV

Sculpture

THE nature of sculpture and the inherent possibilities in the material for the imitation of natural form make it perhaps the most immediately comprehensible of all the arts. Architecture has somewhat the same universal appeal, yet to grasp the full majesty of a great building requires some familiarity with the culture of the region. Painting, limited to the flat surface, has developed stylistic mannerisms of its own; and its forms of expression are so idiomatic that one does not feel the beauty in a fresco or canvas unless he is acquainted with the civilization which produced it. A cloud in a Chinese painting looks very different from one on a canvas by Titian. We are able to recognize and enjoy both because we have learned to understand the pictorial expressions of both Chinese and Venetian schools; but for a person absolutely ignorant in the field, these pictures would have little to tell. A case in point is that of the Oriental with his tradition of placid even lighting. He is irritated and confused by our chiaroscuro; to him the shaded half of the face in a portrait simply looks dirty. Thus, the limitation imposed by two dimensions has enforced artificiality on painting and circumscribed its appeal. Sculpture, on the other hand, less restricted, stands free, awakening a more catholic response. It transcends both time and continents.

In the Eastern Hemisphere, sculptural expression and techniques were interchanged by Asia, Africa, and Europe—witness the Greek influence in some of the Buddhistic statuary—but medieval America had to develop its own principles, drawing on its experience in clay modeling and the carving of wood and bone. The small toylike figurines of the archaic period might be viewed as the predecessors of the superb stucco wall reliefs of Palenque and Comalcalco; the carved bone tools, the precursors of the Maya Maize-god of Copán, sculptured in stone.

One might go so far as to say that the high quality of pre-Columbian art is most apparent in its sculpture. The charm of the crystal frog (*Pl. 256, fig. a*) can be sensed immediately; the figure of the seated Aztec leaning on his arms (*Pl. 61, fig. a*) or of the rattlesnake (*Pl. 60, fig. a*), indolently coiled, requires no explanation. Even a tyro in the arts can see and understand these subjects and will, most probably, even derive some emotional reaction from them.

The pre-Columbian sculptor shows great feeling for his material. Egyptian carving was "conditioned" by the native granite employed; Assyria used limestone; Tanagra, clay; Donatello chose bronze; Rodin, marble as well, while the African primitive carved in wood. The Maya artist worked out his technique and his style of expression in the material locally at his disposal. Limestone was common, which also furnished stucco for his wall reliefs. The Aztec carver frequently used trachyte, serpentine, and other rugged stones. The plastic talent of these peoples found expression also in jade, bone, and wood, which will be presented later.

It is impossible for us to take the full measure of pre-Columbian sculpture, for much of it that we know functioned as ornament, either built in or applied to a building, and what we see today is only a fragment of the original, stripped from its setting. Furthermore, as in many early civilizations, color was applied lavishly to both sculpture and architecture and must be kept in mind in any attempt to visualize the living art.

Our civilization tends to evaluate an art by the way it depicts the human figure. Even according to this standard, some of the pre-Columbian sculpture would rank high. But one factor must be taken into consideration: various cultures have very different ideals of beauty. The flattening of the forehead generally practiced by the Maya appears to us unnatural, but in 15th-century Florence, the beauty ideal of the ladies, as immortalized by Piero di Cosimo and his contemporaries, shows that the hair was shaved off for two to three inches above the brow. In medieval America, besides the sloping forehead, artificially elongated in childhood, crossed eyes, also promoted early, and a receding chin were deemed marks of beauty. Moreover, the grotesque and the horrifying, often repulsive to us but nevertheless strikingly effective, played a much larger part in their art than in ours. Realism is frequently almost submerged in esoteric symbolism, but in many cases truly sculptural talent shines through, making immediate contact with us. Ease and subtlety of pose and balance of movement are often so humanly expressed that alien elements can be disregarded and the sculpture enjoyed without a discordant note.

One type of sculpture did not exist here: that is portrait statuary. Although certain stelae and other smaller pieces, such as the Totonac *palmas,* show individual characteristics, or even features of portraiture, they cannot be accepted as actual likenesses of a particular person; rather they are condensations of racial and traditional trends. In other early civilizations also, a so-called portrait of a person—frequently made after his death—was strongly idealized. Our humanistic and individual approach to the subject was absent in pre-Columbian America. The arts there never went beyond serving a hieratic purpose, and did not reach the level of "art for art's sake."

Not all of our five areas in medieval America were equally articulate in sculpture. The most impressive work in stone is restricted to the Mexican and Maya areas. Parts of the Southwest and Southeast modeled animal and human subjects into their ceremonial and utilitarian vessels. A number of scattered regions offer stone bowls with plastic animal decoration, and the ingeniously carved pipes of the Southeast and Central United States (shown in "Facets of Daily Life") prove command of the medium there. The Andean Area also produced sculpture in stone, but these people never reached the full use of the three dimensional in carving on a large scale, and their work is angular and strongly conventionalized.

Two lines of sculptural development can be observed: carving in relief and in the full round. In the following illustrations, examples of different degrees of both of these will be shown. Some of the earliest statuettes found are already conceived with consciousness of the three dimensional. Elsewhere the subject is depicted by scratching its outline across a stone slab—drawing with a chisel rather than sculpturing. The carving out of different levels to emphasize the contours produced relief. The background, already lowered, had then only to be carved completely away to show realistic outlines in the round, and the subject conceived in such a position that all unnecessary stone could be chiseled off. The statue that resulted, however, was often still flat, more of a cut-out than a plastic body. It will be noted that some regions seem to have found the relief completely expressive and satisfying, without reaching for the three dimensional. In certain instances, such as the Maya stelae, plastic and incised details appear on one and the same stone.

In order to bring out contrasting artistic qualities, a chronological presentation was avoided in this survey, as it would have necessitated showing much from the Maya before the Mexican. The chapter starts with the less articulate specimens of carving. We must not forget that all civilizations developed slowly. The inventions of a prehistoric people advanced at an adagio tempo. More time was needed in that age for the ripening of ideas than in our own, when the pace has been accelerated by the accumulated experience of centuries.

MEXICAN AREA

On the Zapotec-Mixtec site at Monte Albán, Oaxaca, carved stones from the earliest period were found with human and glyphic content.[20] *Pl. 57, fig. a* shows a slab that once decorated the base of a structure. A human figure is the main theme, and a pictograph presenting a bird and other signs is drawn in the upper left corner. In this carving the smoothed and polished surface of the stone was used to high-light the principal features of the subject. In between and around them the lines are deepened, probably by pecking with a primitive stone chisel, and the background worked up into a dull finish. The contour lines are deepest around the head and body; more shallow incision is used for details, such as the fingers. The half-open mouth, strongly emphasized lips, and low forehead are well brought out. An ornament hangs over the stubby nose, and the round ear-plug is sharply carved. Had the ear been merely suggested by a lightly incised line, it would have looked more natural, but chipped out as deeply as it is, the emphasis has disturbed the realism. The struggle to define the three-quarters pose with crossed arms and legs is obvious. Yet there is a feeling of human flesh in the carving. It is not a serialized portrayal, such as occurs, row on row, in Egyptian and Assyrian reliefs, but has rather the terse quality of a cartoon.

The second slab (*fig. b*), presented as a companion piece, has an orderly column of glyphs. In contrast to the first, where the entire surface of an irregular stone was utilized, the subject is neatly framed within a well-defined oblong depression, and instead of a single direct portrayal, the representation, which consists of a serpent head in the upper half and a human figure in the lower, is rigid and condensed. Thus motifs from life became conventionalized into glyphs which had associated meanings. The bar and four dots at the bottom are numerals.

These stones have been classified as belonging to Monte Albán Epoch I. The breadth of the artistic talent of the Zapotecs is documented in the clarity with which, even at that time, both figural and glyphic subjects were executed.

The relief work in *Pl. 58* has advanced considerably beyond mere incision and makes use of several planes. The first illustration (*fig. a*) is of a limestone fragment found at Tilantongo, Oaxaca, where it had been used as building mate-

rial in a Spanish church. The Mixtec god, Five Death, is represented, identified by the skull with ear-flaps and the five dots carved before his face.[24] He
wears an elaborate headdress of sweeping quetzal feathers, with three stiff eagle
quills pointing upward, and a patterned kilt edged with bells. On his right arm
he carries a shield and in his hand three darts. A pouch is hung over his left arm
and in that hand he holds a decorated spear-thrower. His jewelry consists of
bracelets and anklets, a great rectangular ear ornament, and a necklace with a
carved mask and three large pendants, probably of jade. The deity seems to have
faced another figure at the left where the stone is broken off.

Little realistic impression is conveyed in the carving. The most plastic element is the half-veiled eye, so effectively executed in the jades of the region.
From an incised spiral (noted in the preceding plate), the ear has reached a
characteristic conventionalization. Head and feet are out of proportion; most
of the accessories, such as the shield and the three pendants of the necklace, are
exaggerated. The headdress is rigid, with little feeling of feathers in it. The
composition seems primarily concerned in outfitting the subject with all the trappings prescribed by tribal iconography. In its linear conduct we do not yet find
a truly sculptural language.

Warriors in full regalia are depicted on a fragment of Aztec stone carving
(*fig. b*). Although nearly every object pointed out in the Mixtec relief appears
here, differences in the manner of execution are immediately noticeable. Figures are better proportioned, heads and feet more naturalistically represented,
and faces and especially thighs show certain rounded contours. Not only is the
technique more advanced and the outfitting dissimilar, but, in contrast to the air-
less static Mixtec figure, the gestures here are those of human beings, even if
orthodox; their involvement in an action can be sensed by everyone. The undulating serpents above them, besides being of symbolic importance, serve as an
effective and decorative border.

Pl. 59, fig. a shows a sculpture of a woman which comes from the Huaxtec
region, Vera Cruz, the inhabitants of which, though ethnically related to the
Maya, show little similarity in their art. The piece is 26 inches high. Liberated
from the stone which surrounded it, this carving more nearly approaches a statue
in the round than any of those yet presented. Completely three-dimensional delineation is still lacking to a great degree, and, in spite of the cut-outs at the neck
and waist, the impression of a stone slab prevails. While the arms and hands are
flat, the face is quite plastically executed. The half-closed eyes and parted lips

give it the expression of speaking or communicating, a characteristic that is more or less widespread and will be noticed in the best sculptures of the Maya also.

The so-called pulque vessel of the Aztecs (*fig. b*) is carved of green quartz phyllite and is about 14 inches high. The sharply projecting head seems to wear a mouth mask, the edge of which is visible toward the ear, and inlay must have once embellished the eyes. Flowing plumes and dart-shaped streamers make the transition to the cylindrical body of the vessel, the surface of which is covered with a design of human figures, monsters, and glyphs, a decoration full of movement.

Although certain features about the piece point to the Aztecs, it is not certain whether it is a product of those people. The type recalls clay *incensarios,* or incense burners, which have heads protruding in a similar manner from the sides of large jars. (See *Pl. 121, fig. c.*)

The statue of the Goddess of Agriculture (*fig. c*), 21 inches high, embodies many characteristics of Aztec stone carving, with its compactness, its feeling for the material, the angular sculptural lines, and the presence of realistic features among others highly conventionalized. Almost a third of the statue is taken up by her heavy complicated headdress, which has cockades on the sides and a protrusion like a bowknot in the center, typical Aztec decorations. Her face, strongly sculptured, holds its own against the massive plain surfaces that frame it. She carries what are probably two maize ears. About her waist dangles a snake, his rattles shaped like hearts. The feet are carved with naturalism in sharp contrast to the conventionalized hands with their symbolic objects. A proof that the statue has not fully graduated into the three dimensional lies in the superfluous stone connecting the headdress and the shoulders.

How able the Aztec carver was, however, to convey a realistic effect in three-dimensional sculpture is demonstrated in the three animals on *Pl. 60.* All are executed with striking power and are so well composed that they are equally effective from all sides.

A rattlesnake, approximately 2 feet high, is shown in *fig. a,* woven into the knot typical of the reptile. Teeth and tongue are conventionalized in best Aztec tradition, and the scaly rattles, conscientiously portrayed, have been used with good decorative sense against the smooth coils. The various planes of the soft folds in the body are cleanly worked out and, with the light and shadow effects, produce an unusual, yet realistic impression.

The toad (*fig. b*), almost 6 inches long, has the same good qualities. The pose of the body, alert expression, and clean sculptural finish, all contribute to our unhesitating acceptance of the piece.

The animal in *fig. c,* 17 inches high, is generally called a dog, although the claws and stubby fleshy tail are not in the least canine. It is possible that the figure, despite its convincing appearance, is not intended to represent a real animal but a mythical creature, supplely modeled and natural though it appears, as it lazily grins at the sky. If so, the statue documents all the more the genuine artistic ability of the Aztecs, for to carve a figure from their fantasy-world so well that it appears alive even to us is a veritable achievement.

Aztec sculpture at its best is presented in the figure of a seated man (*Pl. 61, fig. a*), more than 2 feet high. His relaxed but attentive pose, showing the same passive awareness that characterizes his present-day kin, is the first thing that strikes us. Headdress and massive ear ornaments are executed in detail, otherwise a general plainness is adhered to throughout the carving. It is this very plainness that clinches the forceful effect of the piece. The human in the figure predominates; in regarding him, we are not overwhelmed with symbols from an alien civilization. The body has the elasticity and vigor of a big cat, and the eyes, though nothing but wedge-shaped slits, seem to be peering into the distance. How much deliberation went into the statue is manifest in the fingertips of the left hand, which, though partly concealed, are still clearly delineated. There is life even in this small detail, for the fingers seem really to grasp the knee.

The next statuette (*fig. b*) obviously comes from a different, though not inferior culture. It shows a recumbent anthropomorphic figure, 16½ inches long. As a whole, it gives the impression of a human, but the ears and pawlike termination of the arms bring animal elements into it. Such adaptations—the Sphinx for one and Mercury for another—occur in many mythologies. The provenience of the carving is not known, nor is it clear just what it represents. According to one opinion, it is classified as belonging to the Huaxtec culture in northern Vera Cruz, to another, as coming rather from the central or southern part of that state. All these regions produced excellent sculpture.

Detached from any culture, however, it can be enjoyed as pure sculpture. Good observation and articulate talent are combined to convey the alert expression in the face and the animation of the body in repose. The back has a smooth, finely curving line, very plastic, and the softness of the body is beautifully brought out. Note the similar attitude in the pottery whistle (see *Pl. 118, fig. c*). There are traces of red on the piece. Holes are bored in the earlobes for the addition of separate ornaments, and the deep-set eyes may have been inlaid, although in their present state they still give a full impression. If the seated Aztec above can be said to be executed in a major key, this statuette might represent a minor.

In the next plate, another non-Aztec carving is coupled with an Aztec to bring out further differences. The first statue (*Pl. 62, fig. a*) is thought to have come from the state of Vera Cruz. A springiness of the legs, an easy position of the arms and hands are immediately perceptible. The head sits firmly on the shoulders and is in perfect proportion to the body. Headdress, earrings, and garment are the only decorations. The teeth are visible, as in *Pl. 59, fig. a,* and again the far-away look is noticeable in the face. Opinions are divided as to whether it represents a man or a woman. The pose is feminine but the slender body and the loincloth could be that of a youth. None of the higher pre-Columbian cultures tended to exaggerate the differences in the sexes.

Compared with the seated man in the preceding plate, the Aztec carving shown in *fig. b* is somewhat inferior. In the former, a more concentrated sculptural mass was produced, yet it has more life. The expression of the face here is dulled somewhat by the blank eyes, which, without the color that once must have completed them, make it rather forlorn. This statue is the least vital of the four, but if considered alone, it has a certain positive interest.

The concentrated quality of much of the best Aztec sculpture may have been due partly to the material used—trachyte or a hard basalt, often dark in tone, in contrast to the softer, lighter-colored limestone that is common in the lowland regions. Straighter lines are employed in the execution, the edges and corners are sharper, the mass is more geometrical. A greater smoothness and fluidity of line characterize the statues of non-Aztec cultures, and more ease can be observed in the pose, although from a sculptural point of view they frequently present more difficult problems.

The Totonac relief (*Pl. 63, fig. a*) shows a section of panel from the northeast corner of the Greater Ball Court at Tajín. The scene depicts a human sacrifice. The victim is laid on a high curving stone, while one priest holds his arm and supports his head and the other wields the stone knife with the point at his breast. A fourth figure is seated at the extreme right, bearing a standard. The Death-god with outspread arms and legs descends from above, between the two officiants, and on the left stands another skeletal figure, with a scroll before his jaws denoting speech. A simpler speech scroll emerges from the lips of the sacrificing priest. The unfriendly content of the relief must not prevent us from noticing the good spacing in the scene and the fine clear outlining of its many details. The fretlike scroll motifs in the border appear frequently in the Mexican and Maya areas, reaching in their application as far south as the Ulúa Valley in Honduras.

In *figs. b* and *c* we have an instance of the same symbolic theme worked up by different cultures into individual stylistic patterns. The plaque of fired clay (*fig. b*), about 27 by 29 inches, is said to have come from southern Mexico. Every detail of the eagle is utilized to a highly decorative effect. The spreading feathers show great variation; the attacking gesture of head and beak is brought out with force and realism. Each talon has its distinct, logical place—one foot grasping the object which the bird is devouring, while its more stable counterpart clutches the perch. The technical difficulties to be surmounted in modeling such a piece were not small; yet it is executed with vigor and freshness. The background is unusually deep and all contours sharply defined. Fret-scroll elements, similar to those on the preceding relief, fill in the empty spaces above the bird.

In *fig. c,* a section from a wall at Chichén, the same subject appears, here transposed into stone and expressed in the idiom of another culture. The technical and stylistic differences in the two works are immediately apparent. In the flatness of this relief and the changes effected in certain details, much of the power of the terra-cotta piece has been lost. True, the same attacking quality is evident in the head and beak, and the tail feathers are in exactly the same position. But the flowing line of the back is broken, and the whole figure is straighter, so that the gesture of the over-size claw becomes exaggerated. The scroll motif appears again above the bird, but in a somewhat different version.

The Totonacs who erected the superb structure of El Tajín (see *Pl. 12*) produced also one of the most sharply minted sculptural styles of medieval America. Their culture, centered in the region of central Vera Cruz, appears to have reached its artistic peak about the 13th century, when parts of the Mexican and Maya areas were feeling the spread of Toltec art. The art of the Totonacs has a special flavor, whether they make use of general themes or those of their own invention.

There are three types of stone sculpture characteristic of the region, two of which are more or less unique. One of these, the strange horseshoe-shaped carvings known as yokes, is presented on the two following plates. They average about 1½ feet in length and are made of polished diorite.[151] Their purpose is still a matter of conjecture. According to some sources, they were found in graves accompanying objects of burial; others would have them used in penitential ceremonies or placed around the neck of a sacrificial victim, although numerous representations of sacrificial scenes show no such shapes. More recently, the yokes have been connected with the sacred ball game.

Realistic and abstract elements are combined in the yoke on *Pl. 64*, one of the most ornate extant. The stone is of unusually fine quality, light and even in color. Above the sharply delineated human head, the muzzle and eyes of a monster-mask are visible. The design is smoothly carried over from the curving side to the flat surface on top, and the hand clasping the upper rim is especially noteworthy. One end of the yoke is reproduced in *fig. b,* showing a somewhat different face and mask. However, a homogeneous style is well preserved throughout.

Although it is the artistic content of the pieces that interests us, the symbolic importance for their makers can be sensed by a glance at the three photographs on *Pl. 65*. *Fig. a* shows a yoke with closed ends, carved in front and on the sides to represent an owl, while the inside is blank. The second one (*fig. b*) is open, with a human face cut in low relief. The third (*fig. c*) bears an all-over pattern, both inside and out, featuring another head, this time in profile, in the curve. Excellent carving characterizes all three, although in each case the prescribed shape of the stone limited the plastic expression.

In the manner of execution, however, they do not fall into a single group. In the first, the subject is carved on the rounded sides in somewhat high relief, with bold thick lines and straight elements predominating in the design. The cameo face in the second is expressed in robust terms, with admirable economy of line. The third shows great refinement, not only in the interweaving decorative stream of the familiar fret-scroll that covers the entire surface but also in the profile, physically little different from the one beside it but carved with a finesse comparable to the jades. The crossing of one branch of the restless pattern over the hair of the figure is a virtuoso touch.

The second distinctive Totonac type, the use of which is unsettled, is found in the axe-shaped heads. They are believed to have been of ceremonial importance or used as architectural decoration.

The one on *Pl. 66, fig. a* is about 8½ inches high and less than 2 inches thick, tapering toward the face. This extreme flatness, a characteristic of all such pieces, makes their purpose still more problematical. The features are clean-cut, with all curved sections emphasized. The protuberance on the forehead indicates, perhaps, an ornament, and the glyphic decoration painted or tattooed on the cheek is said to be Zapotecoid.

The second specimen (*fig. b*), over 9 inches high, not only presents a different physical type but is differently carved. Both pieces, nevertheless, show a certain uniformity in general shape and a relationship in their sculptural build-up. Despite their strangeness and thinness, both have about them something of a portrait; the individuality of their features is clearly seen when one is compared with the other.

Similar wedge-shaped carvings have been found also in the highlands of Guatemala (see *Pl. 97, figs. a* and *b*).

After viewing the so-called yokes and axes of the Totonacs, we come to another type of sculpture peculiar to these people, generally designated as *palmas*. These are usually made of volcanic rock, unpolished, and range from 9 to 24 inches in height. Although only single figures are presented on *Pl. 67,* couples, group scenes, and sometimes even animal shapes occur amidst stylized designs.

Fig. a shows a standing man wearing a large headdress which resolves into a decorative pattern with fret-scrolls. The figure, like the others here reproduced, is kept in perfect proportion—a great advance over numerous other pre-Columbian cultures. Expression and pose are animated, and not a single element is portrayed in that exaggerated manner which not only often disturbs us but prevents the work from being generally accepted as one of high standard. Note the tattooed scrolls at the sides of the mouth which recall those of the preceding plate.

The head in *fig. b* is sharply modeled within a bird's beak. The simplicity with which the flaring plumes of the headdress are treated is a contrast to the involved decoration on the other examples shown.

Perhaps the finest details of all are presented in *fig. c.* The hair, tied with a large bow, is clearly defined and, besides the usual costume accessories, there is a bag held in the man's left hand. Much of the stone, the top part of which is missing, is devoted to scrolls in beautiful permutations.

Neither stiffness nor heaviness is felt in these carvings with their interesting blend of relief and three-dimensional sculpture, and, in spite of the use of common motifs, each shows individuality in its ornamentation. The patterns on the garments, carefully delineated, add their decorative value to the compositions.

Totonac *palmas* always have a flaring top and a definitely concave base—features that indicate a particular use for all of them. It has been suggested that they were applied architecturally; they are, however, completely finished in appearance, with no raw sides or ends. Since some were allegedly found in graves, the idea that they were fashioned as memorials might be considered, a theory further supported by the fact that each has a distinctly different theme. The number of them that have recently come to light with unknown provenience might also point to burials. They give the impression of miniature individual stelae, larger examples of which will be seen in the Maya Area, each also with its distinctive details. These too may have a connection with the ball game.

Sculptured heads from four different regions, all within the Mexican Area, are presented on *Pl. 68*. The first (*fig. a*) was, according to information, removed from a grave near Oaxaca in the last decade of the 19th century. Including the neck, it is 10½ inches high. The carving is remarkable for its terseness of expression. Its plastic language is quite alien to the region where it was discovered. The headdress is simplified, and the ears, pierced both at the top and bottom, show a stylization not met heretofore. Tattoo may be denoted by the five beads at the corners of the mouth.

The head in *fig. b* was part of the legacy of Maximilian of Habsburg. Of dark green stone and about 7 inches high, it might easily be classed among the jades. The unrealistic narrowness of the piece, suggestive of the axe-shapes, is counterbalanced by the virtuoso carving of the features. In accordance with the beauty ideal of a number of pre-Columbian areas, the forehead is elongated. The "flame" medallion between the eyes and the broad outlined "eyebrows" are reminiscent of the jade masks in *Pl. 248,* while the conical form of the sculpture and the extended tongue, together with the sly yet benign expression, recall the puzzling creature in the Tuxtla statuette (see *Pl. 235, fig. d*) and the pottery head from Kaminaljuyú (see *Pl. 132, fig. b*).

Xipe-Totec, the God of the Flayed, is apparently the subject of *fig. c*. Doubtless the bloodiest ceremony of the Mexican religion was that which paid homage to this deity. After sacrificing a prisoner of war, the priest put on the skin of the victim, covering his face and most of his body with the gory trophy. The rite involves imitative magic in its attempt to invoke in nature the rebirth of vegetation, which is looked upon as a new skin for the earth.[25]

The head here is 10 inches high, carved of extremely hard stone, pale in color. Little opportunity for plastic detail is offered by the face covered with the skin of the flayed, but the sagging eyelids are tellingly depicted. The headdress with its cross ridge is ornate, incised with decorations of uncertain glyphic character. Traces of red can be discerned.

A different type of stone, less hard than the one just described, was used for the carving in *fig. d*. It appears to represent a masked head, perhaps an aspect of death, with its emaciated cheeks and startling eyes. The deep corrugations are most effective, carried through to define not only the forehead, brows, and the cheek bones, but even the angular jaw. The mouth has Olmec analogies, discussed in the chapter on jade. A heavy rounded ridge cutting across the top of the headdress in a line similar to that in the preceding picture gives a bold accent. The origin of the piece is not known, but one somewhat like it, found in the corner of the state of Guerrero at a crossroads of several distinct cultures, may furnish a clue to its provenience.

These four heads represent something more than strange or sinister portrayals, for they testify to the spiritual latitudes of these peoples and demonstrate impressively not only the scope of their imagination but their ability to express it in three-dimensional form.

In making the transition to the Maya Area, we present on *Pl. 69* Totonac and Maya reliefs side by side to demonstrate some of the differences in the sculptural languages of these two neighboring cultures. The two Totonac pieces come from central Vera Cruz, the Maya from central Chiapas. Although the first carving represents the best in Totonac, we shall see far finer sculpture from the Maya Area in later plates than that from Tenam.

On the stone slab (*fig. a*), nearly 6 feet high, is carved a chief—evidently a ball player—and his attendant, who seems to be helping him dress. His headgear is complicated, with the sausage-like ridge seen in some of the axes and a cascade of five feathers behind. A double string of beads is around his neck and two sets of bracelets on his left arm. His right arm and hand are bound, as if for a contest of some kind. Knees and feet are heavily ornamented, the right more than the left. His kilt clings to the lines of the body as if of a soft woven material. Dignity and condescension are embodied in the figure. His beard is sharply defined (compare with *fig. b*), and where it meets his upraised arm and the headdress of the attendant, the problem of placement is well solved.

The curving lines of the second figure serve as a good foil to the upright posture of the superior. Although this part of the stone is damaged, enough remains to give a satisfactory impression. He seems to be fastening the belt of the chief, and his hands convey well the action of pulling and adjusting. Note that the fingers of the right hand are bent outward unrealistically, as are also those of the chief's left.

The friezes that frame the top and bottom each carry a different motif, not one line of which is loosely or uncertainly carved. Many of the details in the composition could have been simplified if desired; the double tie of the chieftain's girdle, the natural uneven fall of the drapery both show virtuosity in carving.

The carved back of a marcasite mirror (*fig. b*) comes from the same cultural circle, and one can discover a similarity not only in its etching-like clarity but even in the features of the face. The head here also is shown in profile, turned to the left, and the beard, mentioned before, is sharply defined. Hair, cap, and earrings are made up of ingeniously contrasted lines. The face has life and strong characterization. In the frame, particularly on the left, a fret-scroll pattern, reminiscent of the type of decoration which is used with such fine effect on the Totonac yokes and *palmas* (see *Pl. 65, fig. c* and *Pl. 67*), gives a further indication of relationship.

With the second stone slab (*fig. c*), excavated at Tenam, Chiapas, we enter the Maya Area. In its linear conduct and clarity this low relief is inferior to the Totonac piece. In comparison there is a loss of life and living proportions; the air in the piece stiffens, and the human body becomes a mannequin for the recording of the paraphernalia of Maya full dress. As detailed as it is, the elaborate costume in the Totonac stela is wholly subordinated to the personality of the wearer.

The carving has, however, highly characteristic features of Maya representations. The pomp so typical of Maya ceremonies is very evident; the headdress is spread out to decorate the entire upper portion of the stone; the lavish ear, neck, and breast ornaments are meticulously depicted, together with belt, breechcloth, and footgear. Note the folds in the drapery behind the legs. The left hand holds a spear-thrower or staff, and the right, a pouch, much larger and more elaborate than anything seen hitherto. This profile also is turned to the left, but the body is posed facing full front, with the feet turned outward. The experience and ability of the carver can be judged from the fact that he did not feel himself restricted by the vertical frame of the stela but let some of the decoration overflow into the border.

SCULPTURE

MAYA AREA

The sculpture of the Maya at its best ranks without question among the highest artistic achievements of medieval America. From the earliest times that we are able to reconstruct, these people carved stone and modeled stucco to combine with their architecture. As the preceding chapter has shown, sculptured lintels decorated chambers as well as doorways; busts, masks, whole entrances were executed with a flood of plastic elements. Tablets and panels with fine and sophisticated incised compositions had a place both on the outside and inside walls.

Independent of the structures, though an integral part of the city picture, was the stone monument called a stela, a large slab or shaft that sometimes reached a height of 35 feet and a weight of more than fifty tons. Stelae were erected in the great plaza and before the temples at certain intervals of time—during the Great Period generally every twenty years—and are believed to have commemorated not only the passing of time but also historical events. This Maya custom covered the years between A.D. 328 and 889. The idea behind it is somewhat analogous to that of the obelisks of Mediterranean civilizations, but the sculptural execution is different. They bear the figures of priests or chiefs, always in ceremonial regalia, and hieroglyphs fill the remaining space. Much of the text is still unsolved, but the dates recorded serve as invaluable contributions to our knowledge. While certain dates will be given here, it is not our purpose to provide a chronological sequence but rather to point out the great variety of stylistic and sculptural solutions that this people found for a circumscribed subject.

A comparison of the three Maya stelae (*Pl. 69, fig. c* and *Pl. 70, figs. a* and *b*) will show how sculptural details can differentiate a concept which at the core is identical. In all three monuments a figure arrayed in full Maya splendor is carved in relief and placed within a frame. They all stand in uniform pose, bodies front, feet spread and pointing outward, heads turned in left profile. The left shoulder is higher, and the chin is superimposed on the right. All wear elaborate ceremonial dress, the details of which will soon be familiar to the reader. On the great headdress the casque just above the forehead represents the head of a monster. A mass of plumes, doubtless the shimmering gold-green feathers of the quetzal, tops the headgear. Elaborate bead necklaces with carved pendants deck the chest and shoulders; the wrists and legs are also bejeweled. The clothing consists of a short kilt with heavy ornamented belt and an apronlike "sash" extending down the front. Ornate high sandals cover the feet. Glyphs appear on each stela, but are differently placed in every case.

On Stela 16 from Tikal, dated 711, is carved a dignitary holding a ceremonial bar (*fig. a*). The evolution in the depiction of this ritualistic object has been extensively studied by Dr. Spinden in his *Maya Art* and others after him. The heavy headdress overlaps the frame and feathered ornaments reach out even behind the body.

Stela 10 from Xultún (*fig. b*), a site not more than twenty-seven miles northeast of Tikal, is one of those bearing the latest date deciphered. Its figural decoration is still more involved. While in the Tikal stone, elaboration was lavished on a single person, here we discover several minor figures. A priest carries a miniature jaguar seated on his right hand and holds in the curve of his left a demon with a swinging leg. In the lower left corner an attendant can be discerned. At least seven masks are incorporated into the priest's attire. His broad collar with its carved medallion is especially effective. The upper part of the sandals, as in the preceding piece, are fashioned into masks, here facing toward the heel instead of the instep.

The Tenam stela is characterized by a compositional restraint infrequent in the Maya Area. The sculpture, both here and in the Tikal slab, is executed with a preference for straight lines and simple curves, while the third shows a predilection for rounded pearlish elements and curling loops much more difficult to carve. The larger component parts, more clearly separated units, and greater variety of line give it a more plastic effect.

All these variations of gesture, ritual objects, and garb signify changes in style from one site or period to another. The elasticity of expression within the limits of a strict iconography is one mark of the high artistry of the Maya.

If Stela H at Copán (*Pl. 71, fig. a*), believed to be from the late 8th century, is compared with those just described, a decided sculptural difference can be noted. The dignitary is *en face* and has stepped out of the frame. The outlines of the monument follow somewhat the contours of the figure, so that it more nearly approaches a statue. A beautifully woven and ornamented skirt is discernible, with even the pendants on the edge carefully expressed in carving.

It is characteristic that the Maya never worked out their stelae into figures in the round; although the figural elements experienced considerable change—in attitude, facial expression, and execution—and even the glyphs were modified as their style developed, the monuments never entirely lost their slablike form.

Quiriguá is justly famous for its sculpture. Although the site lies only about twenty-five miles from Copán as the bird flies, the traveler has a much longer journey, for the direct road that existed in pre-Columbian times is overgrown with jungle vegetation. Stela D, like a number of monuments here, has two figural sides, the better preserved of which, that on the north, is shown in *fig. c.* The material is the reddish-brown sandstone native to the site, which adds a somber dignity to its carvings. The height of the sculptured slab is about 20 feet, the width 5, and the thickness 34 inches.

The figure does not stand out so free as at Copán, but the Maya's love of changing plastic surfaces is even more manifest. The only undecorated section is the face; the rest of the stone is an exposition of the sculptor's tremendous skill and arduous labor. From headdress to ankle ornaments a studied elaboration is evident. The glyphs (the east panel visible in *fig. b*) are gems of medallion carving; indeed, according to Dr. Morley, glyphic execution reached its peak in the panels of stelae D and F at Quiriguá.[91] Its date is 766.

Here should be mentioned the strange and inexplicable monuments, like boulders in shape and covered with involved carving, that are frequently found near the stelae at Quiriguá. Called "turtles," these altars are believed to symbolize the earth-monster. Their symbolism is so involved, however, that an intense familiarity with them is necessary for their appreciation. The sculptural talent which executed them is manifest in other types of carving easier for us to grasp.

Monuments with seated figures—a feature rare in Maya stelae—are presented on *Pl. 72.* The type occurs several times at Piedras Negras. In a somewhat damaged state, but with content still clear enough to be enjoyed, is Stela 6 (*fig. a*), which bears the date 687. A dignitary sits cross-legged within a shallow niche. The figure proper is almost 4 feet high. His monster headdress and breast ornament are quite massive, but this stocky muscular personage does not seem weighed down by them. Note the virtuoso touch in the carving of the loose knot just below the collar. Vertical columns of glyphs adorn the frame and smaller glyphs are incised on the drapery above and even in the arch formed by the curving feathers. The figure holds a pouch decorated with a brilliantly executed little monkey-head medallion, which dangles across the lower section, connecting the main subject with its frame.

Stela 14 from the same site is presented in *fig. b.* The much deeper niche, with the looped material above the head, is still more suggestive of a canopied throne. The seated dignitary has much in common with the preceding one—the details of the headdress and the pouch in his hand are more clearly discernible in this case—but here he is a character in a scene. Before him stands a full-length figure with upturned face, an offering in his hand. The pose of the chief, noble and self-assured, is in good contrast to that of the subordinate, who seems to do him homage. A third person, almost obliterated, is suggested in the lower right. The unprecedented blend of different plastic depths not only serves to bring out the central subject but even gives a sense of perspective. Despite the sections that have suffered from exposure, the stela illustrates fully the dignity in Maya art.

The execution of all details is done with the hair-fine finesse of a copper engraving. Great care was given to the dress of the standing figure. Note the decorated band and the knotted fringe on the edge of the lower garment and the openwork band with frets just above it. A single feather of the headdress is swept up with great artistic courage, as if blown by the wind or tossed up by the gesture, making a smooth transition from the upper section of the carving. Another feather, from among those he holds, turns downward, making contact with the headdress below. A series of footprints is just discernible coming from the right and mounting the ladder-like construction that seems to lead up to the throne.

The glyphs, placed unobtrusively and with great decorative effect on the throne, hanging drapery, and the plain section beside it, refer most probably to the ceremony involved. The date is interpreted as 800.

Fig. c shows Stela I at Quiriguá. The shaft is about 13½ feet high and has on the front (not shown here) a chief standing in conventional pose. Our picture reproduces the back of the stela, where amid a welter of plumes a small seated figure is carved. Although he occupies relatively little space considering the mass of the stone, he radiates concentrated power. The flowing headdress is well arranged, breaking out of the niche and guiding the eye to the Serpent Bird hovering above him. The body of a double-headed monster serves as frame, carved with the symbols of various constellations, its heads distinguishable on either side near the dignitary's knees. Below the figure is a grotesque mask as throne, from which hang two outflaring frets.[91] The date is 800.

A lively inner movement connects one section of the carving with the other, and the upward sweep of the feathers at the base close the design effectively, preventing it from running into the ground. Although the composition may have little meaning for us, it has an artistic maturity which holds together concisely the whole world of pattern it contains.

In the monuments from Piedras Negras shown on *Pls. 73* and *74,* the subject matter has achieved real freedom and the technique, great refinement. A full view of Stela 40, which is more than 13 feet high, is presented in *fig. a* of *Pl. 73.* It is dated 746. The central figure is shown kneeling upon a podium that divides the sculpture in two sections. The bust on the lower half offers, in the main, familiar elements and is quite rigid in its inflexible gaze. The great revelation of the piece is conveyed by the figure above with its symbolic action, a representation of the Maize-god scattering corn. We are at once struck by the fact that he has neither the stiffness of pose nor the static weight of body so characteristic of the stela figures already seen; much breathing space is allowed him. This differentiation between the two figures may have been deliberate; facing in opposite directions and so contrastingly conceived, they effect a crescendo through their very independence.

The kneeling pose of the Maize-god (*fig. b*) has the softness and complete linear freedom of some of the Palenque stucco reliefs or the best painted vases, even though the hardness of the medium here made the execution of such a graceful line considerably more difficult. The headgear, with its lacy ornament shaped like a bishop's mitre, rounds out the dignity of this extraordinary figure, and the mask or head attached to the back of the god is executed with fastidious care. Such careful delineation of the hair is unusual in Maya art. The hands are exquisitely expressive in their separate gestures, the left holding a decorated bag containing the seed which the right is dropping. Falling kernels of maize are discernible just before the open palm, and leaves of the mature plant, curling like fleur-de-lys, decorate the border. Dexterity, intelligence, and devotion created this figure—emotionally the most immediate among all Maya sculpture.

Stela 12 from Piedras Negras (*Pl. 74, fig. a*) is perhaps the finest expression in stone relief left by the Maya. The monument is 10⅓ feet high, about 3½ wide, and 1½ thick, and weighs about four tons. Its material is native yellowish limestone, which, when freshly quarried, is soft and easily worked. It was broken into four pieces but is now restored to such an extent that its original appearance can be easily imagined. This and the one just described are uncarved on the back.

The narrow sides of this stela are inscribed with hieroglyphs in accordance with Maya custom. The deciphered date is 795. It should be remembered, however, that in some cases dates may have had commemorative significance and would not necessarily coincide with the time the monument was erected.

On the face of the rounded slab, at the top, is sculptured a person of authority, seated on a dais and looking down upon the scene at his feet. He is probably the one-time ruler of the site now called Piedras Negras. In his hand he carries a long befeathered staff. Two attendants, also richly dressed, stand on either side a little below, and between them crouches in suppliant pose a figure who is perhaps the chief of a conquered people. He is unbound and still wears his necklace and other ornaments, an indication that he has been accorded the honors of war. Eight smaller figures crowd the lower space, possibly captives destined for sacrifice. All are bound with rope and have been despoiled of their necklaces and ear ornaments.

The scene as here presented makes the best possible use of relief. The lack of perspective is compensated for by grouping the units of the story-telling composition on different levels, one above the other; those in the foreground are carved in very shallow relief, while the background behind the main figure is considerably deepened, in the manner already seen in *Pl. 72, fig. b.*

To our modern eye, the group of prisoners is perhaps the most rewarding. Here, on a relatively narrow surface, is recorded a character study of eight human beings with a *triste* future. Their arrangement is completely devoid of any schematic representation—so often encountered when a mass has to be pictured—and in pose and facial expression each one has individuality. The huddling together of their bodies and the jumble of upturned faces alone would convey the desperation of their plight. Especially clear for closer study are the three in the lower right corner (*fig. b*), where the stone is still intact. While the rest look more or less toward the ruler, on whose decision their fate depends, the man on the extreme right lets his head hang. Apparently the oldest among the prisoners, he has lowered his gaze, bitter and without hope. Small details such as the hair, the expressive postures of the hands, and the knots and folds of the breechcloths, excellently drawn (note the third from the right), prove that each figure in the composition, whether ruler or captive, received the same careful attention.

Some of the minute jewel-like glyphs incised on the dais and elsewhere may refer to the occasion here commemorated, while those on the bodies of the prisoners probably give the names of the captives or the town or tribe which each represented.

Our admiration of this piece grows when we consider that it was carved without metal tools, with only the use of flint, obsidian, or other hard-stone implements and abrasives, such as sand. The effect is of an etching in stone.

Palenque, whose great artistic refinement was displayed in its architecture, reveals the same high achievement in sculpture, both stone and stucco. The stone tablet in *Pl. 75, fig. b,* consisting of three large slabs and dated 642, stood against the back wall of the inner sanctuary of the Temple of the Sun. It is carved in very low relief and records a scene from an offertory ceremony. On the right, standing upon the back of a prostrate figure, is a priest—a little under 5 feet tall —holding in his hands a statuette with a demon mask. His body, pulsed through with life, can be picked out from the mass of confusing detail. He is drawn with amazing surety and the gesture of offering is realistically conveyed.

A smaller priest on the left is also occupied in making an offering of a statue. He too stands on a figure, which in this case is kneeling, bracing itself on its outstretched arms. A shield with a mask and two crossed ceremonial darts or lances fill the space in the center, while below is an altar-like construction, supported by two seated figures. All the subordinate persons in the piece are masked. They are posed to bring out a certain symbolic meaning for the Maya and demonstrate for us admirable skill.

Among the glyphs is a date interpreted as 2359 B.C., so remote that it is thought to be some legendary or astronomical reference. It is noteworthy that the framework of dates on all three sanctuary inscriptions of the group (the temples of the Sun, the Cross, and the Foliated Cross) are closely interrelated. The same principals also appear—the tall, somewhat obese priest with his scant garments and mitre-like headdress, and the smaller figure, wrapped in intricately knotted scarves, with a flower waving above his head—but placed in varied settings.

Originally the panels reproduced in *figs. a* and *c* flanked the doorway to the same sanctuary, as shown in *fig. d,* Catherwood's sketch made in 1841. They were removed and are at present set into the outside wall of the village church of Santo Domingo Palenque. The relief at the left shows a young person in resplendent regalia, his headdress branching in several directions, his chest covered with elaborate decoration, and his heavy ornamented belt featuring a jaguar head. His right hand curves downward and his left, upward in a precious manner, which is reminiscent of the symbolic gesture of the Maya Maize-god of Copán. (See *Pl. 90.*)

In the other panel (*fig. c*) appears a stooped old man with a shrewd sly expression. He is dressed in a jaguar skin, over which hangs an unusually long string of beads. Both hands clasp an object held to his mouth, from which smoke seems to emerge. Familiar symbolical decorations, many of them not interpreted as yet, are inserted where space permits. The same sure and animated linear conduct that characterizes the great tablet above is manifest here.

The ruins of Yaxchilán, sometimes known as Menché, lie in Chiapas also, on the banks of the Usumacinta River. This site has become famous chiefly for its masterly sculptured lintels.

On Lintel 53 from Structure 55 (*Pl. 76, fig. a*) we witness for the first time here a scene pictured frequently in Maya art, in which two figures are facing each other. The smaller of the two is represented in full profile. His pompous attire is worthy of notice. The large package that he carries weighs down his right hand, while the left rests on top nearly on a line with his chin in a natural well-observed position.

The individual who receives this offering is undoubtedly the more important personage. He stands in a stela pose, feet spread apart and face in left profile. This three-quarters position is indicated, as is general in Maya art, with one shoulder somewhat raised. All the majesty of his office is apparent in his dress. Many details, usually obscure, are here remarkably clear through the variation of pattern. A broad jade bar hangs across his breast, and medallions and pendants with human faces, both frontal and in profile, are applied liberally throughout the costume. In his right hand he holds a manikin scepter, extraordinary in its clean carving and well-preserved state. As the great headdress demands more space than is available, its top feathers vanish beyond the frame and return to it, a rare feature. Feather ornamentation appears also from behind the figure on each side, and single feathers, curving upward, counterbalance the downward-trending lines. This little-known but very remarkable carving presents Maya iconography at its best, both in spirit and execution.

Lintel 15 from House F, to use Maudslay's nomenclature (*fig. b*), has become well known since his publication. At the right, a worshiper kneels before a huge serpent, from the jaws of which a divine figure issues. It should be noted that kneeling is a posture of reverence which we take for granted but which was practiced in very few Asiatic and Polynesian religions. The hands of the supplicant, holding what is probably an offering in a basket container, are well carved, with the right remarkable for its foreshortening. Although his face is turned in profile, his body is presented nearly full front, enveloped in a heavy robe that is beautifully patterned and edged with a different design. The details of the hairdress are used to a highly decorative effect.

The second participant in this scene is one of the most important of the fantastic symbolic creatures in Maya mythology. Rising from a vessel that contains cone shapes similar to those in the hands of the kneeling figure, it has the body of a serpent but ends in a human head, with a human right hand extended in a communicating gesture. The windings, scrolls, and smaller incised motifs are all taken from a settled artistic vocabulary.

In a comparison of the two reliefs, it will be noted that while *fig. a,* from the year 766, conveys a greater sense of realism in pose and gesture, *fig. b,* with the date 702 ?, surpasses it in decorative quality. In the first, differentiations are made by varying the pattern on the more or less uniform plane of a blocked-out relief; Lintel 15, on the other hand, uses also variations in the depth of the carving, giving a more plastic impression. The diagonal division of the field is unusually subtle. There is another striking distinction between the two tablets: in the first piece the priestly figure dominates the scene; in the second, the dignitary is subordinated to the supernatural.

The contrast between a blocked-out relief on the one hand, producing angular detail, and free-flowing, almost three-dimensional plasticity on the other can also be observed in the carvings on *Pl. 77,* once called lintels but now believed to have served as ornamental wall panels. On Lintel 1 from Piedras Negras (*fig. a*) is carved a chief with an attendant, receiving the homage of six kneeling warriors. He stands in the conventional pose, wearing a rich headdress and feather display, breast ornament, shield, and woven materials finely conveyed. His companion is a pace or two behind him, smaller and of less importance but nevertheless lavishly attired. The great rings around his eyes denote paint or a mask.

In excellent contrast to these two who stand in dignity, anchored by their staffs and theatrical in pose, is the closely knit composition of the kneeling warriors. Their heads and headdresses are distinctly separated, but below the shoulders they blend into one mass. While there is some differentiation in detail, especially in height, we feel that all six of them express a uniform action. The glyphs that frame the scene on three sides are neutral in effect, so dynamic is the figural portion.

Lintel 3 (*fig. b*), also from Piedras Negras, was found in a temple which stood near some of the most beautiful stelae in the Maya Area, including those shown on *Pl. 72, fig. b,* and *Pl. 74.* It is a tragedy that this sculpture should be so seriously damaged; however, like a magnificent fragmentary torso, it still speaks with the eloquence of true art.

The lintel measures roughly 4 feet by 2 and is 5½ inches thick. Almost the entire surface of the stone is carved in relief to a maximum depth of 1½ inches. A ceremony is probably pictured—a less warlike gathering than that just discussed, as no weapons are visible. In the center of the composition, on a rectangular altar or throne, a chief is seated, perhaps the personification of a deity. A number of such built-in thrones have been excavated at this site. On this one the boldly carved back is shown draped with a spotted jaguar skin, and the covering with its tasseled fringe is carefully executed. While the chief's face is mutilated and the right arm, probably raised, is missing, the one detail of his left hand, as it grasps the edge of the dais, is enough to prove the high quality of sculptural talent involved.

The group at the right, judging from the space used and the size of the bodies, seems to have consisted of four figures, two adults and two children. The extended arm of the one on the end is undercut and made fully plastic, a rare occurrence in Maya sculpture. At the left stand three persons cut in very deep relief. Their postures are varied and realistic, their arms crossed over the breast in the Maya gesture of reverence.[79]

In the foreground below the altar, seven others are seated, with a tall tripod vessel placed on the ground in the center of the group. There is rhythmic flow of line and movement in the whole scene; the masterly execution is particularly clear in the harmonious blending of the many different poses. Even in the fragmentary state of the piece, their attentive attitude is evident. Sculptured details, such as hands, feet, fingers, and even nails are portrayed with perfect clarity, and the delicate fabric of their garments is meticulously conveyed. All probably wore ornamental headdresses; the one immediately in front of the chief still shows the outline of a long-billed bird, distinguishable against the dais.

Judging from the existing background, at least four of the heads in the group must have been carved in the full round. The end figure at the right gives an idea of the lightness of the whole composition in the freedom of his pose, as he sits turned expectantly toward the center, leaning on his hand. At the opposite end, enough remains of the first figure to convey not only his gracious carriage but also the refinement of technique in cutting out the section behind the neck.

Delicately carved hieroglyphs are executed in both cameo and intaglio. One hundred fifty-eight characters are inscribed in fourteen different groups, the greatest number known on any lintel.

Upon comparing the two pieces reproduced on this plate, we are astonished to notice such divergence, not so much in ideology as in the plasticity of execution, in carvings from the same site, both dated 761. It would seem that within the autarchic art of one city much individual talent came to expression.

After having seen these lintels, we can more easily imagine the fragment from the same site (*Pl. 78, fig. a*) before it was demolished. In the center, which was probably part of the frame of the composition, stands a human figure, feet apart and back to us. We notice again the sculptural trick of lowering one shoulder to express a more plausible pose. The headdress, although not very elaborate, contains some new features.

The second figure must have been the last person of the scene within the frame. His arms are folded; some details of a headdress and breechcloth are all that is discernible. In its present condition it has an impressionistic softness and, as a fragment, it perhaps comes nearer to us than it would have when intact. Remarkable command of the medium is shown in the juxtaposition of very shallow relief and deep plastic carving.

In a much better state of preservation is a very thin stone slab from Jonuta, Campeche, on the border of Tabasco, Mexico (*fig. b*). It is 38 inches high. This bearded Maya with his sloping forehead, almond eyes, and protruding under lip, executed with the sharpness of a copper engraving, could be a character study. The fact that the farther leg and arm are shown lends a certain plasticity to the shallow relief and more life to the figure. He is draped with a jaguar skin and bears a vessel heaped with objects reminiscent of those on some painted Maya vases. A parrot behind his head is exquisitely drawn—note the ruffled wings, open beak, and the realistic depiction of the claws. Judging from the size of the scroll with the glyph panel at the upper left, the piece may have been a part of a larger composition, one which these details make us long to see.

Relief work in stucco came to its supreme expression in the perfection and flamboyance seen at Palenque. Piers of the buildings are covered to their full height with figures that approximate life size. Within, walls are incrusted with medallions. Each structure carries out a separate theme, yet in style all are homogeneous. Stucco work throughout Palenque, whether figural or abstract, speaks one idiom, not only highly articulate and technically preëminent but one which also approaches those principles by which we judge art.

To produce these reliefs in delicate stucco under tropical conditions was certainly a technical achievement, for the preparation of the background, preliminary and final modeling, and the drying must have been threatened by the general dampness of climate and often imperiled by torrential rains. How well they were executed is proved by the remnants that have survived—all too few, but in relatively good condition, considering the fact that Palenque's latest known date falls in mid-8th century.

It was the custom to refurbish stucco surfaces from time to time with a thin coating of plaster that was then colored, and there are places in Palenque where the face of the original is covered with several layers.[81]

The stucco relief in *Pl. 79, fig. a* occupies a full pier on the west front of the Palace, House D. A figure in dancing pose looks down upon another, kneeling, whose face and body are, regrettably, worn away. Although so much movement is rare in Maya art, it is beautifully and rhythmically portrayed here; weightless, the figure seems to float on its feet. The gesture of the left hand directed toward the kneeling companion is completely independent of that of the right, which carries an ornate ceremonial object.

Fig. b shows a pier on the eastern façade of the Palace, House H. Compare the elaborate bead network on the costume at the left with that in *fig. a* and on the Copán stela (see *Pl. 71, fig. a*). The personage who is standing, undoubtedly the most important of the three, is lavishly garbed. Though the face is destroyed, we detect in his body and carriage a clue to his youth and *noblesse*. His headdress, fantastically flamboyant, is balanced, though not by paired elements. A jaguar skin girds his hips, its tail hanging down the back. The undamaged human head attached to his waist in the back, which may represent a trophy or a mask, is in itself a demonstration of complete command of the medium.

A certain restraint can be sensed in both of these compositions; neither the flamboyant feathers nor the streaming hair is allowed to burst out of bounds. Breathing space is ample in both scenes. The rich frames are proof of great compositional ability, the possession only of a people mature in art.

Of a technical excellence on a par with Palenque's, even if not so ebullient, is the stucco work found in a tomb at Comalcalco in Tabasco, Mexico, only about ninety-six miles distant. This Maya site suffered a dearth of stone and built its structures of baked brick. Even in ruins the extensive area of the settlement can be perceived. Some of its edifices reach a height of 115 feet and a length of 575, but for our survey, the greatest contribution comes from the small burial chamber hidden in the undergrowth of the western part of the dead city. It was discovered on the last day of a Tulane University expedition in 1925.[15]

SCULPTURE

The reconstruction of the tomb (*Pl. 80, fig. d*), which includes even the skeleton that was lying on a low platform, produces something of the impression that the archaeologists received when they broke through the blocked doorway. In the original, both figures and walls show traces of a deep red color, with which the finely smoothed cement floor was also stained. The tomb is believed to date from the end of the 7th century.

Fig. a presents an original detail from the south wall, and *fig. c,* one from the north. Even in their dilapidated condition, both attest to great ability in characterization, for while the pose has more stolidity than in most of the Palenque stucco figures, the two faces are much nearer portraiture. The lean man on the right especially, with his bowed head, deep wrinkles, and penetrating look, is one of the most human documents salvaged from Maya art.

In *fig. b* the entire east wall is shown, more clearly seen in the reconstruction below. This group of three, the best preserved, gives a good idea of the loose, yet decoratively connected sequence of all nine figures that ornament the chamber. Each man is individual in face, figure, and action. The one on the left, in profile, stands inactive, with his arms crossed over his hanging belly. Especially spontaneous is the pose of the left arm and hand of the figure in the center, whose head is shown turned to the right but whose body faces front. The man on the right points, as if in conversation, into the space where a vertical column of hieroglyphs is inserted.

Compared with the figureheads so frequently depicted, these are people. According to tradition, the Maya had actors and jesters.[158] Whom these nine figures represent, whether chiefs, priests, warriors, courtiers, or clowns, we may never know; but it is evident that they are indicative of a grand scale of living.

The next four plates present comparative material. Two different types of stone sculpture from the state of Chiapas, a region preëminent in Maya art, are shown on the first (*Pl. 81*).

The stone tablet from Palenque (*fig. a*) was probably brought out by Captain Dupaix in the last years of the 18th century and is now in the Museo Arqueológico Nacional, Madrid. It was first reproduced by Leon de Rosny, who saw it there and published it as Yucatecan.[116] The late Marshall H. Saville, great American pioneer archaeologist, adjudged its provenience, after seeing it in Madrid, as Palenque.[127] The relief deserves more attention than it has received. It is to be regretted that such a classic example is little known, largely because of its isolation, while many more accessible pieces of weaker quality are reproduced again and again. It is believed to have been connected with an altar in the Palace Group and is judged earlier in date than the stucco figures there.[68]

The carving is executed in the best style of the Great Period at Palenque. The priest or chief admirably fills the space allotted within the plain frame. He is seated with one foot under him, leaning forward. His right arm presses against the frame, while the left, as he holds high a trailing water-lily, reaches into the opposite corner. In the palm of his hand, two of the fingers gracefully curved, he carries, according to de Rosny, a symbol of the sacred serpent. The weight in the composition lies in the left half of the sculpture, as the body leans in that direction, but this is ingeniously counterbalanced by the movement expressed in the exquisitely flowing lines on the right. The carving of all details is precise and varied; especially interesting are the headdress, earplugs with pendants, and the finely woven and decorated belt and cloth, lying in natural folds. His full profile, in characteristic pose, brings out very clearly the sloping line of the flattened forehead.

The whole composition has the same plastic air admired in the stucco-relief fragments and bears a similarity in spirit to the figures in certain jade pendants. The same delicacy of linear conduct and the same masterly use of deep- and shallow-cut detail will appear in some of the jades in a coming chapter.

Through the courtesy of Dr. Spinden, we are able to reproduce the stone statuette in *fig. b,* showing a Maya astronomer seated on a hieroglyph. It is 9 inches high and 5½ wide. According to the renowned Maya scholar, it comes from the Intermediate Period, which would place it at least two or three hundred years later than the stone tablet above. It is noteworthy that individuals seated on glyphs also appear on carved series at Copán.

While relief and full-round sculpture of the same culture and period in medieval American art usually speak the same plastic language, we observe here a strong stylistic deviation. Besides the differences inherent in a three-dimensional piece and the more limited relief, we note in *fig. b* a complete departure from the stylized manner that we observed in preceding examples and saw illustrated in *fig. a.* A robust and dynamic rhythm permeates the carving, and, instead of an aristocratically cool and remote representation, a human of flesh and blood—with even a dose of humor—sits before us. A new plastic idiom is injected into the piece that here is only the expression of power and life, but which in the following centuries changed into hardness and even coarseness. Besides the display of talent in the easy carriage of the turned head, which again faces left, the sculpturally difficult gesture of the arms and hands should be observed. In a statue carved perhaps five hundred years later (see *Pl. 62, fig. b*) they are no longer kept separate but held close to the leg, even though the greater mass of stone would have made it safe to cut them in the round had the artistic stimulus still been alive.

The great virtuosity of the Maya sculptor in composing figures within the limits of a circle recalls the distant *tondos* of early Italian painting. Just as in the case of those great Quattrocento panels, the subject matter never seemed crammed into its circumscribed space, so, in the three examples shown on *Pl. 82,* the content of each relief, no matter how intricate, is artistically balanced and fits into the frame.

A ball-court marker from Copán, 25 inches in diameter, is shown in *fig. a.* As was noted in the chapter on architecture, ball games were played throughout the southern Mexican and the Maya areas, and it is not surprising that the people of these regions set the mark of their genius on the paraphernalia required for this ceremonial sport. Two personages are carved on this piece, facing each other across an inscribed plaque. The one on the left seems to be attired in the protective armor necessary for the game, while the other, judging from his elaborate garb and the masks attached at both front and rear, might be an officiating priest or chief.

The density of composition transmits even to us something of the tension that must have preceded such an occasion, upon which at times even lives were forfeit. The creation of a ground line gives to the two individuals firm footing. Although available space is limited, they do not have to stoop to fit within the circular border, and even the headdresses have freedom of movement. Unobtrusive and subtle are the four points on the inside rim of the frame, forming in effect a quatrefoil for the relief. With its unbelievable variety of sculptural lines and shapes, this marker can be considered at present the most superb example of its type. It is dated about 600.

On a small round altar from Tonina, also known as Ocosingo, central Chiapas (*fig. b*), a priest making an offering is the sole subject. He is placed in the circular field with complete command of composition, without a ground line or other plastic element to stabilize or bind him on this difficult shape. The outer frame of hieroglyphs and the deep undecorated background set off the figure in the center admirably. His face is clean-cut, his gesture easily understood, and his pose has lightness and grace. There is in the carving dignity, maturity, and general appeal.

A second ball-court marker, one from Chinkultic, Chiapas, is shown in *fig. c*. It is 18½ inches in diameter and also bears a disk with a glyphic inscription. Here there is no ground line for the figure to rest upon. A quite unrealistic pose is depicted, and there is less subtlety in composing for a circular frame. Many straight lines cut across the field, and although they furnish interesting contrast (as in the case of the rectangle formed by the legs), they also introduce considerable restlessness. The two blocks of glyphs seem awkwardly placed, but those in the rim are spaced with remarkable facility. The date is 591.

The recording of the dress and certain technical details in its delineation do not seem purely Maya. (See *Pl. 69, fig. a*.) In fact, in the plastic language of the whole piece influence from another culture is evident. There is a flatness about the whole, a rigidity of line and a certain lack of geniality.

In their build-up the three pieces manifest somewhat a common ideology; in all of them the chief figure in the scene turns toward the left and similar details of costume can be detected. But the longer we compare each with the other, the more pronounced become their differences and the more clearly we sense a diversity of background. In the first, besides the human element, a composite mythology had to be served; in the second, the calmness of maturity and a virtuosity in expression simplified whatever had to be recorded; in the third, the idea is not crystal clear, but tinged with an elusive alienness.

Three stone fragments, each portraying a human head, are brought together on *Pl. 83* to show those considerable stylistic differences that appeared in localities relatively not too distant from one another and all connected by trade and ethnic threads. Copán lies about two hundred twenty miles from Piedras Negras, and Piedras Negras some four hundred fifty from Tajín. All three examples present the left profile, which, as may already have been observed, is the position of an overwhelming majority of high dignitaries in carvings and must have had iconographical significance.

The spirit, however, of each is characteristic. The first two are highly Maya. The Piedras Negras work (*fig. a*) dates perhaps from a later period than the Copán piece (*fig. b*), which shows a much greater simplicity in approach. Aside from this, Piedras Negras was master of relief and remained within the bounds of that technique, perfecting it to a decidedly individual degree. Copán, on the other hand, produced some of the most liberated sculpture in the round, and even this fragment shows a tendency in that direction. In *fig. c* a section of a column from El Tajín is seen. Its plastic units and the spreading of design, outspokenly Totonac in type, are utterly different from the other two.

A comparison of the eyes in the three pieces will show in the first a circular deepening, in the second a lidded half-moon shape, and in the third, a deeper hole with convulsive overhanging eyebrows. In addition, the decorative background and other accompanying features, such as ear and earplug, document how distinctive was the recording of a similar theme in a similar medium.

Pl. 84 also offers comparative material, for it is by placing examples from two cultures beside each other that we are best able to mark the differences, sometimes subtle, sometimes obvious, that characterize individual styles.

Fig. a presents a lintel from El Chicozapote, a lesser-known site in the valley of the Usumacinta River that lies between Yaxchilán and Piedras Negras. As we have already seen, this region produced superb carvings. The scene here features two people, a stooped older man and a youthful figure that might be a woman. Each is gesticulating with one hand, in both cases that on the inside, which may be a concession to compositional and decorative considerations. Both faces have portrait-like features. Here it might be remarked that the majority of early portraiture is executed in profile. Seemingly there were technical reasons for this, for individual features are more tellingly brought out in outline than in full-face representation. Even the Italians—far later than Piero della Francesca—show this predilection.

This lintel, dated about 690, is one of the few that still retain their original colors. The skin of both figures is a burning red; necklaces, earplugs, feathers, and the empty inscription field are emerald-green, while the body of the headdresses is a flame-red. Loincloths are green and blue, and the background is dark red with a blue border above and below.[74]

The Zapotec stone relief (*fig. b*), about 15 by 24 inches, presents an obvious contrast in style that requires little further comment. Here also persons are seated facing each other, on the ground or low cushions in the upper half and, in the lower, on daises.

The two figures on the right are men, judging from their cross-legged pose and flowing feathers, the other two, women, seated in Indian fashion. Note the feet under the fringe of the skirt. Both wear a headdress very similar to that found even today in Oaxaca (where it is called *tlacoyal*) and in certain parts of the Guatemalan highlands. It is made of heavy strands twisted around the head in the manner of a turban, with the loose ends left to hang down the back of the head like a tassel.[89] Woven fabrics are designated on all four figures, with the shawls around the shoulders of the women and the breechcloths of the men especially clear.

The top section of the carving is devoted to the open jaw of a monster with six large teeth. From it emerges a figure, a garland in its hand and a bubble coming out of its mouth signifying speech, probably an emanation. In the lower panel, this part is occupied by a small monkey.

In contrast to the blank background of the preceding lintel, the remaining space is filled with signs and symbols, like a page of Zapotec manuscript. Glyphs are inscribed even over part of the margin. The content is said to be calendrical, with an unusual number of day signs.[20] The two carvings, with so much similarity in theme and so little in iconography, come from sites about three hundred seventy miles from each other.

Beginning with *Pl. 85* a series of three-dimensional Maya carvings comes to discussion. The fragment from Copán (*fig. a*) was undoubtedly built into a structure, judging from the tenon at the back, and appears to be the reared head of a reptile. Even in its damaged state the piece is fresh and alive, with something of the primeval power of a Romanesque gargoyle. The surety of execution in all details attests to an iconography so established that the carver knew exactly how to give shape to an image of the Maya fantasy-world.

The human head (*fig. b*), also from Copán, was likewise probably applied as decoration to a building. The almond cut of the eyes, the somewhat aquiline nose, and half-open mouth are all details which will be found in the sculpture of Copán and regions influenced by it. In this head the upper teeth are clearly visible, while in those that follow they seem to have been conventionalized until they appear to be the end of the tongue. The rings around the eyes, denoting a mask or paint, were met in Lintel 1, Piedras Negras (see *Pl. 77, fig. a*). The wooden brace below the chin was fashioned to keep it in balance on the museum shelf.

Heads made of stucco (*Pl. 86*) were also frequently used as a decorative element on Maya buildings. Although because of their friable material most of them today are in poor condition, their importance warrants their inclusion here.

Real modeling in the features and a good feeling for the natural curves of the face are revealed in the head salvaged from Palenque by Maudslay (*fig. a*). Of the four, this quietly human piece stands nearest to our esthetic principles.

With its open mouth, teeth, and hanging under lip, the head from Piedras Negras (*fig. b*) approaches a mask in idea. This is the only one of the four in which enough of the headdress remained to make a restoration of this part possible. In the execution of all these heads certain similar plastic tricks are noticeable, but this specimen has, nevertheless, its own style. It is larger than life size and is said to have been part of a heroic figure.

Even more individuality is apparent in *fig. c,* from Uxmal, Yucatan. A fortunate preservation of some of its coloring gives us a clearer idea of the original appearance. Here we have an example of one way in which eyes were painted in pre-Columbian America: it was done by giving a light color to the eyeball, a strongly contrasting dark to the iris, and even adding a dot in the center to suggest the gleam of the pupil. The slight cast, plainly depicted, was to the Maya a mark of beauty. The painted rings recall the Copán head of the preceding plate. The face may have emerged from a monster jaw—the fragmentary remnants around it, especially under the chin, would suggest some such frame. Drawn with proportioned clean-cut lines, the aristocratically closed lips give a severe and uncommunicative expression. Baffling plastic details are visible above the nose and upper lip. But the longer we gaze at this face, the more we glimpse of the life which lies today shattered and in chips.

Fig. d comes from Louisville, British Honduras, and is about 9 inches high. Closer in expression to what might be called the Copán type, it shows a fine sense for light and shade. A tendency toward remoteness is noticeable in the veiled eyes and the abstract expression.

Among the larger examples of Maya sculpture that were incorporated into their architecture, a special place is due the imposing trachyte figure, larger than life size (*Pl. 87*), which once occupied the second place on the Hieroglyphic Stairway at Copán. The low dais upon which he sits is embellished with symbolic decoration in keeping with Maya ceremony. On the left, tassels can be discerned, with lattice-work below them similar to that noted on the Piedras Negras stone stelae (see *Pl. 72*).

There is dignity in the statue even in its mutilated state. His massive headdress is fashioned in the shape of a monster's upper jaw. The cape, meticulously carved, shows intricate textile patterns and tassels, and an elaborate belt can still be distinguished. A heavy jade necklace and bar with mask rest on his chest, and earrings almost hide his ears. The legs, too, are decorated with well-defined ornaments and the ceremonial apron hanging between them is enriched with a large bold design.

As already mentioned, every step of this great structure is covered with glyphs, and most of it, if not all, was painted. (See *Pl. 21, fig. a.*) Five statues, each different, punctuated the majestic sweep of the stairway. They must have been a splendid sight against the plastic background, vibrant with color. In no other civilization is there anything quite like it. This statue, even as it stands, uprooted from its original setting and forlorn, is still a worthy match for many a Hindu or Chinese figure in our museums, whether a 6th-century Buddha or a Judge of Hell of the later Ming Dynasty.

A number of related stone heads exist which also were not independent statues but ornaments for the entablature sections of buildings. The type was found at several sites but most are known to have come from Copán. On the three plates that follow a series of them is presented.

A head from Copán (*Pl. 88, fig. a*) shows the typical features, executed according to a well-established sculptural language. Eyes are almond shape, drawn out at the corners; the slender nose is long and straight, and a somewhat curling upper lip discloses part of the teeth or tongue. The head is pleasantly elongated, and locks of hair are represented by groups of two or three chiseled lines leading away from the face.

Another stone head from this site, nearly life size, is pictured in *fig. d*. Although the sculptural build-up is at first glance strikingly similar, there is less softness in the expression. Its shape is not so elongated, and the cheek bones are emphasized a little more. The hair is more rigid and is drawn with different strokes. The earring, here undamaged, shows the style associated with the type. In this piece the tenon at the back is visible that served to fix the sculpture into the wall of the building.

The provenience of the carving in *fig. c* is unknown, but it has positive Maya characteristics. The ear ornament, though smaller, is similar to the one just mentioned, and the open mouth also suggests the other heads. But there is no indication of hair, and the large protruding ornament applied on the forehead is a new element. The eyes have a slit line and not an almond shape; the nose is shorter, and the cheeks are more oval.

Fig. b comes from Quiriguá. Despite outspoken plastic differences, the kinship is obvious. However, it no longer has the radiation of the others. Slight changes in each feature bring about a coarsening of the expression: the eye line is drawn more toward the temples, with deeper carving in the corners; the chiseled line of the hair is much more conventionalized and less artistic; the nose is stumpy, and the mouth smaller and not so finely drawn; also, the aristocratic elongation of the head is gone, and the chopped-off lower half of the face gives to it a sullen unfriendliness. Throughout the piece the expression has narrowed down and darkened; this is the head of an idol.

In the two examples on *Pl. 89,* the carefully arranged hair that frames the youthful face is topped with the curling leaves of the corn. It is partly because of this feature that these sculptures are usually called Maize-gods. They were all created to be viewed from below, and the dramatic effect of the powerful tropic sunlight from above was carefully calculated.

The limestone bust pictured in *fig. a* is about life size for an Indian. The treatment of the hair and headdress is the same as that seen in the Copán heads of the preceding plate, and the face has the same oval shape. But here for the first time the upper part of the body is represented. The shoulder line seems somewhat abrupt and rectilinear. From the large necklace placed over the chest is suspended a grotesque mask, on the snout of which is carved another face. Pendants suggesting snake heads hang down from the jewel. Both hands were extended, the left now broken off, the right turned downward—a gesture associated with the Maize-god, as will be seen in the next plate. The face has an inward-turned expression, giving the whole piece the atmosphere of an incantation.

Fig. b presents another young Maize-god, also from Copán. Its height is 18 inches. In this side view is seen most clearly the characteristics that mark the type. A crest of softly curling maize leaves surmounts the oval face. Strands of hair, brushed back from the forehead and temples, fall in front and behind the great earplugs, creating a soft and pleasing frame for the face.[43] The head has a stronger, more impassive expression than its companion on the plate.

After observing these several examples, we are inclined to conclude that whether the sculptor worked as an individual or whether he merely conformed with the demands and restrictions of a hierarchic tradition, he gave to his work a living rhythm that was his own.

Maudslay's great contribution to pre-Columbian archaeology is not found in his books alone. During the long months that he passed in the cities of Maya splendor, he made casts—and under what difficult circumstances—of important inscriptions on stone monuments, thus enabling scholars of later generations to work on the problems of many glyphs, generally inaccessible or now even obliterated. For the cause of art, perhaps one of his greatest contributions was the transportation to England of sculptured fragments from Copán, through hundreds of miles of jungle. In London these have served as inspiration for scores who never could have seen them in the forsaken valley in Honduras.

In this collection is the crown jewel of medieval American sculpture, the bust of the Maize-god shown on *Pl. 90*. Life size, it is said to have been one of a series that decorated the exterior wall of the Temple of the Sculptured Doorway (Structure 22).

The date of the temple appears to fall in mid-8th century. Here a comparison with the Europe of that time is recommended. After the migratory waves of Asiatic nomads had swept over that continent, monumental art there was in eclipse, and we must turn to the large Buddhistic statues of Asia to find great sculpture contemporary with this period of Maya art.

This bust of the Maya Maize-god has suffered many misfortunes, but luckily the general sculptural lines are not too damaged for our enjoyment. Even though the top section of the headdress is broken, it still tends to enhance and elevate the figure. The smooth forehead, somewhat flattened in accordance with the beauty ideal of the Maya, is emphasized by the upward sweep of the hair. The eyes look down in a baffling and fascinating way. Note that they have no realistic outline; the upper eyelid protrudes slightly, showing no actual rim, a great and crucial difference when compared to the others, naturalistically finished. The carved half-circle of the eye sockets helps bring out the desired expression, which changes with the variations of light. The upper lip is drawn up a little, giving a definite impression of speaking or chanting.

It is the mouth and eyes that decide the success of a sculptured face, whether the subject be an actual portrait or an idealization. And probably the softness of the eyes and the enigmatic character of the mouth in this carving are responsible for the title, "The Singing Girl," which clung to the statue until the early 20's. One is apt to interpret the ingratiating gesture of the figure, its supple rounded proportions—deceptively un-Caucasian—as feminine, while actually they are evidence of the feline grace that is a characteristic of the Maya even today. The soft merging of the shoulders into the upper arms is not only a good piece of realistic sculpture but gives to the figure the sensuous radiation of a young body.

All the ornaments represented were probably of jade, for metal was rare in the Great Period. The large protruding beads that form a necklace and frame the monster-mask set off the smooth surface of the body with their light and shadow effect. They also furnish us with unquestionable evidence of a genuine Maya style of stringing jade beads. A wide cuff adorns each wrist, and a belt and loincloth are suggested at the waist. A comparison with the bust on the preceding plate, the plastic principles of which are identical, will prove the superlative quality of this carving.

Consideration and clarity are manifest in the execution of the arms and hands. The palms show even the life line. The right hand curves downward in a condescending and inviting gesture, while the pose of the left conveys at one and the same time divine blessing and admonition. A similar position, implying both invocation and restraint, is met in Asiatic art, but there the right hand points upward and the left, down. In Buddhism this is interpreted as signifying "without fear" and "charity."

The spell of the Copán Maize-god is strengthened by the spiritual message conveyed through it. The longer we look at this serene figure out of an alien world, the more we are loosed from the beauty ideals of our own civilization. The radiation of a spirit expressed in so overwhelming a manner takes hold on us. We are aware of a communication being delivered and feel the poorer because of our inability to understand it. He seems to be a link between mankind, transitory and restless, and the celestial Creator.

After this chapter was already written, an appreciation of this statue appeared in the posthumous volume of essays by the great English art-historian and critic, Roger Fry, among lectures on Egyptian, Mesopotamian, Aegean, Negro, Chinese, Indian, and Greek art. We quote:

"In the finest works of the Maya culture which preceded the Aztec, we find a much more surprising freedom from the rectilinear geometric bias . . . , a plastic sensibility of the rarest kind. I do not know whether even in the greatest sculpture of Europe one could find anything exactly like this in its equilibrium between system and sensibility, in its power at once to suggest all the complexity of nature and to keep every form within a common unifying principle, i.e. each form taking up and modifying the same theme. The oval is of extraordinary beauty in its subtle variations upon the main idea—you will note how a too exact symmetry is avoided by bringing the lock of hair on one side further over the cheek than on the other. Here then we find the expression of a sensibility of a very high order. There is also I think undoubtedly vitality, a powerful suggestion of the inner life—of a strange tension of spirit—of an almost tragic cast."

In an attempt to avoid an anticlimax after the Maize-god bust, we turn to some aspects of architectural relief that offer a contrast. A few relief carvings used to embellish the bases of buildings were shown under architecture. *Pl. 91* presents other examples, included here under sculpture because of their hybrid character and the fact that they are considered independent of the structure.

Fig. a pictures a detail from the base of the Palace at Palenque. Artistically these figures in stone fall far below the gracious stucco reliefs that appear exactly above them, and they are dated earlier, in the beginning of the 6th century. They are well worth study with their modeling, sometimes grotesque but always expressive, reminding one in their linear conduct somewhat of the Comalcalco stucco work. (See *Pl. 80*.)

An interesting parallel takes us out of the Maya Area to the Zapotec-Mixtec site of Monte Albán, about three hundred miles from Palenque. Here among the ruins of an early temple, stone slabs were found bearing incised figures referred to as "Los Danzantes." The first illustration in this chapter (see *Pl. 57, fig. a*) presented a close view of one of these; *fig. b* shows several others. These figures are not recorded in the plastic style of Palenque, but rather are crude and petroglyph-like. Yet, power of observation, surety of line, and humor are noticeable in them. What a veritable cycle of cartoons they must have formed, ranged one beside the other in their architectural setting.

In Yucatan, the type of decoration on the base of buildings changed. The human figure was forced into the background, and, as a result of a more barbarous ideology, animals and monsters took over the field. A section of a stuccoed wall from the Maya site Acancéh, in northern Yucatan (*fig. c*), shows this trend. It is dated in the early 8th century. Projecting cornices covered with patterns of the same iconography leave a broad zone in the center for the main decoration. This space is further divided by double stepped bands into panels, and a figure, a fantastic blend of the human and animal, is placed in each. Prominent are the bat, serpent, and squirrel in human pose and gesture. The speech scroll occurs several times. As grotesque and strange as they are, they bear the unmistakable mark of good craftsmanship and are highly decorative. When first uncovered, the whole was brightly painted.

Artistically the most uncouth carving on this plate is *fig. d,* a section from the base of the Temple of the Warriors at Chichén Itzá. The panel here is also framed but the protruding bands are this time undecorated. Again the subject is animals in somewhat humanized poses, but the brilliant individuality of earlier Maya art, its free and spontaneous character are no longer in evidence. The eagles and jaguars that alternate in flat relief, with glyphic signs strewn among them, follow a stereotyped pattern, identified with the Mexican occupation of this town.

Because so often the exact purpose of an excavated stone object can only be guessed at, it is a special occasion when an original painting can be produced to document its use. *Pl. 92, fig. a* presents a restored mural found on the north bench of the filled-in Temple of the Chacmool at Chichén Itzá, showing a warrior chief seated on a throne that is carved in the likeness of a jaguar. The head of the beast is depicted looking toward the spectator, and the two forelegs are clearly drawn; his curling tail hangs down at the other end.

This very type of seat was found in a chamber of an early structure that was encased within the temple-base of the well-known Castillo, where it may be seen in its original position today (*fig. b*). It is 33 inches long, 27 high, and carved from one block of stone. The animal was painted a brilliant red, and applegreen jade disks of remarkably fine quality were inlaid for spots and eyes. A large turquoise mosaic was inserted in the middle of its back. Its white teeth, remarkable in their ferocity, are all intact. A comparison of the two photographs will show how well the mural complements the statue, giving us an authentic glimpse of an episode in a Late Maya ceremony. Waldeck publishes another jaguar throne in the so-called "beau relief" stucco at Palenque.[166] Attention should also be called to the jaguar seats of the Inca Empire. (See *Pl. 277, fig. a.*)

Before closing this review of figural sculpture in the Maya Area, it seems appropriate to bring examples of carving in the round, in which the human shape was frozen into a highly unrealistic pose. It is interesting to note that this deterioration is coincident with the non-Maya period of Yucatan. Both of the following specimens come from Chichén Itzá.

Pl. 93, fig. a shows two atlantes which served, as the photograph clearly indicates, as entrance pillars for a small building. Certain parts are blocked out of the mass to suggest the human figure, its hands upraised, as if holding up the lintel of the door and, ultimately, the roof. Despite the clumsiness of the general impression, the columns appear less heavy in effect than they would have uncarved. Smaller figures in atlantean pose are found at this site supporting the slab of an altar or dais.

The monolithic statue illustrated in *fig. b,* nearly 5 feet long, is designated as

‹ 143 ›

Chacmool, or the Red Tiger. Such semireclining figures, with knees drawn up and upper body raised on the elbows, are quite common in northern Yucatan and are also found from the Totonac region in the Mexican Area as far south as El Salvador. They seem to have served as a sort of altar and are believed to date from the 11th or 12th century. The round concavity clasped by both hands was apparently used for offerings or incense. The breast is decorated with a conventionalized bird, a motif seen on other sculptures at Chichén Itzá. In comparison with the other ornaments, the headdress and earplugs are executed with more detail, showing serpent heads in low relief among other patterns.

The statuary presented on this plate is the uninspired ending of a long and rich artistic vein and represents one of the several low points that every civilization doubtless experiences. The power and monumentality we have seen have here become, for the time being, stereotyped mass production, static and earthbound.

As the main consideration of this survey is to display artistic highlights of the various cultures, selecting subjects that would appeal to the general reader's esthetic sense, certain material of specialized interest and occasionally even carvings well known among archaeologists have been omitted as delaying factors. The line of artistic development often does not follow along anthropological and ethnic borders, and therefore a survey from the esthetic point of view has sometimes to work from a different angle.

There are, however, certain types of sculpture in the Mexican and Maya areas which should be mentioned, although they are not illustrated here. Among these are the mammoth heads and reliefs, problematic but articulate, found at Tres Zapotes, Vera Cruz, and at La Venta, just across the border in Tabasco. From the scant material available at present, this region, fertilized by several first-class cultures, seems to have produced an interesting art of its own, not only in stone but in pottery and jade. A fuller knowledge of this territory will doubtless throw light on several problems of pre-Columbian archaeology.[141]

Mention should also be made of the colossal heads and crude human and animal figures, reaching a height of 5 feet in certain cases, found in the department of Escuintla in Guatemala and still farther down the Isthmus in El Salvador. Although rarely of great artistic merit, they display good carving ability and are significant as cultural milestones. The recent excavations in the region of Cotzumalhuapa in southwestern Guatemala—in the same district as well-known El Baúl—have brought to light sculpture of an amazingly fine quality.[155]

The next illustrations take us into the southern periphery of Maya influence to the Ulúa Valley in the northern part of Honduras. Here the arts that developed in Yucatan and Guatemala blended with those of the highlands of Honduras and were tinged with Chorotega influences from the south.

Among the most interesting manifestations of this district are the calcite vases, executed so perfectly and with such artistry that only some of the alabasters from the Mexican Area (see *Pl. 257*) may be said to rival them. The material, indigenous to this region and generally classified as a marble, is milky in tone with a delicate bluish-gray vein. Although the cylindrical shape occurs in early Maya pottery and, in smaller size, even occasionally among the early Mexican cultures, there can be little doubt that the pieces of this type originated in a single cultural circle.

Pl. 94, fig. a shows a low tripod bowl, about 4 inches high, with grinning heads, probably monkeys, as handles. Two scaly bands inclose the decorative panel, the top one running to the right, the bottom, in the opposite direction. Between them, in the center, is carved a conventionalized mask or head. An oval mouth with teeth is the first feature to be noticed; just above it are almond eyes and a headdress of scrolls, perhaps stereotyped puma ears. The additional eyes, one on each side, are discussed under *fig. b*. The rest of the panel is filled in with two rows of fret-scrolls, generally interpreted as serpent tails, which occur in a more loosely knit pattern in various Maya carvings and can also be traced in decorative designs from even farther north. (See especially *Pls. 76, fig. b*, and *274* for Maya and *Pl. 63, fig. a*, for Totonac examples.)

Lately this single itinerant motif has been torn from its indigenous *milieu* and presented as proof of direct Chinese influence in pre-Columbian art. A closer comparison of it with patterns that appear in Asiatic art is undertaken at some length in the chapter, "Evolution or Influence"; here we are concerned only with its development as an organic decorative element of a Middle American culture.

Fig. d presents another low tripod of ingratiating form. It is about 5 inches high. The legs of this piece are carved into puma heads, and the handles project from the sides of the vase like gargoyles. The double row of scrolls appears again, the pattern forming two gaping serpent profiles, the curling snouts of which meet above a mask similar to that in *fig. a*. In these we find an explanation of the separate eyes that were carved at the right and left of the face in the other piece. The general effect is less concentrated than in the first example, because of the change in the framing bands. Carved frets interrupt the sequence of scaly motifs in the upper border and occupy the lower one exclusively.

The vase in *fig. c* is about 6¼ inches high, without legs but with a raised base embellished with openwork. The whole decorative outlay resembles in principle the two pieces already discussed. A larger and more angular scaly band runs again without interruption to the right at the top and to the left at the bottom. Bats' heads form the handles and below them bodies are suggested. The mask in the center of the scroll pattern is omitted, but one eye is carved just below the top border, a detached and floating motif, and a foot appears beneath it among the scrolls. The larger surface may account for the use of three instead of two rows of scrolls to fill the panel, or this addition may be due to some technical limitation or a disinclination to carve bigger elements. This larger surface, which could take more plastic decoration, may also have inspired the button-like centers in which the scrolls end. It should not be forgotten that all these marble vases were fashioned with simple stone tools.

The vase in *fig. b* is 7⅜ inches tall and has a diameter of 6½ inches. It also stands on a raised base. Two jaguar heads, one looking up and the other down, make up each handle; conventionalized feet grasp a ball between them. A second pair of feet for each head is carved in relief on the surface of the vase at the side and may serve as a clue to the floating foot just mentioned. This piece carries more decoration than the others; even the base is ornamented with relief, and the openwork is more complicated, suggesting a fret. The scaly band flows away from the inserted rectilinear motif that interrupts it at the top and toward it at the bottom. Three rows of serpent-tail scrolls encircle the main body, among which, on the photograph here shown, four eyes are visible. Doris Stone points out that these are connected with heads in profile, two on each side.[142]

One of the most beautiful specimens of the Ulúa vases is reproduced on *Pl. 95, fig. a.* It is 9⅝ inches high and also has a bottom rim with openwork. The handle represents a puma clasping another animal. Five rows of scrolls ranged about a mask in the center cover the main body of the vase. In none of the others is the fanciful play with the spiral carried through with such logic. Faces in profile are easily recognized beside and below the mask, and even feet are inserted here and there. The scales of the top band move to the left and those at the bottom to the right.

Fig. b is a very shallow basin, less than 2 inches high, without a base and with only one handle. Here a single band of rectangular scales is present in the upper border and one row of spirals in the main panel. The manner in which the spirals are combined into a ∽ shape is suggestive of the undulation of a serpent body, an impression that is carried out in the plastic serpent head as handle. Single scrolls form the blunt end of the reptile's snout and the hinge of the jaw, while a smaller spiral emphasizes the protuberance above the eye. This scroll motif, which is an outstanding feature of all Ulúa vases, belonged to the inner core of the artistic imagination of these people, and wherever there was an opportunity to apply it, they have done so. (Compare the composition of the serpent profiles in *fig. a.*)

That these elaborate marbles were highly prized—their use was probably restricted to the ruling class—is proved by the fact that pottery imitations have been found over a wide area, with, in certain instances, even the handles fashioned into animal form. (See *Pl. 143.*) These shapes from clay, however, have nothing of the arresting beauty of their prototypes. Crude marble vases were unearthed at Kaminaljuyú in the Guatemala highlands and in quite late stratifications in Petén and British Honduras.[152]

INTERLYING AREA

Of the two seated figures on *Pl. 96,* one is from Guatemala, the other, from Costa Rica. The first (*fig. a*) is 11 inches high and shows a kneeling man, without ornament, both hands at his chin. Whether it is a prayerful gesture or only a contemplative pose we do not know, but we cannot escape its human appeal.

The second piece (*fig. b*) belongs to the Guetar culture, which occupied the Costa Rican part of the Isthmus and carved its statues from lava of varying fineness.[167] Note that the pose here is the same as that in the Aztec statue (see *Pl. 61, fig. a*) with even the fingers suggested clasping the knees. The curve of the back and the distribution of weight in the figure make him come alive. The headdress composed of three small lizards in relief is unusual; customary headgear for such stone statues is a conical cap, probably representing the pointed, wadded-cotton helmet of the warrior, which will be seen on the next plate. A comparison of the sculptural details of the two carvings will show that the eye in the Guatemalan piece is egg-shaped and encircled by chiseled-out surfaces, while in the Costa Rican both eyelids are separately indicated.

It would be easy to say that these two statues are "primitive" carvings, but closer inspection will reveal an innate subtlety in them. There is a human softness and sincerity about them which makes them sympathetic at first glance.

The shape called ceremonial axe-heads for lack of a better designation has already been met in the Totonac culture of Mexico (see *Pl. 66*). Now, far to the south in Guatemala, this form appears again in the first two pieces illustrated on *Pl. 97*. The theme of the carving here, however, is not the human head; it has become a more condensed and considerably more mystic subject.

In *fig. b,* 11 inches high, a man is shown leaning backwards in a decidedly forced position against a flight of steps. He may be a sacrificial victim, whose breast is to be torn open to cut out his heart; the steps then would represent the stairway before the temple where this bloody rite is performed. The carving, even in its strongly angular lines, is executed with power and expression. A vulture tearing at a skull is the subject in *fig. a,* an axe 12 inches high and extremely thin. A similar theme was used in a pottery vessel from the Andean Area (see *Pl. 163, fig. a*). In contrast to the Totonac axe-heads, the stone in both of these is pierced. Little elaboration is spent on either, but every line is tellingly placed.

The man with arms akimbo (*fig. c*) presents another example of an independent statue from Costa Rica, boldly executed, with good plastic feeling especially in the legs. He is a little over 4 feet high. The style of headdress is interesting, with its coiled snake and amphibian figure. In this connection it may be noted that the alligator or crocodile is a primary motif in the art of the entire Interlying Area. The combination of the two reptiles, the simple tattoo marking over the body, and the changed features in the face are evidence that we are out of the region where Maya influence made itself felt directly.

Still more novel in sculptural expression is the piece in *fig. d,* about 14 inches high. The two figures, connected by their linked arms, represent "the dual officiants" at a human sacrifice. The one at the right holds a human head, while the other carries an unidentified object in his uplifted hand. Neither shows much individuality in expression. This statue is unique in that two persons are carved from one block of stone. The piece is said to have come from the region of the Guetar culture. From the artistic affiliations found here, the district seems to have been a meeting ground for influences from the south rather than the north.[65] (Compare with *Pl. 225*.)

Although household objects doubtless received artistic attention, few of them remain for our consideration. Fortunately some stone implements have survived to add to the incomplete mosaic of pre-Columbian life. In *Pl. 98* three *metates,* or mealing stones, are illustrated, upon which maize or cocoa beans were ground with a stone roller.

The first (*fig. a*) is Chorotegan in type, although it comes from Santa Lucía Cotzumalhuapa in Guatemala. Its length is 47 inches and its height 21. The serpent head is finely stylized, and the smooth transition of the head into the body of the piece is effected with much suavity. Note the roller shaped to fit the grinding surface.

In the second *metate* (*fig. b*), from Costa Rica, the animal is more realistically brought out, with a puma head, four legs, and a curling tail. The diamond pattern here is reminiscent of the carved figures just discussed from this region, and the ∽ motif on the edge recalls the Ulúa vases.

Openwork introduces variety into the execution of *fig. c*. This *metate*, 29 inches long and 12 high, comes from Nicaragua and seems to represent a puma or jaguar. Quite expressionistic in manner, it conveys a remarkable sense of life, even potential movement. The arabesque on the back of the head, the dissimilar bands that ornament the grinding surface, and the elaborate openwork feet are all highly decorative. So much was undertaken here in stone that the piece was too fragile to withstand the centuries and was discovered in fragments.

All three of these objects served an identical purpose but what individual approach and execution are manifest in each.

In this same area and on somewhat the same artistic level were the low chairs, almost like footstools, upon which it was the privilege of the ruling few to sit. An example of the type in pottery is shown on *Pl. 149*. Ecuador had larger U-shaped stone seats supported by a crouching human figure.

ANDEAN AREA

On our route to the Andean Area, those pre-Columbian sculptures deserve mention that are found around the town of San Agustín, Colombia. This district, some three hundred miles south of Bogotá, has now been converted by the government into a national park. The statues represent human and animal figures in static, often cubistic shapes and in some cases are 14 feet in height. They are crude when compared with the material illustrated. It is noteworthy, however, that they possess certain ideological expressions characteristic of the carving of other areas, though distorted through lower mental and technical abilities.

The sculptor's art in the Andean Area should not be measured by the same standard applied in the Mexican or Maya. Pottery, weaving, and metal-work here were so highly developed that even had this region used stone only in its phenomenal architecture, its place in medieval American art would be secure. There are, however, certain examples that should be presented, not only because they offer new styles but because they broaden the horizon of artistic achievement within the Andean Area itself.

The stone slab in *Pl. 99, fig. a* is about 8 feet high and comes from Cerro Sechín in the Casma Valley (northern coast of Peru). Upon it is drawn a figure with head turned to the right and feet pointing in the same direction; the torso is in more of a frontal pose, further clarified by the position of the two arms. The left hand, grasping a ceremonial bar, is notably unnatural in drawing. As in the Maya stelae, the left shoulder is lower than the right, seemingly a sculptural trick, applied also here to foster an optical illusion.

The carving as such is rather in the nature of incision, without any pretense to plastic effect; nowhere is the superfluous stone cut away. The purpose of the whole composition seems to be simply the recording of a powerful and ferocious personage, although our eyes see mostly the grotesque in it. The style shows affinities to the Chavín culture.

In the high mountains of central Peru lies a small village called Chavín de Huántar. This is the site of extensive ruins consisting of high platforms faced with dressed stone and containing an intricate series of galleries on three distinct levels. A considerable amount of stone carving has been found about the site, and while it may not actually be the center of distribution of the style, all pieces of this flamboyant type are designated as Chavín. Thus, as in the case of Tiahuanaco, the term "Chavín" refers both to a site and to a culture or style.[8] The granite monolith from Chavín shown in *fig. b* is considered to date before the 6th century. This stone, also known as the Stela Raimondi after its discoverer, is 6½ feet high with a greenish cast. A short standing figure is represented wearing a lofty headdress, a veritable tower of masks. Certain motifs of this carving—the branching snake heads, jaguar masks, and claws—appear also in the works from this region in other media (see *Pl. 195*). The ceremonial staffs in both hands and the feet, turned outward, remind one of the god in the center of the Gateway of the Sun at Tiahuanaco, except for the fact that the two scepters here are identical. The stylized detail work is finer, and, since the head is not protruding as in the Tiahuanaco carving, the plastic effect is different. An abundance of masks and conventionalized decorative elements make the monolith a rich ground for students of Andean iconography.

Somewhat clearer for the untrained eye to grasp is the massive statue illustrated in *fig. c.* It was found at Tiahuanaco, and the boy at its head gives an excellent idea of its colossal size—nearly 24 feet in length, including the base. The mass of the stone was carved down into a rectangular block with little allowance made for the arms and hands. Familiar Classic Tiahuanaco patterns are strewn all over the piece, and some of the figures in profile, especially those on and below the arms, resemble closely motifs on the side of the Gateway. One is struck with the condensed and complicated artistic ideology, though its full meaning is problematical to us. A certain organization and refinement can be observed in the decoration, which with its sometimes abstract designs is reminiscent of the textiles of this area.

Smaller objects from these cultures bridge more easily the way to our imagination. The stone animal bowl (*Pl. 100, fig. a*), 13 inches long and 6½ high, is classified as belonging to the Chavín style. It has the shape of a puma. The head is quite realistically portrayed with bared fangs and eyes that were originally inlaid, though its body is made somewhat overweight by the demands of the receptacle placed in its back. The several motifs applied all over the creature may point toward a sacrificial or ceremonial use; besides straight, "clover," and ∽ elements, the Greek cross appears several times, another argument that motifs can be and are invented independently in localities isolated from one another.

The second stone bowl (*fig. b*), about 5 inches high and 26 long, including the handles, is of later manufacture. The piece came from the highlands of Peru and is of Inca style. As will be seen in the chapters on pottery and weaving, the Inca rule established a high level in conventionalized patterns and forms. In this stone bowl the ornament, although originating in nature, is distilled into an agreeable but unindividual decoration. Its appeal is in its suavity and meticulous finish rather than in its design.

It is an enigma why a people so able as those in the Andean Area in modeling clay or casting metal or in shaping intractable stone at will for their building did not easily achieve the higher manifestations of sculpture.

In reviewing the sculpture of the Mexican and Maya areas, we recognize details of orthodoxy surprisingly similar, such as the animal-mask and feathered serpent; yet stylistically, that is, in the matter of sculptural language, these peoples show great temperamental differences. As the Mexicans tended toward mass in their architecture, so they revealed the same feeling for mass in their sculpture. The Maya, on the other hand, perfected the relief in its many aspects, displaying a love of elaboration, of broken surfaces and curving lines that is characteristic of all their art. Dealing less with planes and solid masses than with balance of detail, their work shows greater refinement though less pungency than the Mexican, and reaches its greatest height in its rare three-dimensional statuary.

Like most of the earlier non-European civilizations, the pre-Columbian peoples in their artistic expression seem to have appreciated the beauty of youth without worshiping it, to have respected age without sentimentalizing it. The more terrifying aspects of nature, which they must have had to face in their precariously balanced life, are not shunned in their art.

V

Pottery

MEDIEVAL America fashioned its pottery vessels by building them up of coils of clay, smoothed with the hand or a small implement—a bit of gourd or a sherd. In books on the subject, the absence of the potter's wheel is usually remarked upon apologetically. However, we venture to say that in some ways it worked to an advantage. In those ancient civilizations that employed the wheel from early times, pottery shapes were soon standardized to a few highly refined and universal types; the disappearance of the human figure in utilitarian ware can be ascribed to this factor. The pre-Columbian potter, on the other hand, unhampered by a mechanical device, was proficient in a wider range and variety. His rounded shapes show the life of the hand which fashioned them, and his talent for modeling had free rein to create some of his most original and artistic work. It is this manifestation of genius which will be given the most space here, for a stratigraphic and strictly chronological presentation is not our purpose.

Mention should be made, however, of the inestimable value to archaeology of the amassed material of pre-Columbian pottery. The making of pottery was universal in all our areas, and most excavations reveal at least sherds. Fragments found about a settlement or in its refuse heap frequently lie in layers representative of different periods of time. Thus, the potsherds can be tabulated into a general comparative scheme by their stylistic distinctions, and objects found in close proximity to them correlated. One of the important results of this has been to modify some of the dating derived from stelae, for the pottery has given a much broader view. Laboratory investigations have advanced so far that now, through the analysis of the basic material, the sand or pottery bits used to temper it, the type of slip, and manner of decoration, local and traded ware can be identified, an important factor in tracing cultural interrelations.

In certain regions of the Southwest, household utensils were first made of baskets, sometimes daubed with clay to make them water-tight. Later clay alone was used for bowls and pots, but with the traditional conservatism of primitive man, features of the basket persisted for centuries; not only the shapes were retained, but even the texture was imitated in the design. We find the same tendency to cling to tradition in our own lives. Although columns are no longer necessary to support the roofs of our public buildings they nevertheless adorn many façades, and although the necktie has been reduced from a protective scarf to a mere band without any practical purpose, it is still considered essential to our costume.

The range of pottery production in medieval America is broader than that of most early civilizations in the rest of the world. Here, within the span of a relatively few centuries, an amazing variety was produced, from the basket imitation to the inimitable fresco vase. This chapter, therefore, has the most illustrations in this survey, because each of the five areas offers beautiful and distinctive examples of the art. Besides an overwhelming display of bowls, jars, pitchers, and plates, with countless styles of rims, necks, legs, and lugs, we shall see earthenware painted, carved, stamped with molds, modeled, and sculptured into rare inventions, and, as a crowning achievement, even emerging as individual portraiture of a sort. The choice would be still greater had it not been for the practice of "killing" pottery to release its spirit before it was interred in a grave, or, among the Aztecs, at the lapse of the 52-year cycle. As we review the great variety of these vessels, it is interesting to contemplate the large share that women had in the craft.

The ceramic production of the New World was highly praised by the Spaniards. At this time, because of the tradition of the Moors who had brought the full flowering of Persian art with them to Europe, Spain led in this field. Indeed, the Italian word *majolica* is derived from the Spanish island of Majorca, whose inhabitants had much to teach the Italians in glazing and coloring. Sahagún writes, after seeing the markets of the Aztec Empire, that all the techniques and shapes of the motherland were to be found here. Glazing was unknown, but a high durable polish was obtained by applying a wax preparation, which still keeps its sheen after centuries in the ground.

THE SOUTHWEST

The tradition of basket-work, already mentioned, is corroborated by a large pot (*Pl. 101, fig. a*), 13 inches high, found in Apache County, Arizona. The piece is built up in coiled bands from the bottom and the basket imitation goes so far as to suggest the sustaining frame.

The smaller and more shallow bowl in *fig. b* is constructed on the same principle, but incised frets suggestive of an interwoven pattern were added. In comparing the two, a certain smoothness and refinement in the later one is noticeable, though the first has power and directness.

In the group of bowls from Arizona (*fig. c*), all bright in effect, linear motifs appear as decoration. Except for the one in the center, they are said to date from the 9th or 10th centuries. In form they show less skill than the first two; there is about them an air of groping and uncertainty, as if their makers even in the act of fashioning them had not known how they would turn out. These simplest of shapes are far from perfect, and the same lack of assurance is evident also in the patterns, which show unremitting struggle with the decorative impulse. It is not surprising to find the center bowl dated 13th century; it offers the most complicated design in an execution most nearly approaching good standards, although even here the pattern elements are still far from orderly and the circle in the center shows an unskilled and irresolute hand.

In *fig. d* the human figure appears as decorative element. The human and animals strewn on the inside of the bowl are executed with a really primitive hand, which even had difficulty in spacing them to advantage. The general impression, both in design and shape, is of hesitancy and unevenness.

Another type of pottery is presented in *fig. e.* This round heavy-walled piece is thought to have been an incense burner. It comes from the Hohokam district, which also produced the fine bone carving illustrated in *Pl. 285, fig. a.* Hohokam means in the language of the Pima Indians, "the people who have gone," and is used today to denote one of the most powerful early cultures in the Southwest. The successful working of both clay and bone, together with a manifest ability to represent animal life, is proof of advancing civilization. Round, well-shaped medallions on the jar bring the repetition of a young bird in a gay mood. The hopping, leaping, little figure has the naïve charm of a Walt Disney cartoon and forms a rhythmically moving pattern around the piece. The color is dull red on a buff ground.

Pl. 102 presents jars, or *ollas,* running as large as 16 inches high, from the 12th and 13th centuries. The shapes vary from the round to the elongated, but all five are settled in form. The decorations make use of the most involved permutations and variations—generally of the zigzag used as a fret or in checkerboard, triangular, saw-tooth, and rectangular patterns, with the always grateful contrast of solid white against solid black, sometimes lightened by hatching. Particular skill was required to adapt the meandering designs to the bulging shape. Each jar has attraction, vigor, and an amazing amount of individuality. It will be observed how refined the same shape and same pattern elements have become in the time-span of a few centuries. Such ancient Pueblo *ollas* are known to have been kept long as heirlooms.

Here (notably in the center jar of *fig. a* and in *fig. b*) we first meet a "negative" design, in which the pattern appears in the natural light color of the body of the piece, while the background is painted. Startling and ingenious effects are sometimes achieved by using this "reverse" method in interlocking patterns.

Pl. 103 shows widely diversified types of various periods from pueblos in New Mexico, Arizona, and Colorado. The rather shallow bowl from Apache County, Arizona (*fig. a*), is 9½ inches in diameter and dated between the 10th and 12th centuries. It carries a conventionalized body of a reptile, with two heads only suggested. The diamond design is flat and very much simplified so that its effect is predominantly decorative. Note the same idea in the brocade on *Pl. 175, fig. b*.

Fig. b, from Sikyatki, Arizona, shows a more advanced talent and bears a later date—14th century. The hand in the center is introduced here not as realistic representation but as a symbol, perhaps of magic. It shows observation and skill in the spacing of the fingers and the exact drawing of the cuff section with its ornament. The more or less abstract design, suggestive of a bird, that starts at the lower left of the arm and circles around the bowl, terminating on the right at the wrist, is deliberately placed and heightens the feeling of esoteric meaning. The outside of the bowl is also decorated. Here we meet the same elements of stylized drawing that have survived in the sand paintings of the Southwest and furnished the primary inspiration to modern Hopi ceramics.[73] The colors are brownish black and red on a yellow ground.

The deeper bowl in *fig. c* is tentatively dated in the 14th or early 15th century. The outside has a long fret design in black, outlined in white, on a slip of clear red; the inside shows a light-colored negative scroll bedded in shaded sections. In spite of the countermovement of the elements, the whole pattern gives a revolving impression. This piece is also from central Arizona.

Fig. d, from near Deming, New Mexico, is more advanced in its pattern development—the most sophisticated of the group. A curving fishtail can be discerned attached to a semicircular figure with four dark feet or fins. Bands in the natural light clay of the bowl are used to outline all the elements of the design. Fine parallel and crisscross lines give variation. Its appeal is apparent, independent of its symbolism.

The water container from the ruins of Mesa Verde, Colorado (*fig. e*), demonstrates how skillful the Cliff-dwellers had become to fashion successfully such a vessel of friable clay. Carried to work in the distant fields on a band, it kept the water fresh for a long time; even our age utilizes the cooling property of unglazed pottery. The decoration has two main motifs: the interlocking step design in the middle and the linear embellishment in the zones at either end. Good feeling for balance is shown by the placement of the heavy, more involved panel in the center.

Whether intentionally or not, *fig. f,* an early gray-ware piece from Arizona, has the drollness of a toy for grown-ups. It is 8 inches high and also a water carrier. The body is constructed on the same principle as that in the preceding jug, but the addition of four stocky legs, an animal head, and handle proves greater originality. It reminds one of the *aquamanile* (bronze water carrier) of medieval Europe from about the same time. The long zigzags in black and white give life to the static shape, and its spontaneity makes sure contact with us.

The mug shape must have been quite common in the Southwest, as many such pieces exist in various collections and museums, although no two have ever been found identical in design.

The three illustrated on *Pl. 104, fig. a* come from the heart of the Cliff-dweller region, and date from about the beginning of the 11th century. The tallest is nearly 5½ inches. There is enough difference in decoration to demonstrate the extent of individual artistry among these people. Considered from left to right, the first has a combined design of three different elements in a large zigzag; the second skillfully varies one motif, the oblique fret; the third is the most complicated, with its central panel of repeated rectangles (in itself a clever management of the negative white and positive black), as well as an upper and lower border and decorated handle. The similarity of the form to the European tankard is evident.

The double jar (*fig. b*) from Mesa Verde is smaller and dates from about the middle of the 13th century. The coupling of two pieces into one is an advance, and the pattern has become routined. It should be noted that the oblique lines in the panels of each side run from the handle toward the outside edge, producing a centripetal effect pleasing to our eye. The flaring rim is also interesting and unusual.

The pottery dipper in *fig. c* is intricately decorated with motifs now more or less familiar. On the handle, the progression of the design from a simple double-outlined meander to a series of interlocking step-frets in black and white is accomplished with delightful ingenuity. The fret appears again in the bottom of the bowl combined with spirals that harmonize with the curve of the utensil.

The cream of Southwestern pottery is displayed on *Pl. 105.* The earliest piece among them is on the left in *fig. a.* This jug, with the curious animal head as handle, dates from the 9th century and comes from the San José River in western New Mexico. What intricate motifs are here applied and how well they are harmonized. The sweeping composite elements of the main body are counterbalanced by the more rigid and controlled checkered band around the neck.

The bowl beside it repeats a single pattern in the three bands. It is a finely executed design, one difficult to space. There is subtle counterpoint in the shifting of the pattern that emphasizes the saw-tooth white line running obliquely across the vessel.

In the piece at the right a completely new decorative approach is introduced. The upper half is bare except for the lacelike star around the mouth; the lower varies two motifs that cross each other on a dark ground. Two stubby handles indicate that the jug was made to be suspended on a cord or band. Both of these pieces are from the upper Gila River, New Mexico, and date from the 13th century.

The three kiva jars from Mesa Verde (*fig. b*) are all Pueblo III, a period of high attainment. In each case the shape is perfected without being cold or impersonal. The patterns show the routined application of motifs developed throughout the centuries, and the jars still retain their glazelike polish after all these years, a contrast to the chalky surfaces of older pieces.

Attention should be called to the analogy in the designs in this row to those directly above them. The one on the left shows the spiral in combination with single hatching; the jar in the center uses parallel bands of step-frets, this time with a more horizontal effect; the light pattern on the dark upper half of the vessel on the right outlines the same star that encircles the rim of the earlier one above it. All three have precisely wrought rims, set back a little from the openings and decorated.

In *fig. c* a jar of a very different character is presented, another Sikyatki piece from the 15th century. (See *Pl. 103, fig. b.*) Although the shape is one of the most difficult to form, it is the design which makes the piece outstanding. The butterflies or moths alternate with geometric elements, placed with mature artistic sense. Burnt tones of tan and red brown on buff, outlined in dark brown or black, make up the color scheme.

Although from across the Mexican border, the polychrome jar in *fig. d* belongs organically to the Southwest through its language of shape and pattern. It comes from Chihuahua and is dated in the 15th century. It is of a creamy highly polished ware and about 8 inches high. The band with its pennant-shaped detail running obliquely across the bulging body of the piece probably denotes a textile. The two beady-eyed parrots, one upright, the other upside down, in the triangle at the left are completely stylized, yet drawn with very good feeling for the subject.

Even more striking is the head, fashioned with a minimum of modeling and emphasized by color. Although the face is not all-important, the simple trick of leaving it white above the variegated surface of the rest of the jar draws our attention to it. The hair-fine line of the eyebrows contrasts with the heavy strokes on the cheeks, which probably denote paint or tattoo. Note that the eyes are cut in such a way that they seem to look at one from any angle, a characteristic that is brought out in the photograph. This little vessel combines the humor of a toby jug with considerable native dignity.

In the pottery of the Southwest a special place must be reserved for the bowls from the valley of the Mimbres River in southern New Mexico (*Pls. 106* and *107*). The population here did not live in cliff-dwellings or in community apartment buildings—at least, no remnants of these exist—but in pit houses. Their humble architecture would not lead to the expectation of any special artistic manifestation. They made the usual corrugated pottery and other common types, the shapes of which were also conventional. But on the matt inner surface of their food bowls they developed a style of silhouette, human and animal, that is unique in pre-Columbian ceramics. Only at Coclé, Panama, 2800 miles to the southeast, do we find a somewhat related approach. Naturalistic representation was apparently not intended; the figures serve as decorative motifs and a story-telling quality of rare charm emerges from these bowls.

Besides the human figure, birds, deer, antelope, dogs, rabbits, fish, insects, and reptiles are used, as well as fabulous creatures who step out of the fantasy-world of these potter artists. The bowls have a fragile appearance, and with their chalky surface recall to mind the naïve but expressive Rhages bowls of 13th-century Persia. Mimbres pottery is not colored; the ground is without exception a whitish slip and the figures are applied in black.

The basket-weave piece (*Pl. 106, fig. a*) shows a well-spaced pattern, covering the inside without margins. The unevenness of the hand-drawn lines lends vibration to the design.

In *fig. b,* the composition fills the entire space, regardless of the large amount of "air" left about the figures. The two men are primitively drawn, but their placement, whether intentionally or not, gives a sense of perspective. The fish-monster, much larger, dominates the scene. A human arm and leg emerging from the body may denote a masked figure. In contrast to the solid black of the two men, the fish is decorated with an S design and other patterns. Of the three fine black threads issuing from its ferocious jaws, the lower ends in the hands of the first and smaller figure, while the two others continue on to the second. These lines are all that connect the three characters in the scene, and one feels that the artist who put them there knew how to bind loose elements into a whole. This piece is dated about 1100.

The swallow (*fig. c*) is completely stylized, his bill unrealistically drawn in profile. The saw-tooth edges of the wings and the cloudlike swirls give a sense of poise and airy ever-changing distances.

Humor is apparent in the mosquito bowl (*fig. d*). The eleven pests buzzing around are really to be sensed. They are depicted with little variation, although some of the legs are pulled in more than others to avoid overcrowding. From whatever side the design is viewed, it shows a swarming movement around a center.

A ring of fine square meanders edges the turtle's shell (*fig. e*), and wavy lines are used to suggest its accordion-like neck. It seems to swim across the plain surface. The mouth is depicted in profile, as was the swallow's, and, as there, the scalloped margin is eased in with a series of fine lines and wider stripes.

The bowl with four grasshoppers (*fig. f*) is divided into lozenge-shaped fields and a squared center. The insects are well caught, although not strictly naturalistic. Their delicate transparent wings are crisscrossed vertically in two cases and obliquely in the other two.

It is regrettable that most of these bowls were "killed," thus impairing their appearance.

The "rabbit wheel" (*Pl. 107, fig. a*) presents an involved use of the zigzag, with the animal heads fitted neatly into each irregular field. The ears are stylized, one above the other, and the whole pattern gives a feeling of rotation.

In the grasshopper bowl beside it (*fig. b*), the zigzag and square coil are combined in an effective border. Although quite differently portrayed than the insects in the preceding plate, details are marvelously well observed, notably his jagged hind feet and cutting jaws.

In contrast to the first piece on this plate, the bowl with the four turkeys (*fig. c*) is quite static. Its squared center and rounded white fields are similar to the divisions seen before. The birds are recognizable, although composed largely of rectangles and diamonds with a few contrasting curves. Their fan tails are especially striking.

In *fig. d,* another of the unusual geometric-patterned bowls, the familiar sawtooth design is featured within a wide margin. A heavy black band outlines the edge of the vessel, while the decorated area is confined within three narrower circles. The fine square coil in the center is characteristic of Mimbres drawing; it has already been seen in the grasshopper and turkey dishes above.

Fig. e shows a less stylized turkey, penned in with two heavy margin lines. It is drawn with linear economy and an observant eye, and is perhaps the most pictorial of all.

A few pottery specimens from Arkansas and the Southeast (Gulf States) are incorporated here (*Pl. 108*) to show what was produced in a neighboring region and to illustrate the great diversity in concept and approach. If we compare this pottery with that on the preceding plates, we are astonished by the profound differences in the people whom we group under the one general term "Indian."

Fig. a, from Arkansas, some seven hundred miles from the heart of the Southwest, presents a completely distinctive shape, a long-necked bottle on a vertical base. The straight neck carries a static step design, the convex body a swirling pattern, both blended in the one piece with good feeling.

Fig. b, also from Arkansas, noteworthy for its fine ovoid form and slender shapely neck, is definitely related to the other, yet brings enough divergence in form and decoration to be illustrated here. It is 10¼ inches high and done in ochre-red and cream.

‹ 161 ›

The small bowl from Louisiana (*fig. c*), only 2¾ inches high, offers another original shape, even after the many variations in the Southwest. Considerable technical skill is revealed in the execution of the design, characteristically Mound Builder. The crisscross background, against which the smooth double bands are laid in S-shaped patterns, produces a lacelike effect, and the rim is decorated with separated, well-proportioned motifs.

Fig. d, a burial urn, 17 inches high, comes from Georgia. It is of dark brown color and has a spiral pattern stamped all over the outside. The ingenious application of the stamping block lends a continuous wavy movement to the repeated pattern, not only avoiding monotony but giving strength to the whole. The vigor of the ornament, as well as the shape of the vessel, reminds us of the capacious bronze *gulyás* kettles (more easily recognized when spelled "goulash"), which were commonly used by Asiatic migrants as they moved on Europe.

A precipitation jar is shown in *Pl. 109, fig. a,* probably used in salt making for removing impurities from the mineral springs near the place where it was found in Missouri. Although there is nothing remarkable in the material or its surfacing, considerable skill was necessary to make such a long piece with its relatively narrow opening. There is suavity in the form of the cap and the way it fits the top.

The two incised water bottles (*fig. b*), 7 and 6⅛ inches tall respectively, come from Arkansas. Original shapes and a beautiful black polished finish make these pieces outstanding. The novel technique of incision made after firing and the fine adaptation of the decorative patterns deserve mention. In the shallow channels traces of red paint can be detected.

The brown effigy bowl (*fig. c*), also from Arkansas, is a little over 8 inches high and has a burnished finish. The head and tail of a horned snake are worked out at the sides for handles. One could not expect these additional elements to be too realistic, limited as the potter was by the undistinguished cooking-pot shape of the bowl, but a certain attractive naïveté must be admitted, which elevates the piece above the purely utilitarian.

As a shape, the incised bottle (*fig. d*), 7 inches high, from the Mound Builder culture in Louisiana is again distinctive, and in its incision it too demonstrates a slightly different approach. There is a virtuosity in keeping the lines always equidistant while covering the whole surface with its swirling motifs; where they are interrupted, the modulation of the motif occurs without any trace of hesitancy, guided by a sure talent.

POTTERY

MEXICAN AREA

The Mexican Area, as well as the Maya which follows it, presents an amazing versatility in handling the humble clay. Here can be seen simple shapes taking on sophisticated proportions or lavish decoration; toylike figurines, primitively conceived, grow into life-size images. Certain representations of human subjects were made with the use of baked clay molds, but, as a result of this technique, were seldom highly artistic.

Pl. 110, fig. a, a jar 15 inches high, comes from the Zapotec-Mixtec site of Monte Albán. Although the shape is not complicated, it is anything but "primitive." It is somewhat similar to the one in *fig. b,* but the neck is longer and hobnail protuberances add plastic effect. The dignified line of the two "handles," actually spouts, betokens real civilization. Burnished but apparently unpainted, the vessel has something of the primeval strength of an early Chinese bronze.

Fig. b shows a jar of baked clay with polychrome design on a stucco ground. Again, the apparent simplicity of the piece should not mislead us to underrate the artistry embodied in it. There are centuries of development behind the deliberate contours, the bulky body, and flaring neck. The decoration, applied with much skill, shows a monster-mask and other fantastic elements belonging to the iconography of Teotihuacán. It reminds one of an early cloisonné of the Eastern Hemisphere.

The funerary urn in *fig. c,* about 9½ inches high, also comes from the Teotihuacán region. In comparison with the other two, it shows a number of advanced features. With its three legs and lid, it is a composition of several elements. The broad rim of the cover, extending well beyond the wall of the vessel, creates a roof effect that gives it finish and individuality. The cylindrical knob on top, in harmony with the sturdy legs, is a new idea. Both urn and lid are decorated with motifs cut out and engraved. A mask with a broad feather headdress can be discerned in the center, and other designs of glyphic content are strewn over the sides. This piece too could find its counterparts in earlier Asiatic civilizations.

The three pitchers illustrated on *Pl. 111* come from three different Mexican states. *Fig. a,* about 11 inches high, was found in the Toluca Valley, west of Mexico, D.F. With its geometric decoration on a henna ground it is rather somber in aspect. Because of its size and the convex band below the rim, it was the most difficult of the three to shape. *Fig. b,* over 8 inches, is a Mixtec product from the Oaxaca region. Its polychrome motifs show a healthy enjoyment in the play of color and line and great surety in applying geometric units to a spherical surface. The third *(fig. c),* although not so finely proportioned as the first, has the most charm for our eyes because of the colorful butterfly frieze on the shiny chocolate-brown of the body. It is smaller than the others and comes from Puebla, the center of the renowned Cholula ware.

Of the three tripod vases in the lower row, the first *(fig. d)* is Zapotec and 7½ inches high. The negative-painted step-fret in the central band recalls the composite stone panels at Mitla. The body is yellow, the upper section cream, and the "background" lines and markings are dark brown; inside it is painted red and chocolate. The other two *(figs. e* and *f)* both come from the Mixtec region. Note the use of serpents to represent the legs on the smaller. They are hollow and contain clay balls or pebbles to make them rattle. The last of the three shows a mature hand in the unhampered application of the glyphic decoration. The ground is red; the figures are white and applied with fine fluency and spacing. The tripod form was a favorite in these parts of the Mexican Area, and the numerous finds show much variation.

Pl. 112 presents two single figures and a group from the country of the Tarascans—a people who, even at the time of the most powerful Aztec expansion in the 15th century, were successful in maintaining their artistic independence. How long they inhabited the region northwest of Tenochtitlán, in what is today the state of Michoacán, is not known. An outspoken and characteristic flavor can be observed in every piece which has come down from them. In their long-headed, flat-bodied figurines, they succeeded in catching a remarkable variety of expressions and attitudes, unusually striking even when compared with the talented work of the rest of the Mexican high plateau.

Fig. a represents a woman in miniature, only 4½ inches high, leaning over her *metate,* grinding corn or making dough. The face with its absorbed smile is very expressive. The bend of the youthful body, the caplike headdress, and the necklace are all more suggested than realistically depicted, but, as always in Tarascan modeling, the whole figure is transfused with a communicative spirit. It could be enlarged considerably without losing any of its vigor.

The seated man *(fig. b),* 28 inches high, is said to have come from Jalisco and dates from about the 12th century. The head has received the most attention and carries through the weary pose suggested in the body. Although the figure is rather shapeless and the arms and legs are out of proportion, the piece makes immediate contact with us through its genuinely human content. Even in their utter strangeness, these pottery representations show us people as human as we are, with the same universal appeal as the more famous Tanagra statuettes.

The group of dancing women (*fig. c*) demonstrates even more forcefully the talents seen above. On a disk about 9 inches in diameter, nine figures dance about three others seated in their midst, yet the piece does not appear crowded. The arms of the nine are interlaced, creating a long rhythmic line. There is tension in the circle as the women lean forward looking with animation toward the center. Again, it is not realism that arrests us, but the peculiar story-telling quality that knows no boundaries in art.

Miniature figures are grouped on *Pl. 113*. The first one (*fig. a*), a mother with an infant at her breast, has certain characteristics seen in the Tarascan work, especially the grotesquely sharp nose, but there are differences in the manner of modeling. The eyes and mouth are represented by deep concavities instead of rolls of clay, and the general outline is more broken. Not only does the baby give the impression of a doll, but the whole piece seems toylike.

Fig. c is even more reminiscent of the examples on the preceding plate. It shows a figure lying on a litter or bed, bound by bands around his chest and ankles. The facial expression is stereotyped, but the aliveness of the extended legs and imprisoned arms is well communicated.

Although among the oldest in pottery types, with their roots in the archaic period, the "pretty ladies" of *figs. d* and *e* show an amazing number of individual details. Certain plastic features place them close to the Tarascan region. The tallest is 5 inches high. The arching eyebrows and large slanting eyes are applied rolls of clay, while the mouths, sometimes protruding, sometimes concave, are formed by incision. Hairdress, ornaments, and pose of the hands demonstrate the enjoyment of their makers in equipping each figurine with the whims of momentary inspiration. Traces of color—which must have added considerably to the effect—may be seen on some of them.

The little man in full regalia (*fig. b*), slightly enlarged as shown, is different in type, probably nearer the center of the Aztec Empire. From his posture, he seems to be dancing. The modeling introduces several new touches to our group, with the free handling of the swinging arms and flowing headdress especially noteworthy.

In the Colima region, which lies beyond the Tarascan, on the west coast of Mexico, dogs were frequently modeled (*Pl. 114*). Some breeds of this animal were raised in Mexico for meat. They are frequently found in graves, perhaps intended as guides to the after-world.

The dog in *fig. c* is about 11 inches high and 15½ long. The deep tomato-red color of the piece is highly burnished. Softness of line and liveliness are apparent from the first moment of observation. The intent eyes, alert tail, and hanging belly of such an animal are familiar to all of us.

The naïve humor of this ware is emphasized by the arrangement of the seated dog and baby, two liquid containers (*fig. b*). The saucer-like rims around the openings on the heads make them still more amusing. Remnants of paint are visible in the eyes of the boy.

The recumbent dog, 7½ inches long (*fig. a*), is made of a brownish clay. Here the characteristic high polish is considerably damaged, but its condition cannot detract from the interest of the vase. The difficult pose chosen for the animal is executed with simplicity and shows the ease with which these potters handled such a problem—as if modeling were a favorite pastime.

The tripod jar (*fig. d*) comes from this same locality and has the same squat plumpness that characterizes the sagging body of the dog beside it. A vegetable is probably represented, with feet in the form of parrots. The neatly turned rim is noteworthy. All of these Colima pieces are unusually three dimensional in quality and bear looking at from any angle.

With *Pl. 115* we come to examples of clay modeling on a larger scale. *Figs. a* and *b* show two Tarascan warriors handling some sort of weapon—clubs or spear-throwers. The first is 2 feet high, the second even taller. They are similar in general posture, and both wear helmets and protective armor with high collars, but there is considerable difference in details. *Fig. b* has perhaps more facial expression, and parts of his armor (which may have been painted in *fig. a*) are worked out plastically. Some of the clumsiness of both statues may be due to the difficulty of shaping such large and asymmetrical pieces out of clay. Nevertheless, definite action is conveyed by the expectancy reflected in their faces as well as the swinging pose of hands and bodies.

The two lower figures take us into other regions, where we find quite another approach to the subject matter and very different techniques of modeling.

Fig. c is only about 6 inches high, but commanding none the less. This little warrior comes from Chiapas, near Palenque, where, as we have seen, there was abundant tradition for working in soft plastic materials. In contrast to the Ta-rascan type, suggestive but never really elaborated, there is rich and effective detail work here. Considerable skill was necessary to build up the statuette out of many little elements, added one by one. Small as it is, the face is a character study, and the exaggerated stance and defiant gesture are admirably caught. The resplendence of the attire is augmented by the mask with its spreading head-dress, suspended upside down on the breast like a war trophy. From the stand-point of design, the incised lines that flare from the pectoral and are repeated in the figure's cropped hair and on the fringe of his sash contribute much toward holding together this ebullient portrayal.

The large seated figure, 13½ inches high, comes from Vera Cruz (*fig. d*), a region also where clay modeling and stone sculpture were equally well advanced. It has neither the naïvely conceived gestures of the first two nor the salty individualism of the warrior, but rather the composure and restraint that inevitably appear as a people become bound by the conventions of a hierarchy. The shoulders and arms have agreeable plasticity and the hands and feet are carefully detailed (compare with those above). It was once painted, as were most of these statues.

As an intermission in the rich succession of ceramic statuary, we offer four pieces that are primarily shapes. *Pl. 116, figs. a* and *b* show the infrequent shape of large plates. They come from Cholula, not far from the city of Puebla. The talent of the potters in this district is manifest again in the varied decoration of this relatively late form. The plates are dated mid-14th century.

The round jar over 8 inches high (*fig. c*) represents the body of a coiled snake. The convexities, difficult to shape, are emphasized by the narrow brown-and-white band that denotes the belly. We have no information on its proveni-ence, but the row of glyphs on the collar-like rim of the jar, which show a strong similarity to those on *Pl. 111, fig. f,* and the painting of the serpent head indicate late Zapotec or even Zapotec-Mixtec style. A remarkably similar example, with the addition of tripod legs, is to be found in the Museo Nacional of Mexico, where it is identified as Mixtec.[100]

The cylindrical vase (*fig. d*), about 15 inches high, comes from the state of Vera Cruz, supposedly the Huaxtec region, which bordered on the Totonac. The material is baked brown clay. There are four panels on the sides, each pic-turing two human figures with headdress, one above the other, holding ceremo-nial objects. The design was first cut out and then orange, brown, and cream paste inserted in somewhat the manner of cloisonné. The work was done with such masterly craftsmanship that even with the vessel in sherds the coloring remained intact. Artistic deliberation is evident in the alternation of the shades.

The five heads on *Pl. 117,* all from the Mexican Area, demonstrate the amazing variety that found expression there in clay. *Fig. a,* about 1¾ inches high, was part of a figurine belonging to the early period of culture at Zacatenco, a site near Mexico, D.F.[162] The body to such a head usually had round tapering legs and short arms, somewhat similar to the figures shown on *Pl. 113.* Despite the fact that modeling is restricted here because of size, a pleasing aspect has been achieved. Outstanding is the Y-shaped ridge serving as nose and eyebrows. In the eyes, the hollows representing pupils in a suggested iris are conscious sculptural additions, their effect calculated. The deft coiling of the hair or headdress finishes the piece successfully. It does not yet have intellectual content, but is very close to it.

The female bust opposite it, with arms only indicated (*fig. c*), comes from Guadalajara in Jalisco. It is about 5 inches in height and has a slip of color. The elongated head, augmented by the tall headdress, and the aquiline nose place it in the group of Tarascan types. The ragged line of the ears is unusual. This piece also lacks real spiritual quality.

Different, artistically mature peoples exchanged inspiration in that sector of Mexico where the styles of Yucatan, Oaxaca, and the lowlands of Vera Cruz meet. The head in *fig. e,* about 8 inches high, would seem to come from this region. The slit eyes with their painted button-like centers are a rare feature, as are the protuberances on the headdress. It is probable that the color around the mouth denotes actual painting of the face.

Similar plastic characteristics appear in the much more realistically modeled head of *fig. b,* about 11 inches high. The same type of eye is present, though it looks more natural here. The face emerges from a monster's jaws, the upper teeth of which are clearly discernible, although the protruding snout is broken off. Involved decoration is applied with virtuosity—almost daring—in this brittle material. The lozenge-shaped spirals above the ears are decorative elements found also in Maya and Toltec art. The youthfulness of the face and the maturity of its execution lead us to accept the piece without hesitation.

The pottery head from Vera Cruz (*fig. d*), 6½ inches high, is one of the type commonly known as "Totonac laughing faces." All are rather square, with large caplike headdresses that extend to the ears, and many bear frets. The monkey in relief is an unusual addition. The achievement of a definite facial expression is a sign of a high artistic level, and the obvious smile spread over this piece gives it real spiritual content.

Aside from the differences that are apparent at first glance, it is worth while to observe the different plastic treatment of the eyes on this plate, from those formed by the archaic fillet technique (*fig. a*) to the realistic (*fig. b*) and the sculpturally mature (*fig. d*).

The little figure from Tempoal (*Pl. 118, fig. a*) belongs to the Huaxtec region. The face is stolid; what slight emphasis it has is given it by the modeling of the nose, mouth, and high cheek bones. Its decorative effect is due to its painting, which lends real meaning to the somewhat clumsy clay body.

Fig. c is a pottery whistle, about 9 inches long, from central Vera Cruz. The droll toylike little figure lies in an unusual attitude. (Compare with *Pl. 61, fig. b.*) Despite a rather heavy execution in the hands and feet, it is done with a good shot of realism. With the rounded modeling of the features and the tight-fitting headdress, reminding one of a medieval jester's cap, the head bears some resemblance to the Totonac laughing head of the preceding plate.

The terra-cotta masquette (*fig. b*), 6 inches high, comes from the Tuxtla district in Vera Cruz. It represents the moan bird, the Yucatecan screech owl, popularly associated with death. Its glyph is used in the Dresden Codex, generally with evil import.[137] This piece, though relatively small, makes a positive impression, strengthened by its rocket-like build-up.

Another terra-cotta masquette of the same provenience (*fig. d*), only 3½ inches long by 2 high, depicts the leaf-nosed bat as the Death-god. If it is compared with the figure above it, a similar sculptural language will be noted. The holes for the eyes, nostrils, mouth, and ears are executed with calculated effect, and the succession of rounded surfaces is subtly varied by plastic and incised detail. The precision in the piece gives the impression of lapidary work rather than modeled clay.

In the last centuries before the Conquest, the potter grappled with larger subjects, also with ease. *Pl. 119* presents two life-size figures of baked clay, both from the high plateau of Mexico in Aztec times, made in several pieces, then put together. According to the accepted interpretation, *fig. a* represents a priest wearing the flayed skin of a sacrificial victim. There is little beauty for us in this piece, with its dull eyes and gaping mouth. Yet it embodies a high degree of technical ability in both the modeling and firing, so expertly done that it has withstood the vicissitudes of the centuries.

Although the face in *fig. b* has not much more expression, in idea it approaches more closely our comprehension. The figure stands nearly 5½ feet high. The rounded turban-like headdress is an unusual feature, as are also the very long ear pendants. The costume is typically Aztec, especially the armlets, which were made of gold decorated with feathers, and the sunburst at the groin. This was fashioned of a thin plaited material and originally had a cone in the center, since broken off; a similar ornament was often worn on the head. The whole chest is hung with necklaces, and the sandals are faithfully represented. While certain details may recall the terra-cotta statues of the Etruscans, a closer observation of the piece moves it back into the almost impenetrable realm of pre-Columbian ideology.

Equal virtuosity in modeling clay is revealed when the high plateau is left behind and we move south into the Oaxaca region, from which the material for the next four plates is selected. Especially typical of this district are the effigy funerary urns and incense burners that feature human and animal figures. In most cases the base is broad, and behind the main figure is a large empty pocket or jar in which incense was placed or, as the case might be, the bones of the deceased for secondary burial. These vessels were usually covered with a red wash, and sometimes as many as four colors are found painted on a single piece.[151]

On *Pl. 120* the two jaguar cave gods, 19¾ and 16½ inches high respectively, are presented, said to have been found in a cave temple near Guila, Oaxaca, facing each other on opposite sides of a funerary urn. The Indians called them "messenger dogs of the gods," and indeed they have certain doglike characteristics. They are, however, fantasy creatures, combining features both of jaguars and bats, executed and transmitted with an expression startling in its clarity of concept and richness of detail. The faces with their glaring eyes and open mouths, the heavy necklace cords, pendants, and bells, as well as the fantastic claws, are all worked out with care. Although these pieces were purchased at the beginning of the century, experts, basing on knowledge accumulated in the last decades, have lately expressed doubt as to their authenticity.

The feet of the next figure (*Pl. 121, fig. a*) are much like those of the "dogs," though the upright posture, the torso, and arms are distinctly human. The head is animal, but it wears the earplugs and headdress of a dignitary. Pierced eyes and mouth lend ferocity to the statue, and the rich necklace of bells and the loin-cloth add to the baffling representation.

The second illustration (*fig. b*) shows an older man in full regalia, holding a glyph or symbol in one hand and a small shield in the other. His expression is as pointed as any cartoon's: smiling to himself, he seems to know much that we can only guess at. There is a certain top-heaviness in the piece, an exaggeration of the head and headdress. Although the figure is interesting, with its lively expression, the present consensus is that, while some sections might be of pre-Columbian origin, as it stands today it shows signs of considerable tampering.

A blending of realistic features and fantasy elements is excellently demon-strated in *fig. c.* The piece is 32 inches high and comes from Tomb 77, Monte Albán, dated in Epoch II. A well-defined head is the center of the composition, crowned by a monster-mask, the nose and eyes of which are clearly visible. This is one of the few human faces which one feels might be portraiture. The some-what cross-eyed look, the arrogant half-open mouth, and high bald forehead pre-sent in quintessence a high priest who stands well toward the top of a powerful hierarchy. Unfortunately the photograph cannot show the subtle build-up of the various planes in the modeling, all serving to emphasize the head. The plain semicircular collar and the wide undecorated "wings" of clay, like a screen in the background, stress the sharp characterization through contrast. The flaring rim at the top, skillfully incorporated as part of the headdress, is the mouth of the incense burner or urn.

A number of subjects were used in the decoration of incense burners. The human figure generally constituted the main motif, but variations in pose and embellishment exhibit a rich and modulating fantasy-world.

The seated human wearing a strange mouth mask (*Pl. 122, fig. a*), 33½ inches high, was excavated at Atzompa and is placed in Monte Albán I. It is a representation of the Rain-god, who is characterized in Maya iconography also by a long hooked nose. Primary attention is centered on the head, although the upper part of the body, arms, and hands are worked out well. The lower part is only suggested and the feet, in their stiff horizontal position, have only four toes. Incised lines on the headdress—unusual with its flaps—reduce the preponder-ance of blank surface.

Fig. b, also an incense burner, comes from a later epoch, Monte Albán III. It is 16½ inches high. Here the main body of the piece is frankly utilitarian.

The lower section with its painted decoration may represent a temple platform, upon which three human figures are performing a ceremony. The main person, with shield, is seated on a block or altar, while two elaborately dressed attendants, carrying ritual objects, stand on either side. In its idea, the piece has a certain analogy to the story-telling pottery jars of the Andean Area.

Figs. c and *d* present seated personages. While the second dignitary is executed on the whole with more decorative skill, the representation shows greater conventionalization—note again the four toes. He wears a fine carved mask on his breast and his cape is edged with braid—a serpent symbol in Zapotec-Mixtec grave finds—very effective in pottery. The whole obligatory paraphernalia of his costume is so much more lavish that, compared with the first, he appears a rich man beside a poor one. In the characterization of the faces, both pieces are equally strong. The flaring "wings" of the two headdresses serve as excellent frames. *Fig. c* is a peripheral example of the type above it. He wears a monster-mask and wide collar, suggestive of the last head on the preceding plate. There are traces of blue paint on his beads and red on the tongue and nose.

The utilitarian purpose of the first three pieces on *Pl. 123* is so subordinated in the design that the urn proper cannot be seen in any of the photographs. All the subjects are human figures in natural three-dimensional representation.

It is doubtful if another piece showing such a delightful buffoon as that in *fig. a* could be found among all the effigy funerary urns and incense burners in the Oaxaca district. He is a little over 16 inches high. His cross-eyes, snub nose, and open mouth, and the lines of his carefully combed hair all draw attention to the face, but shoulder cape, hands, legs, and the ornamentation are executed with rare consideration and skill. As he sits there, so well behaved with his hands on his knees, he confirms the description of some of the early chroniclers who reported these people as jolly and credulous before the maltreatment of their conquerors changed them.

The war chief in full regalia (*fig. b*) carries a thick staff in his right hand and a shield with mask and pendent feathers in his left, both interesting features. His head is placed within the beak of a bird-mask and his costume shows an unusual detail in the birds' heads on the breast, probably of metal.

The same bird-mask headdress reduced to a mere shape appears in *fig. c.* The statuette is 20 inches high. Although the position of the hands adds to the stiffness of the pose, the wavy outlines of the circular skirt and ruffled anklets counterbalance any rigidity. The spirals on the garment and the ornament above the nose are new details to us. As a composition, this figure has more line and vibration than the preceding one.

In *fig. d* (not an urn) we have a nude figure, 13½ inches high, of tannish color, without any decoration except a tall headdress that bears glyphs, the lower one of which is the Zapotec sign for 13. In contrast to the preceding pieces, laden with ornament and symbolic appendages, it presents simply a young human body, treated with a good sense of realism and proportion. The cross-eyed expression and open mouth of *fig. a* have here lost their grotesque character, and the position of the legs, with hands resting on knees, familiar in various manners of execution on other plates, is here graceful and natural. The arms and shoulders are beautifully modeled; fingers and toes, carefully detailed. Signs similar to those on the headdress are incised on the breast. He appears to be watching intently, perhaps as an onlooker or waiting to take part in an initiation ceremony. Here we have the first case in which decorative elements were omitted which might detract from the subject—a live youthful human creature.

The clay representation of a warrior (*Pl. 124, fig. a*), 23½ inches high, is dated in Monte Albán II. Both posture and gesture here are new. The pushing movement in the whole figure—perhaps a dance pose—is in contrast to the static pieces that have preceded it. There is ease in the modeling, not only in the general attitude but in the small additional decorations. The eyes are somewhat similar to those on the Atzompa vessel (see *Pl. 122, fig. a*), also of an early period. Plain surfaces behind the headdress and in the loincloth serve as contrast for the embellished sections.

In the various examples presented, the free treatment of the subject will be noted: figures are met both standing and seated in widely varying poses.

Fig. b is a small cylindrical vase, 5½ inches high, from the excavations at Atzompa. A vessel of this type must have been used as a container for small offerings, perhaps jade, turquoise, or pearls. Important for us is the cameo-like sharpness of the relief, showing a human head surmounted by a bird-mask. The most difficult lines and planes are achieved without a sign of hesitation.

The uniqueness of the large pottery statue (*fig c*), nearly 3 feet high, begins with its pose, some details of which can be reconstructed only by guesswork. The flexed legs are most infrequent in pre-Columbian modeling, as is also the position of the arms, the left resting on the knee, its hand grasping the broken right, the direction of which may have been forward or upward. Besides the posture, another unusual feature is the number of small decorative ornaments, applied with the greatest skill yet observed. Particularly impressive in their exactness are the armlets with mask and beaded frame. The proudly held head is masterly, not only in execution but in expression, and crowns a mature and dignified body. The sharply demarcated line in front of the ear suggests that the figure is wearing a mask. Such a grotesque "harlequin" nose as his appears on the small jade in *Pl. 251, fig. c,* which comes from El Salvador, as well as a jade mask from the Guatemala highlands, now in the University Museum at Philadelphia. The headdress seems to be a band with long ribbons hanging down the back.

This piece represents a peak in the pre-Columbian artist's modeling in clay. Few strange details are present to disturb our enjoyment. His dash gives him universal appeal; his litheness is comparable to that of a gladiator. However, where the figure belongs stylistically is a puzzle; it has few characteristics of the region where it was found.

MAYA AREA

In the pottery of the Mexican Area the human figure is frequently seen in combination with vessels of utilitarian purpose, a practice which also carries into the other areas to the south. The ingenious blending of the abstract and realistic noted here is found among all pre-Columbian peoples.

The first two examples in *Pl. 125,* one from the Mexican and one from the Maya Area, show an incense jar worked into each piece as an integral part of the composition. *Fig. a,* from Puebla, Mexico, and 7 inches high, is a tripod fashioned to represent a crouching man with a large round jar strapped to his back. Its conception is true to life; even today the traveler may encounter such a figure bearing a burden held by a cord across the chest. The disproportionate belly and uneven length of the legs serve primarily to stabilize the vessel. (Compare with *Pl. 297, fig. a.*)

In *fig. b* the *incensario* is in the form of a large bowl or kettle, held on the lap of a man whose legs have been simplified into two crescents, drawn one over the other, to constitute a base. This piece, our first from the Maya Area, is of dark red fired clay and about 9 inches high. It comes from Lake Amatitlán in Guatemala. The head seems uncomfortably pressed between the heavy head-dress and its vertical "wings." (See *Pl. 122, fig. c.*) Large earplugs, a very long breast bar, and beadwork directly under the chin are added. The incense bowl and the figure are blended with a freedom that reconciles us to the alien artistic impulse that created it.

In the shaping of the large jar from Guatemala (*fig. c*), 16 inches high, its utilitarian purpose predominated. However, the addition of the animal snout and suggested ears convert it at once into a living subject. The two low handles take on the semblance of arms akimbo, and the brown and black design painted over the white slip gives the impression of a textile blanket.

The two lower vessels of *Pl. 126, fig. b* from Chiapas and *fig. c* from Isla de los Sacrificios, Vera Cruz, are used as connectives between the Mexican and Maya areas, coming, as they do, from sectors where characteristic artistic influences mingled with one another.

The rounded contour of the jar just discussed is met again in *fig. b,* although this piece has no zoömorphic elements; the three handles and painted motif leave no place for an association or suggestion of human or animal form. It is simply a utilitarian vessel, which, when found, contained remains of cremated bones and cloth. It is nearly 12 inches high and has a flat base. Besides the decoration, which is quite conventionalized, hasty but fluent, the most artistic feature is perhaps the finely finished curving lip.

The painted beaker (*fig. c*) ranks higher from all points of view. The more involved form, complicated as it is by the pedestal, shows a development. A deliberate continuation of the dark stripes, which run parallel on the vessel but are splayed on the base, accenting its line, proves that the craftsman well understood the modulation of pattern. The vertical lines are good contrast for the outspokenly horizontal frieze at the top, where a serpent-like monster is represented with elongated gaping jaws.

Three ochre-red pottery pieces are presented in *fig. a.* The beaker at the left has complete stability and perfect proportions, enhanced by its rounded rim and the flange just above the base. (Compare it with the crystal cup from Monte Albán, *Pl. 255, fig. a.*) The plate, the largest of them all, measures 13½ inches across. Its shape is remarkably symmetrical, and the even rim and clean precision of the depressed center, olive-green in color, are noteworthy. Especially unusual is the conical bottle (right), with its body flaring from the vertical base only to narrow sharply again at a completely different angle—one which must have been difficult to fashion with the hand. There is a suggestion of a painted band at the neck, above which the piece seems to have been finished in a darker tone. In this group there are only plain surfaces, no decorative patterns, yet what refinement is apparent in the shapes—all made without the use of the potter's wheel.

The effigy vessels on *Pl. 127* are constructed in such a way that the upper part with the head forms a cover for the lower hollow section, used as a container. Those in *figs. a* and *b,* together with the covered tripod vase (*fig. c*), come from Kaminaljuyú, an early Maya or even pre-Maya settlement in the highlands of Guatemala.

Fig. a, 8 inches high, represents a hunchback, generally an omen of evil. The shape of the body may have been influenced by the desire to create as much hollow space as possible. However, other parts of the figure, particularly the detail work in the face, counterbalance any distortion and make of the piece a striking characterization. Headdress, ear ornaments, necklace, belt, and loincloth are green, the body is crimson, and the mouth, scarlet. Ingenious perforations in the headdress, one of which is visible just above the ear, were arranged to light up the eyes and mouth.

The seated woman (*fig. b*) is not handsome but certainly an excellent bit of caricature. She is 11 inches high. Finer incision work than that on the boy below her adds to the interest of the jar. Her garment is a burnished olive-green, very effective against the dull rippled gray of the rest of the piece. A playful enjoyment in decorating, whether with applied strips of clay or incision, is evident in the exquisitely executed bowknot of the skirt. The belt also is tied in front with another carefully depicted bow.

The covered tripod jar (*fig. c*) is 18 inches high and dark brown in color, with a single incised panel on the front that shows traces of red paint. The bird on the lid is a novelty. A duplicate in design, although about 5 inches shorter, is owned by the Museum of the American Indian, New York. In an art where some individual touches are nearly always present, the existence of such a striking counterpart is worth mentioning. Another similar vessel is in the museum at Teotihuacán.

At the site of Uaxactún, already discussed in the chapter on architecture, the Carnegie Institution of Washington, under the leadership of A. Ledyard Smith, made important discoveries in the field of pottery as well as in other arts. Through the great generosity of the Institution, we are permitted to reproduce here some of their unpublished material, which adds new aspects to the unfolding panorama of Maya art. A publication of the Institution has appeared that treats the archaeological finds in detail.

The first of these objects to be presented here is the effigy jar in *fig. d,* about 8 inches high. It shows a cross-eyed boy whose eyes are lighted from behind in the manner described under *fig. a.* The material is blackish in tone and highly polished, with the incised decorations brought out in white paint. It is note-worthy that the pose of the legs and hands in each figure on this plate is different though equally well defined.

One of the greatest artistic achievements of the Maya was their painted pot-tery. Vessels of fired clay, not particularly distinguished in shape, were covered with a thin coat of stucco and the smooth inviting surface then decorated with painted figures and glyphs, frequently of story-telling character. Although the scenes represented were composed for the limited circumference of a pottery piece, they have the space-filling quality of a fresco.

The same iconographical concept prevails in them as in all the other products of the Maya, whether of stucco, metal, wood, or jade, in flat or in the round. This use of an identifiable language is found in all high civilizations before the Renaissance. Chinese, Babylonian, Egyptian, and Cretan art each had its distinctive manner of delineation, which enables us to assign a single piece, ac-cording to its characteristics, to the civilization which produced it.

In the Maya and Andean areas particularly, as in Greek vases, painted scenes of story-telling content give us revealing glimpses of the life. Because of their pictorial decoration, these pieces might be discussed under painting, but since they are primarily vessels, they will be considered here, as one of the crown-ing achievements of pre-Columbian pottery. Neither the porcelains of China nor the majolica of the Mediterranean would be placed in any other category than that of pottery, regardless of their painted themes.

Here it should be pointed out that although each artistic product of the Maya bears the distinctive Maya stamp, it is nevertheless treated with a clear realiza-tion of the qualities of the medium in which it is created. The Maya were the only people of medieval America who developed a distinct artistic idiom for each material. In their best works they made full use of the monumental possi-bilities in stone, the modulation inherent in clay, the shapes slumbering in a raw piece of cloudy jade, and the potentialities for flowing decoration in the fresco, whether on a wall or a clay vessel.

One pottery piece from the Teotihuacán culture has already appeared with a mythological subject painted on a stucco ground (see *Pl. 110, fig. b*), but the technique will be more readily discerned in those on *Pl. 128*. In *fig. b*, from Kaminaljuyú, the form is not simple. The sides of the jar are slightly concave and it stands on three slab legs; it has a lid, the knob of which is strikingly like that on a Mexican vessel found nearly seven hundred miles away (see *Pl. 110, fig. c*). Such resemblance provides renewed stimulus to consider the connections between the early cultures of the Mexican and Guatemalan high plateaus. Remnants of a monster with flamboyantly drawn feather decoration are clear on the painted surface, even though somewhat battered. The subject flows freely over the cylindrical body of the vessel, and an equally artistic pattern appears on the lid.

Among pre-Columbian pottery of this type, none ranks higher artistically than the fresco vase in *fig. a*. This vessel, 7 inches high, is one of those found at Uaxactún. The bottom of the piece flares out with a sharp edge counterbalancing the overhang of the cover. Its tripod legs are a little shorter than those of the Kaminaljuyú piece and are better digested into the body. The lid is smoothly rounded, without a knob, and its solid black surface, together with that of the legs, sets off the delicately colored composition.

The unrolled design of this vase is shown in *fig. c*. It consists of two panels of unequal size, each of which shows two personages seated on jaguar skins, facing each other. The man on the extreme left is the figure seen on the jar above. Their gestures are of iconographic significance, and the columns of hieroglyphs, if deciphered, would probably shed light upon the subject.

The amazingly refined designs must have been executed by artists of calligraphy. The whole decoration recalls the finest technique of manuscript illumination (see *Pl. 266*). There is ease and lightness in the depiction of the dignitaries, and all glyphs, inside and outside the frames, are placed with an outspoken feeling for their decorative effect. Delicate tones of yellow, red, jade-green are used with black outlines. When in perfect condition, with its colors alive, the piece must have been the equal of any ceramic product of the Old World.

Other cylindrical vessels with painted story-events were found in early Maya sites. The pieces pictured here, however, differ from the Uaxactún fresco vase in that the background is usually colored and the design is built up in a less delicate way—more like a wall-painting than a page of manuscript. One may presuppose formative stages for this type of pottery, despite its apparently early date, for modeling would seem to have preceded painting, and simplification of the vase form for the purpose of receiving picture records must be regarded as a later development.

Pl. 129, fig. a presents another Uaxactún vase, cylindrical in shape and 9 inches high. The ground is a rich red and below the rim a cream-colored band bears hieroglyphics outlined in black and painted, some in red, some in pale orange. Five human figures and a jaguar constitute the main characters in the scene (*fig. c*). A chief wearing a wide collar of feathers, or perhaps of jade, and a large headdress is seated cross-legged on a dais. Behind him stands a smaller person in a fringed cloak, bearing an object in his hands, while the next in line carries a ceremonial standard of splendid feather-work. Two imposing figures face him, both arrayed in colorful textiles and rich headdresses, with feathered insignia at their backs. Faces and bodies are painted. The first carries a baglike object; the second, a long staff. Between them sits a jaguar, who holds a neat package bound with a ribbon, similar to cache vessels with votive offerings found in excavations. The two rows of glyphs inserted in front of the seated chieftain give a date equivalent to A.D. 140, as deciphered by Dr. Morley, and must refer to an event that took place centuries before the vase was made, which perhaps commemorates the occasion when the two ambassadors appeared before the ruler here depicted. Other glyphs scattered about the piece may identify the individuals.[132]

The scene is strange, but we cannot escape the drama in it. A meeting between two different peoples is evident from the detail of their dress and ornaments; the figures are far from standardized and gestures and colors also serve to differentiate the characters. The whole painting has splendor, dignity, and movement.

Fig. b presents the painting on a tripod dish from Holmul, a site not far from Uaxactún. Its decorative composition reminds one strongly of that on the preceding vase, not only from an iconographical point of view but also through its facile and flamboyant spirit. The center of the bowl contains a definitely framed tableau, in which stands a high priest in full regalia, his profile turned to the left and his right arm outstretched in a ritual gesture. A small figure faces him in the left corner, and at his back is a stylized feathered serpent, in which are submerged a human figure and, just below it, a jaguar swinging a censer. The inside rim of the dish has a row of precisely painted hieroglyphs around the edge, with eight "snake-birds" spread out below them. Despite the delicacy in the construction of the central figure, it has static weight, in contrast to the circular motion of the design in the border. This effect is enhanced by the bold use of solid black in the square that frames it.

The cylindrical painted vase in *Pl. 130, fig. a* is 9 inches high and comes from Chamá in the Alta Verapaz district of Guatemala. A decorative band of chevrons replaces the glyph border of the preceding vessels and is repeated at the bottom. The meeting of seven persons is pictured, two of them apparently leaders, judging from their darker painted bodies and the concentration of action in and around them (*fig. c*). The bald-headed chief at the right, whose forehead is markedly flattened, is draped in a large jaguar skin and carries a decorated lance. Several of the protagonists show sparse moustaches. Their dress is quite different from that seen in the vases just described, and attention should be called to the fan shape some of them carry. The scene radiates tension and displays more action than is usually depicted. There is restlessness in the curling lines of the drawing and the many cross angles. The vivid portrayal of grotesque features is as powerful and sure-handed as in Chinese art.

A vase 8 inches high from Ratinlixul, also in the Alta Verapaz district of Guatemala, is shown in *fig. b*. Between the chevron border at top and bottom is pictured a dignitary borne on a journey in a litter carried by two men (*fig. d*); five more individuals make up his entourage. His necklace and turban-like headdress stand out from the others and the jaguar, or dog, below the litter may be further indication of his rank. He also carries the woven fan insignia seen above. The bearers and the porter, who follows with a large pack held by a tump line, are depicted as smaller persons with humble attitudes. The four officials beyond are painted with enough detailed decoration to differentiate them from the others. Three of them carry paddle-shaped clubs, while the last in line bears a small round package in his left hand and rests his right on his left shoulder. The cylinder shape of the vessel makes the procession endless. Only three glyphs occur. The curved lines used in the preceding vase are recognizable here, but the expressive vigor is lacking. Poses are repetitious and there is no sense of action. However, the longer we look at the unrolled design, the more we catch of the atmosphere of pomp and ceremony. The ruler in the litter has the sensual and autocratic appearance of a maharajah.

Pl. 131, fig. a shows a vase about 6½ inches high from Nebaj in the Guatemala highlands. On it is painted a chief sitting cross-legged, his right hand holding a ceremonial object and his left bent in an amazingly deliberate and free gesture. His costume, which resembles those on the vase just described, is worked out in detail, even including the fringe on the cloth. The attendant behind him could have stepped out of an Oriental fable illustration, as he stands with arms crossed looking toward the low altar with its basket-like object. Glyphs appear above the kneeling figure, others are framed in columns, and a panel behind the attendant contains a longer inscription. The colors are quiet in tone, with the designs in red and orange against a yellow-buff ground and outlines and details in black. The drawing has real dash. Executed in a manner that was practiced also in the Near and Far East, its assurance of line could not be improved upon even there.

In the other three illustrations, the story-telling theme is diluted into decorative and finally degenerate patterns. *Fig. b* is another Chamá vase, but not a simple cylindrical shape. The form with its fluted lower half, suggestive of a vegetable, is an early Maya type.[40] The neck of the vessel above the chevron band—which runs, as may have been noticed, nearly always from left to right—presents a cylindrical surface upon which a seated figure is painted. The headdress, flowing in two directions, is so arranged that despite the "low ceiling" its decorative effect is fully realized. A particularly brilliant detail is the left hand as it rests on the hip, the fingers curling most preciously.

On *fig. c,* which is about 7 inches high, a quetzal is featured below the band of glyphs and between the framework of two light ribbons, with plumage so spread as to fill, in a highly artistic manner, half the main field. The depiction is not realistic, but is satisfying none the less because of the virtuosity of its transformation into a stunning decorative scheme.

Fig. d is a peripheral example of this art. From its style it may be surmised that it comes from El Salvador, the southernmost region of direct Maya influence. First it will be noted that instead of the cylindrical form a keg shape is produced, which is much more difficult to decorate. The depiction of the face and dress is different from those just considered; the presentation is less calligraphic and more "painted." The staring eye, the angular features, the lack of abundant facility in the drawing, and the large surface of undecorated background are characteristic of the pre-Columbian pottery of this section.

In *Pl. 132* we have the utilitarian cylindrical shape fashioned into human heads. *Fig. b,* from Kaminaljuyú, is 11 inches high and pinkish buff in color. Two elongated ears serve as handles, and the lower end of the piece, superfluous for the representation, resolves smoothly into decoration. A turban-like headdress marks the rim, going all the way around; otherwise, the back is plain. The eyes are wise and living, and the nose has a fine narrow bridge. The problematical lines that characterize the mouth have already been met in sculpture (see *Pl. 68, fig. b*) and will be seen again among the first of our jades in the Tuxtla statuette (see *Pl. 235, fig. d*).

Fig. a, 7 inches high, comes from the early Maya site of Quiriguá, best known for its excellent stone sculpture. It was found in a dark corner of a ruined structure, broken into twenty-three pieces, but as only one small fragment was missing, a perfect repair job was possible. The elongated line of the other head is here modulated into jovial roundness, and the shape is further removed from the cylindrical form, following instead a curving line that flares slightly toward the base. The face is clearly outlined at the sides and finished with a short beard. A smooth inset rim suggests that there was once a cover. In color, the eyes, earrings, fillet, and mouth are a dull bluish white, the beard and fillet decorations, red, and the body is a rich cream. The jar reminds us of Mochica portrait vases (see *Pl. 160*).

The whistle fashioned in the likeness of a Maya standing with arms crossed (*Pl. 133, fig. a*), 6¼ inches high, is allegedly from Yucatan. One runs across this passive yet alert pose even today in the Maya Area. The piece bears traces of yellow paint. Behind the arm is the mouthpiece of the instrument.

The fragment 4¼ inches high (*fig. c*) is another whistle, also said to come from Yucatan. When intact, the figure must have had a pose similar to the one above it, but with the left arm crossed over the right, showing the hand and fingers. There are also differences in the headdress and breast ornaments. But the facial build-up is the same, even from the point of view of modeling, although intricate tattooing makes the expression here bewildering.

Fig. b, 7 inches high, was found at Palenque by William H. Holmes in a tomb in the base of the Temple of the Cross. The flowing headdress with its loop is done with especial virtuosity. Executed in the best tradition of the site, the figurine is the finest of this group.[49]

Another whistle (*fig. d*), 4½ inches high, comes from Tabasco, a state that borders on Yucatan. This piece is chunky and less plastic than the others, and the pose and headdress are different; nevertheless, all four possess a strong inner relationship. Each is individual, yet all are held together by the framework of Maya characteristics.

The theme of mother and child, perpetuated in many arts and universally understood, also engaged the talent of the pre-Columbian potter. Four cultures are represented on *Pl. 134*. Two examples (*figs. a* and *d*) from the Mexican Area are included to show the technical and stylistic differences in various regions not too widely separated to be influenced, at least indirectly, by one another.

The toylike piece (*fig. a*), from the state of Morelos, not far from Mexico, D.F., is without doubt the least advanced of them all; at first glance it appears little more than a monkey that clings to the shoulders of the mother. The long slanting eyes, the heavy legs, tapering to a point at the feet, are archaic characteristics. Gesture and movement are limited in the struggle for articulation. Yet the theme is clear enough to have appeal.

The figurine (*fig. d*), 6½ inches high, speaks a very different language in its modeling. The contours are no longer uncertain, and a definite mood is transmitted through the clarity of its plastic execution, typically Tarascan. It is a contented scene; the protective curve of the mother's arms is very expressive.

A still different pose is seen in *fig. b,* from Solcajá, Guatemala. Here the mother clasps her child about the waist, and the baby holds both hands to its mouth in good international fashion. The crude modeling gives her a somewhat anxious expression. This statuette is only 5 inches high and is fashioned from coarse brown clay without a trace of other coloring. The ears of both mother and infant are pierced for the addition of ornaments.

The mother with a child and dog (*fig. e*), a little more than 6 inches high, was found near Palenque. She has a broad stance and complacent expression. The child, his hand held firmly in hers, seems to be seated at her side. An unusual feature is the hair that hangs about his shoulders. The puppy clasped at her hip is amusingly realistic and brings to us a new glimpse of Maya life.

While Maya talent created the large and magnificent stucco reliefs of Palenque and Comalcalco, we have no clay statuary of large size from this region, such as was seen in the Mexican Area. The figure of a goddess and warrior (*fig. c*), only 12 inches high, is one of the largest pieces yet found. It comes from the state of Campeche in Mexico, within the realm of the Old Empire, and is said to date from between the 7th and 10th centuries. It is a masterpiece of modeling and carries within it deep spiritual content. No longer the simple mother and child theme, it shows a female deity with a warrior nestling at her knee. Even with the disturbing effect of the broken arms and cracked face, we can realize the young body, beautifully proportioned and enticing. She must have worn originally an elaborate headdress, only the center of which now remains. The curving lines of her shoulder, breasts, and lap radiate great sensuality, an impression that is enhanced by the ecstatic expression on the warrior's face and the gesture of his hand as if he would lose himself in her sheltering presence. The heroic proportions of the goddess in comparison with the warrior's figure are an indication of the transcendental import of the piece. The pair are inclosed in a magic circle permitting no intrusion. In the slight protective bend of her head and the upward turn of his, there is evidence that the Maya, too, realized the existence of that mystic borderland where the mother and lover in woman merge, inseparable.

The artistic dash that we enjoyed in the painted pottery appears also in lightly incised figural compositions on similar shapes (*Pl. 135*).

In the 5-inch vase said to come from Yucatan (*fig. a*), a single figure dominates the jar. His upturned right hand is making a significant gesture, pointing perhaps to a column of conventionalized glyphs on the opposite side of the piece, shown in the photograph on the left. Flesh and bone are suggested throughout the slender body, which has life and elasticity, nobility and grace.

The cylindrical chalkware jar, 4¾ inches high (*fig. b*), is said to have been found in a tomb at Zacualpa in the Guatemala highlands. On the inside, it was painted black, with red pigment rubbed into the incised lines; on the outside, there is no trace of color, except for the creamy tone of the clay. Again a single figure is depicted—interpreted as the young Maize-god.[69] His elaborate headdress of flowing feathers and flowers seems almost to mark off a margin below the rim of the vase. He too looks toward a column of glyphs incised beyond the lines of the waving headdress. The foreshortening of the right hand is perfectly indicated. The figure has a hurried wind-blown rhythm, and shows a talent which knew how to produce lines at once vigorous and expressive in a limited space. (Compare the gesture with that on the gourd-shaped Chamá vase, *Pl. 131, fig. b.*)

Fig. c, a slightly flaring cylindrical vase, comes from Asunción Mita in southern Guatemala, near the border of El Salvador. It is yellowish buff in tone, 8 inches high, and its entire surface is covered with incised decoration. The figure here is standing and his headdress fills the space at either side. The same impetuous gesture of the hands occurs again. His left arm, raised to shoulder level, reaches beyond the flowing feathers as if pointing, and his right moves downward, the outstretched fingers turned toward his body. This vase shows a condensed etching-like design, while in the other two a higher degree of fluency and a more virtuoso touch are apparent.

After seeing these revelations of the sound and versatile ability of the Maya potter, it is not surprising to find him master of still another type, the vase with relief decoration (*Pl. 136*).

It required technical perfection and stylistic maturity to produce the gracious egg-shaped vessel from Uaxactún (*fig. a*), excavated in a burial. It is 8 inches high. The surface is divided into two decorated parts, representing in both instances two seated persons gesticulating to each other. The upper part of the relief is once again framed by a band of glyphs, a characteristic of certain fresco vases already noted. A well-proportioned base adds suavity to the composition. Coming from one of the oldest settlements, this piece testifies to early mastery in this field also.

Fig. b shows a brownish jar, 6 inches high, from Zacualpa. Its chief decoration consists of three human figures, depicted from the waist up, with large headdresses that are expanded to ornament all the free space. As the figural content is by now familiar, we are free to consider how the relief was produced. There are vases which seem to have been made in two halves with the help of a mold or stamp and then fitted together. In such a case, a rough uneven line shows clearly the imperfectly welded edge, particularly on the bottom. But even then the blending of the relief decoration in the two halves is admirably done and only very close study reveals the slightest break in the continuity of the design. In other examples of this type, no joint can be discovered. Even though the reliefs may have been executed by another method, as yet unsolved, the term "carved ware," which is often applied to this type of pottery, is not completely satisfactory, for it implies a deeper background and more sharply cut detail.

The technique of incision on the tripod vase in *fig. c*, as well as its shape, reminds us of the funerary urn from Teotihuacán (see *Pl. 110, fig. c*). It comes from Kaminaljuyú and shows three mask sections, each different, surrounded by affluent decorative elements. The material is a fine black ware with a high polish. Red coloring matter was painted on or rubbed into the sunken background to make an effective contrast. The slits in the feet are noteworthy. A much stronger stylization in the design can be noted than in the other pieces on this plate. While in all cases there is a tendency to cover the available space, two different plastic effects are evident. Here the relief is blocked out, with extensive flat surfaces, and plasticity is indicated by incision.

The bowl in *Pl. 137, fig. a* is rounded in shape and rimless. It bears two medallions in relief, each with a human figure as central subject. Columns of glyphs, lightly incised on the pale buff surface, flank the panels. The side here illustrated shows the marks of restoration, but even so we can delight our eye on the facility of line. A figure, half lying, rests his elbows and right knee on what appears to be a couch, his left leg extended and raised almost as if in flying. His hands support a small vertical tablet inscribed with glyphs. Above him, on the right, is poised a bird, apparently a pelican, executed in a decorative though unrealistic pose. The two lozenge shapes coming out of the open beak—or going in—connect it with the human. The medallion on the other side, composed in as masterly a fashion although somewhat simpler, shows a man in profile seated on a low stool before another panel of glyphs. In each case the frame is rigidly observed, with not a single detail breaking over the double line of the border.

For this piece we have no provenience, but surmise that it came from Yucatan. We have seen a similar bowl in a private collection in Mérida. The fact that an object was found in a certain locality, however, does not necessarily mean that it originated there; many articles were traded for their beauty and rarity, both in pre- and post-Columbian times, traveling far and passing through many hands.

Fig. b, an interestingly shaped bowl presenting a jaguar seated within a medallion, comes from Yucatan. It is of pale yellow material with traces of red sizing and black spots painted on the animal. The creature wears a cape tied around its shoulders, a loincloth, and a headdress with the familiar image of the Long-nosed God, as well as wrist and ankle ornaments and a noseplug.[137] The head is modeled plastically to a certain degree, while details on the animal body are emphasized by incision. The feet and part of the headdress trespass upon the compositional frame. Such liberties, far from impairing the artistic unity of the medallion, actually enhance it, showing talent and experience. The relief here is worked out more deeply and decisively than in any case seen hitherto. With its sharp outlines and compact composition, it bears a telling resemblance to a jade carving.

The medallion frame probably represents a water-lily stem coiled and knotted, with two blossoms branching out at opposite sides.[137] These framing lines are more deeply incised than the jaguar. In this connection, it might be mentioned that the water-lily is associated with the style of Palenque, appearing, among other carvings, in the panel from the Temple of the Sun (see *Pl. 75, fig. b*) and the relief at Madrid (see *Pl. 81, fig. a*).

The Guatemala lowlands, not far from the border of Honduras and El Salvador, is given as the provenience of the heavily decorated jar in *Pl. 138, fig. a,* long famous as one of the most outstanding pieces of Maya ceramics. It is 7¼ inches high and presents an intricate pattern composed of deities in human

POTTERY

and animal form, with ritualistic paraphernalia and symbols so coagulated that it is difficult to separate the individual decorative elements. In the illustration, we see two heads turned toward each other, typically Maya in feature, surrounded by a baffling maze of detail. The plastic variety in the piece, emphasized by the shadow effects of the unusually deep relief, make it alive, and the smooth band of the rim does much to "tame" it and hold it together. This vessel must have been really sculptured, since only this technique could have produced the different levels. It was found in a vaulted tomb not far from Quiriguá, and its sculptural compactness and ideological impenetrability place it certainly very near to the enigmatic stone altars of this early Maya site.

The tall cylindrical vase in *fig. b,* 11¾ inches high, came to the National Museum at Washington from a private collection in El Salvador. It is said to have been found at Ataco in northwest Salvador and is one more example of the intermingling of styles in that part of Central America where Guatemala, Honduras, and El Salvador meet. In this corner lies the ancient shrine of Esquipulas, a pilgrim center even today that draws Indians with offerings from all directions, the Catholic prayers adapted to their own rites. There is no doubt that pilgrims traveled this same road in pre-Columbian times and that an exchange of artistic influences resulted.

The vessel is of a shiny brown ware. Two plain zones at the top and bottom set off the plastic center, where two double rows of human heads, elaborately framed, encircle the vase. The same hatching was seen on the sunken background of the jaguar bowl in the preceding plate. Above, below, and dividing the composition are series of delicately incised glyphs, non-Maya in character. All these decorative elements are knit together with endlessly winding and interlacing bands. The heads, all facing right, show little individuality. Admirable is the unobtrusive virtuosity which created this spectacular piece.

As to its technical build-up, we may only conjecture. But whether it was put together by applying clay rolls or sculptured out of half-dried material, whether it was stamped with variously applied clichés or, as is most probable, produced by a combination of techniques, it is unique.

The foregoing illustrations have demonstrated amply that there were periods when Maya pottery approached in quality real sculptural art. If bowls, jars, and vessels of such exquisite workmanship have survived, how rich and amazing must have been the realm from which they were drawn.

Pl. 139, fig. a displays a sculpturally stunning relief executed on a somewhat concave cylinder. Its two panels, bound together by a band of Mayoid glyphs, present almost identical subjects—the only known instance of a full standing figure appearing on a relief vase. A chief in full regalia is shown against a relatively deep background, which enhances the plasticity of the figure. Many details are recorded that are generally indistinct. In his upraised hand he holds a ceremonial baton; in the other, a shield. Tightly woven cords with tassels hang from his waist in the front and rear. Another feature that has not appeared so sharply defined before is the tall fanlike ornament, which seems to be affixed at the back of the waist and extends above the head, its feathers distinguished from those of the headdress by different treatment. This is probably the same ornament used to such decorative effect in *Pl. 129.* Suspended below it is a human head, a trophy, with upturned face and hanging hair. A very rare feature in Maya art, it is here extremely realistically portrayed. The mottled coils of an immense serpent body are suggested near the lower frame, affiliating the work even more closly with stone and wood sculptures. The piece was bought in El Salvador.

Fig. b, said to have come from the Salvadoranean border in Guatemala, also makes use of a horizontal band of plastic glyphs, Mayoid in type but heavy-footed symbols when compared with the precision of those just seen. On the main panel of the vessel is an incised design representing a fantasy animal with a long curved neck and a head that hangs almost vertically from the upper frame.

In the examples shown in *figs. c* and *d* the formerly strong artistic trend is petering out and changing into new forms and patterns. The first, a jar from El Salvador, 9 inches high, has a fine matt finish. Its glyph band, better carved than that of *fig. b,* is quite plastic and well spaced, and the alluring tactile quality of the surface below it compensates for the lack of other decoration. The piece has a solid line and is by no means degenerate.

The shape in *fig. d,* from Honduras and 9 inches high, shows a divergence from the cylindrical type. The band of Mayoid glyphs is still a feature, but here they lack plasticity and appear incised rather than carved. Painted patterns in red and black, somewhat faded now, make up the main decoration against the orange color of the ware. The two handles with small animal heads protruding from them are a non-Maya addition, an element that we shall meet frequently in the next area on our way southward.

The diminutive flacons, or flasks, shown on *Pl. 140,* some no higher than 2½ inches, come from the southern Maya border. They are comparatively rare and belong to a type distinctive enough to indicate some specific purpose, as yet not definitely known. Traces of mercury and cinnabar, materials highly prized in pre-Columbian America, were found in some of them.[14] Cinnabar was used in paint; mercury, for magic and perhaps in metallurgy. The flasks also might have carried medicines. From the carefully modeled rims, stoppers may be assumed.

Fig. a, 3 inches high, from Honduras, is not only beautifully executed from a technical standpoint but has the most story to tell. Two seated figures, identified as Fire-gods, face each other, separated by a column of glyphs. Other glyphs appear as decoration on the narrow side panels. The two deities show strong similarities to mythical figures from Maya codices, and some of the symbols appear to have come from such a source also. However, the characters on the convex sides are classified as pseudo-glyphs.

It is not necessary to analyze each decorative element to appreciate the admirable skill displayed in this small flask. The even finish of the contours and the perfection of the bottle form show it to be the product of an expert and routined hand. A stamp was probably used for molding the ornamented surface. The workshop must have been in southern Maya territory, from where the type spread as far as Yucatan in the north and El Salvador in the south. Because of its small size and the valuable liquid it must have contained, it would have been likely to travel far. George B. Gordon found several examples, one especially elaborate, in the Ulúa Valley.[41]

The influence of this shape and decorative scheme manifests itself in an unexpected variety. Obvious imitations of coarser material and cruder execution have been found in various parts of the region. The other three flasks pictured in the first row (*figs. b, c,* and *d*), all from El Salvador, show such derivation and are of interest because of their provincial craftsmanship and peripheral design.

In *fig. b,* an oblong form with one figure on the side, the outline is less graceful and the framing band heavier. The face and body have little expression, recalling the small heads of the tall vase in *Pl. 138, fig. b.* On top there is a peculiar recumbent skeleton figure which seems characteristic of this brick-shaped type and is found also on the next example (*fig. c*), in which a higher artistry is evident. This flacon, 2½ inches high and without a trace of paint, is made of fine-textured, putty-colored clay. Not only is the shape well proportioned but glyphs appear—apparently conventionalized glyphs that are purely decorative. In the next flask (*fig. d*), a crude local pattern of animal elements makes up the panel. This piece is noteworthy for its covering of brilliant tur-quoise paint.

In the second row, the orange-ware bottle in *fig. e* comes from Yucatan and bears an impressed design of a figure with flowing headdress. The edge is inter-estingly corrugated and the decoration is unusual, but the imprint is shallow and degenerate when compared with the precise work in the piece above it. *Fig. f,* 5½ inches high, is deep red and presents a departure in shape. A human head is modeled in high relief—an unusual feature—and there are lightly incised pseudo-glyphs on the narrow sides. A very distant cousin of the first flask is shown in *fig. g,* 7 inches high. The neck is fashioned into a human head and the two handles are shaped to represent arms and hands, bringing a completely dif-ferent concept into this series. The doughnut form is very unusual—we have to go to the Central Coast of Peru to find a similar shape. *Fig. h,* 3 inches high, is a likeness of a tomato or a squash, plants indigenous to this country. With its rich red color and its neat naturalistic modeling, it runs a close second in workman-ship to the flacons with the best figural relief.

All of these specimens demonstrate once more how versatile was the creative genius of the pre-Columbian potter, even within the confines of one area, and how widely local tastes or artistic limitations changed and varied one utilitarian shape. The flask form is an ancient one. Chinese pottery has known it from prehistoric times, and from there pastoral peoples have carried it into Europe.

When utilitarian vessels were fashioned in the shape of animals or humans, a kind of grotesqueness resulted (*Pl. 141*). The right half of the buff, 8-inch double jar (*fig. a*) is modeled to resemble a *pisote* (a member of the raccoon family), holding its snout with its paw. The legs, both front and back, are slightly plastic, with paint added to emphasize them and decorate the body. The jar is so constructed that it makes a whistling sound when a liquid is poured from the spout at the extreme left. This peculiarity, its double form, the con-necting tube, and the bridge handle are characteristic of the Andean Area (see *Pl. 158, fig. b*). The fact that the piece here was unearthed in Kaminaljuyú and is made of a local clay gives a further clue to possible influences between dis-tant areas of pre-Columbian civilization.

The bowl with tripod legs representing human heads (*fig. b*) is a large piece and comes from the Quiché region of the Guatemala highlands. The broad, somewhat humorous features of the faces recall the Tarascan figures of the Mexican Area.

In *fig. c,* 6 inches high and from Zacualpa, Guatemala, a turkey forms the body of the rounded jar. The blackish ware has a high polish, and remnants of dark red paint are still visible, portraying very well the puffed-up creature with its spread wings dragging on the ground. The neck of the jar carries a fluent glyph-like design. Similar ware was fashioned by the Chorotega, indigenous to Nicaragua[69]—again evidence of the movement of styles and shapes from distant cultures.

The clay sarcophagus (*fig. d*) is 3 feet long and comes from Nebaj in Guatemala. It represents a fantasy animal with wide-open mouth. Four feet, resembling bear paws, are suggested on the cover, and the whole piece rests on four animal legs. Despite the clumsiness of the shape, a sense of proportion was maintained. The piece is very rare. It would seem to be influenced by strong non-Maya traits, although it comes from the heart of the Guatemala highlands where many interesting Maya customs still prevail. With its bulbous snout, thick coffee-bean eyes, and the little ball decorations applied near the mouth, it has at least an ideological relationship to the first incense-burner cover illustrated on *Pl. 144.*

On the southern border of the Maya region, where peoples with very different cultural concepts lived, the meeting of two strongly characterized creative streams produced amazing results. Patterns once spiritually significant were conventionalized to mere ornament. Pseudo-glyphs applied as decoration on flasks have already been seen, and such symptoms will be more frequently observed as we enter regions where the Maya influence thins out. On the other hand, new decorative schemes make their appearance and new subjects rise to dominance, so that the work still remains vital—showing divided influences, but not degenerate.

In *Pl. 142, fig. a* we have a jar from El Salvador, 6½ inches high, with a bird as central design, probably a pelican, holding some multiple-armed water creature in its beak. It is not naturalistically represented: the wings are divided symmetrically on either side of the body, as if viewed from above, and the legs are thick and of the same color as the feathers. Dots are effectively used to set off the head and breast. The ability here displayed in spreading the subject so skillfully that it fills the surface without demanding additional decoration is a non-Maya trait.

Also from El Salvador comes the tripod jar (*fig. b*), 5½ inches high. The protruding handle is modeled into a monkey head, and black and red paint are used to represent the other parts of the animal against the buff surface of the vessel. The abstract design below the rim is interesting, as well as the checkered pattern on the legs.

In *fig. c* another monkey jar is presented for comparison, this time from distant Coclé in Panama. The head is a small button, defined by paint, and the monkey claws have been ingeniously abridged in black on white. The form of the vessel is more complicated and is divided with good decorative sense into two main sectors. Circles, not squares, are the outstanding ornament.

On the cylindrical shape of *fig. d* a bat with outspread wings is drawn on a dark ground in each of four square medallions. Here, as in the bird above, the use of the primary theme to its best decorative advantage is apparent. Symbolical elements and aberrations of glyphs encircle the vase as minor motifs, and dark spots are used as accent throughout the design.

Fig. e shows a vase, about 9 inches high, from the Ulúa Valley. A loose representation of two figures clasping each other is the main theme. The dot outline, noted also in the first jar, appears, extending from the headdress down the back. All the other elements, repeated constantly in "running bands," are here mere line and color, their one-time symbolical import now hazy. The rhythmic whirl of the design is refreshing and delightful.

All the vases on *Pl. 143* come from Honduras and show different versions of the style which reached perfection in the more permanent marble.

The transformation of symbols, so diluted as to be practically unintelligible, into a lively decorative pattern is illustrated in the first (*fig. a*). Plastic detail enters in the shape of two reptilian heads as handles, their painted bodies spread below them. The other decorative units are so drawn out and interwoven that little of their meaning can be disentangled. This piece, 10¼ inches high, comes from Lake Yojoa, only about twelve miles from the Ulúa River where the exquisite marble vases (see *Pls. 94* and *95*) were found.

In *fig. b* incision with no coloring furnishes the decoration for the same cylindrical form. A loose mask with a plastic nose occupies the center of the piece. The scrolls, wavy lines, and the slanting-S motif show kinship with the more condensed patterns on the marble vases, and the two bird heads, projecting like handles, also suggest a common ancestor. A flaring base and rim give the jar a certain finish.

In *fig. c* we have a vessel of the same type, 9½ inches high. Here the details of the central mask are not so much incised as indicated by perforations. How strictly certain features were retained, in spite of the break-up of the primary idea, can be observed in the horizontal slit eyes of the two masks, as well as the swirls of the headdress. An animal that might be a monkey is applied at the sides. Although less artistic and more poorly executed than the other two, this vessel, with its simplified form and the step-design band around the rim, makes a still better connection with the Ulúa marble vases.

INTERLYING AREA

Trade influences as well as the general versatility of the potter make it difficult to lay down stylistic borders along the bounds of ethnic groups. *Pl. 144* presents three pottery covers of incense burners (the first, from a Maya region), which, though all serving the same purpose, vary greatly in expression and manner of execution.

The most massive in body and sinister in composition (*fig. a*) comes from the Alta Verapaz region of Guatemala. We have already seen examples of the excellent ceramic art of this district and this piece likewise shows good workmanship in modeling. The open mouth, the stumpy nose, and other details in the face recall the animal sarcophagus on *Pl. 141, fig. d;* even the finger-pinched border is similar.

A crocodile is modeled on the cover of the *incensario* from Nicaragua (*fig. b*), his curving tail forming a handle. There is something amusingly human to us in his attitude. His features, though caricatured, are well conveyed.

In the crocodile from Costa Rica (*fig. c*), the ornamental indentation seen on the last piece is transformed into openwork. Despite the stylization, the impression conveyed is realistic, and the same living creeping quality is expressed as in the one from Nicaragua.

It is interesting to compare the eyes of the three specimens on this plate. Those in the Guatemalan piece are elongated "coffee beans." In the Nicaraguan, they bulge from the cheek, while in the Costa Rican crocodile they are cut around, with a sharply indented pupil.

The first two vessels on *Pl. 145* are both from Costa Rica. In the tripod effigy jar (*fig. a*), 12½ inches high, the two heavy legs and the tail, which serve as feet, are rattles. Plastic additions of an animal head and two shorter "arms" are tied into the piece by the skillfully applied designs in batik-like negative painting. In this process the pattern is covered with a protective layer, and the rest of the surface painted, so that on removal of the covering the design stands out in the natural color of the jar. The expanse of undecorated surface on the body of the animal produces good contrast. This form is a favorite in the region, but the minor details of embellishment are always varied. The colors, as in all four examples given here, are tones of orange, orange-red, and dark brown on buff.

In shape, *fig. b,* more than 9 inches in diameter and 13¼ inches high, is built on the same principle, but with the elimination of the zoömorphic. Instead of the tripod feature, this large egg-shaped vessel has a hollow base, which contains the rattle. The protruding edge just above it is modeled with great subtlety. Motifs in negative painting are spread over the entire surface, with even the blank medallions used with decorative interest in the brown ribbon that encircles the jar. Bird and animal designs, some of them similar to those in *fig. a,* can be detected in the ornamental bands, which, in a clever variation of width and content, are deftly applied to bring out the complicated form.

The shallow tripod dish from Nicaragua, not far from the Costa Rican border (*fig. c*), shows relationship to the other two both in concept and decoration. The shape again manifests skill and ease in modeling, and the plastic monster heads are particularly expressive. Clay balls that rattle are visible in their mouths. The painted elements are less concentrated, and a sort of dilution of the former warm and pulsing talent is apparent.

Fig. d, 8 inches high, was found in the Zacualpa region. The shape was undoubtedly inspired by the type from Costa Rica (*fig. a*), though it is clumsy and less in proportion. Its somewhat spreading design recalls pieces from Honduras and El Salvador (see *Pl. 143, fig. a*). Nothing could show more clearly the infiltration and exchange of artistic ideas. The Zacualpa region produced highly individual pottery of its own as well as specimens that show very strong Maya influence. What powerful fountains of non-Maya style there must have been in the south to assert themselves here.

The site of Coclé, named after a river in Panama, was put on the archaeological map by the expeditions of Peabody Museum of Harvard University, joined later by Brooklyn Museum and the University of Pennsylvania. The narrow isthmus that connects two vast continents served as a bottle neck for many stylistic movements. Individual development, however, was not crowded out in this funnel; on the contrary, the region produced an outspoken style of its own, although certain influences from the north and south are evident. On *Pl. 146* we see a variety in both shape and decoration which, even if not completely unprecedented elsewhere in medieval America, nevertheless documents the high degree of individuality in the art of Panama.

The bottle (*fig. a*), 8 inches tall, belongs among the élite of pre-Columbian pottery. Form and decoration are harmonized with rare artistic judgment. To shape the body of the vessel, with its rounded lower section slanting off toward the neck at a sharp angle, was in itself not an easy task (compare *Pl. 142, fig. c*), and to add the funnel-like neck required as clever a hand. Still another sign of thorough artistry is the variety and spacing of the vertical panels. We find the familiar spiral motif, a favorite of the Coclé region, executed in white and outlined with black on a red-brown ground. The heart-shaped design in white on the neck appears on other Coclé ware and may be a conventionalized mask, upside down to us as seen here. The balanced yet lively impression of the piece is the result of the fortunate union of a highly satisfactory shape with decorative patterns attractive in their geometric build-up. In some of its details it reminds us of Near Eastern ware. So universal is its esthetic appeal that it could be smuggled in among pottery of distant civilizations without its identity being detected for a time.

The bowl of the pedestal vase in *fig. b*, with its deep symmetrical grooves, seems to have been inspired by a plant shape. In its lines it has such proportion and ease that, despite its monotone brownish color and the absence of applied decoration, it appears a finished product. Even in the company of the superlative piece at the left it holds its own.

In *fig. c* a vague little animal head protrudes from one side. Legs are painted on the body of the piece on a larger scale and the ringed tail forms the handle-like spout. The spiral used in *fig. a* appears again, painted on the neck.

The low open bowl in buff color (*fig. d*) is decorated with a winged motif in red that might even have been inspired by a hand print. While the vessels described above show distant affiliations with the north, this one could be connected by certain characteristic motifs to the Andean Area (compare *Pl. 164, fig. c*).

The small bird effigy (*fig. e*), decorated with the spiral pattern, is in its humorous effect also closer to the south. Spirals, absolutely unrealistic as feathers, enhance the naïve charm of the little figure.

The presence of a variety of shapes in Coclé, particularly of the relatively infrequent plate, gives additional importance to the site from our point of view.

Pl. 147 shows five round specimens and one oblong, adorned with widely varied patterns.

The first (*fig. a*), about 12½ inches in diameter, is divided into four rectangular fields by two broad intersecting bands that contain the drawn-out spiral motif on different-colored backgrounds. Stylized "rampant" birds are placed within the fields. The combination of negative and positive painting in the design is noteworthy.

What appear to us to be purely geometric elements on the oblong shape (*fig. b*) doubtless held certain symbolical meaning for the maker, for the same mask idea seen on the neck of the bottle in the preceding plate may be discerned here also.

A wheel pattern is used as structural division for four fields in *fig. c*. Within them are painted stylized monkeys with outspread arms and legs, looking from the position of their faces as if they were hanging upside down. As in the first plate, the lively decorative effect absorbs us, leaving us without any desire to search too closely for realism in the animal representation.

In the stag plate (*fig. d*) a singularly poetical feeling for design is manifest; the head is spaced with such radiation that it fills the whole piece. Its contours outlined with black give a new artistic expression when compared with the other Coclé work. The amazingly good job of restoration should not be left unmentioned.

A zigzag design in three colors covers the entire surface within the narrow border on *fig. e,* and the lack of exact repetition makes the pattern more striking. After a moment's observation, one can feel in it the climbing crawling movement of a row of reptiles.

Fig. f is the most refined. The eight medallions are disposed on the brownish-colored plate with an interesting lack of symmetry. In five of them, crabs are depicted on a light ground; in the remaining three, a pattern resembling a four-leaf clover is placed on a dark. The various positions and angles in which the motifs are arranged give a rhythmic connection to them all. How easy it is to enjoy the production and to try to appreciate its art, but how difficult even to approach the concept which inspired it.

The talent of these people is curiously parallel to that seen in the Southwest, particularly Mimbres, not only in the artistic language of their imagination and the evident enjoyment of the potters in their work, but in the adaptation of plant and animal forms to geometric fields. There are, however, positive differences when the two regions are compared—notably in the limited breathing space and more luscious curves of Coclé.

In this Interlying Area, impulses of an artistic nature from local, neighboring, and distant cultures produced fantasy shapes that are not found in either the adjoining Maya or Andean areas. These impulses may not be expressed in so articulate a manner as in the greater cultures, but the pottery has importance, as it embodies the swirling cumulative ideas of the region and documents for us a quite different approach from that of the more powerful northern and southern neighbors.

Fig. a on *Pl. 148,* from Nicaragua, is a vase with polychrome surface and slightly modeled face. There is still much Mayoid in the manner of painting, but the use of scalloped lines from the corners of the eyes and the nostrils is outspokenly local.

The piece with four human figures, male and female (*fig. b*), probably served as a pedestal for a large bowl. It is classified as coming from Colombia, but it should be remembered that this state until 1903 also embraced what is now the Republic of Panama. The figures are elongated, like early Romanesque statuary, and arranged in couples, each holding hands as if for a dance, with the unengaged hands on their hips. The long garment of the woman in the foreground suggests an intricate textile art in this region, not one example of which has survived.

The tripod vessel in the shape of a jaguar (*fig c.*) is slightly more than 14 inches long and comes from Chiriquí, Panama. No doubt influences from Costa Rica played a part here, but while in Costa Rican ware conventionalized animal elements are woven together into one pattern, in this piece the decoration is composed of small sharply defined geometric fields connected by a red network. The expression is playful and toylike, especially when compared with the mature formidable jars of the other region. It should be noticed that realism was sacrificed to produce a three-legged vessel.

The squatting human in *fig. d* comes from Costa Rica and introduces an entirely different manner, both in modeling and painting.

Fig. e, from Venezuela, Colombia's eastern neighbor, shows a figurine with a disproportionately large canoe-shaped head, which it supports by tiny arms. It is about 18 inches high, hollow, though not a vase, and in spite of its size and top-heavy appearance, stands without support. The coffee-bean cut of the eyes is similar to that in the Colombian piece above it, but otherwise it speaks its own language. The perforations at the sides were probably for additional ornament. (Compare with the nude figure on the gold helmet, *Pl. 220, fig. b.*)

With *fig. f* we return to the Chiriquí province of Panama. This strangely shaped pottery vessel is 14¾ inches long and shows a female figure at either end, the head of each forming a wide spout. It is far from realistic and conveys a complex idea. The decorations on the neck and side of the jar are the typical animal representation of the region, in red outlined with black. Some similarity to the more brilliant work from Coclé may be seen in their rampant poses, the decorative spreading of the different elements to gain balance, the use of dots, and the comb-tooth feet. Four-footed jars such as this are rare in pre-Columbian America.

Peoples not sophisticated but artistically sound sometimes produce as striking objects as their more civilized neighbors who are bound in taste and expression by hieratic rules of orthodoxy. All pieces on *Pl. 149* show the enjoyment of the potters in modeling and embellishing their ceramic ware.

The open bowl from Chiriquí province (*fig. a*) is 5 inches high, and the light color of the clay, like a fine bisque ware, is left natural with no painted decoration anywhere. It makes a delightful impression with its miniature "atlantes."

In *fig. b* the clay stool, 10¼ inches high, must have been produced not far from this same district. Three creatures, a blend of human and animal, support the platelike top. Little animal heads are applied as edging to the seat, and a rough hatching breaks the monotony of otherwise plain surfaces.

Fig. c presents a tripod from Costa Rica, 6½ inches high. The urn shape is very fine, and the perforated legs are unusually long. We have seen tripods from other regions where the form alone, with painted decoration on the legs, seems to have been found satisfactory, but here the playful talent of the potter added the little monkey figures in a "thinker's" pose.

A similar inclination to decorate with grotesque elements can be found in the example from the Santarém region of Brazil (*fig. d*). We know little of these people on the middle Amazon River, whose artifacts, mostly ceramic, are just now beginning to be studied. Although they were apparently on a rather low cultural plane, their pottery is ornate and highly plastic. It is believed to have been made for mortuary purposes only, as it is too fragile for general use. The work shows analogies to that of the West Indies, Marajó Island, and other parts of the Amazon district.[80]

The bottle pictured here is 7 inches high and nearly submerged in exuberant detail. Two lateral branches representing slightly opened crocodile mouths extend from the body of the vessel. Each bears a veritable procession of human and animal figurines—on the end is a human with his hand to his forehead, behind him clings a jaguar, and following him is a bird. Other animal representations are modeled on the base. Every creature is shown in action, which gives the whole piece a particularly lively appearance. The mouth of the bottle is well turned and ornately decorated with various incised designs.

Below Panama, certain pottery shapes begin to reflect influence from the south. The larger mortuary urn from the Ocaña district of Colombia (*Pl. 150, fig. a*) stands over 2 feet high, including the lid. Besides the human figure seated on the cover, the decoration consists of reptilian heads and forefeet applied on the urn proper like handles—although there are also rounded grips (see center). The modeling of certain elements shows a close relationship to metal objects produced in the same country. Whether cast or clay representations, the same imagination and expression come to the fore; the lumpiness, the use of globular forms on ears, breasts, even fingers and toes are unlike anything presented so far and are suggestive of work with wax. The face of the figure shows traces of paint; otherwise the natural light color of the clay is left.

Fig. b, about 8 inches high, comes from the Quimbaya region of Colombia, famous for its metal-work. The design on the vessel proper was done in negative painting. The three quaint figures sitting on the three stumps are as hazy in expression as the face in the piece just discussed. Here there is a hint of coastal Peru.

In *figs. c* and *d* we again step over the frontier of our five areas into Brazil, but the pieces warrant it. The first is a large burial jar, 2 feet high, from the Amazon Delta. Its beautifully rounded shape is covered with a small fretlike pattern—the conventionalization of a reptile—that has given the name "alligator ware" to pottery with this type of surface decoration. There is also a creeping alligator depicted in relief on the side, the rakelike feet of which recall those of Coclé. This jar speaks a more powerful language than many of the specimens of the Interlying Area, and the lack of data concerning the region of its provenience shows how much there is to learn about these primitive but fascinating cultures.

The second alligator-ware jar (*fig. d*), 18 inches high, shows a cylindrical form rounded toward the bottom. The flaring rim with its low plastic decorations relates it definitely to the other, but the conventionalization of the pattern here is far advanced. The angular outline of the "alligator" is recognizable in the center, and the pronglike feet, as well as the dots used to represent scales, are also present, but detached and employed only as decorative elements. Its finely turned lip provides an adequate finish to the urn.

The region around the Esmeraldas River in northwestern Ecuador has revealed pottery that cannot be overlooked. On *Pl. 151* we offer for study eight small heads of clay, ranging from 3 to 5½ inches high. Except for the first, which is from Venezuela, all were excavated in this district.

The first two (*figs. a* and *b*) show so-called archaic traits. In their modeling, they are somewhat reminiscent of the figurines of the early cultures on the high plateau of Mexico, and in expression some features even bring to mind those of Egypt and China. *Figs. c, d,* and *e* have more spiritual content. These could have been fashioned in some peripheral region of Middle America. The last three (*figs. f, g,* and *h*) move toward a local style that is growing stronger and more bizarre. The faces are losing their realistic features, and a grotesque and stylized air makes itself manifest. The feeling for decoration becomes articulate, producing masks which can hold their own with those of the Greek theater.

The pottery of the Interlying Area does not bear the impress of completely civilized living and a broad established hierarchy, but rather of awakening, powerful, artistic energies and untapped resources of imagery.

ANDEAN AREA

In the Andean Area we are confronted with such new types of pottery that it would seem as if we had stepped into another world. Not only is the technique of decoration distinctive but, what is more important to us, the artistic formulation of the idea is new. Here a separate fantasy-world found expression during the centuries, creating its own pictorial language. The whistle jar, a peripheral example of which was seen on *Pl. 141,* is common in this area and also the vessel with a stirrup spout. One of the most unusual manifestations is the portrait jar from the Mochica culture, and nowhere else does story-telling pottery reach such novelistic proportions. Finally, when one tribe, the Incas, organized all this region into one vast empire, there was a tendency for their style to permeate the individual and diverse arts of the various subjugated nations.

Pl. 152, fig. a shows a stirrup-spout vessel of the Mochica, or Early Chimú, culture, which flourished along the northern coast of Peru from about A.D. 500 to

800. The piece is 8½ inches high. A man blowing on a shell trumpet, his head thrown back, forms the neck. Conchs were much valued as trade goods throughout medieval America, and such instruments were common among the peoples along the coast. The headdress is plastic and the textile pattern of the clothing clearly defined in paint. There is a sense of sound in the general attitude of the trumpet blower with his upstretched arms.

Fig. b, slightly over 10 inches high and also Mochica, is built up in a similar fashion, but the figure on the neck is a warrior in full regalia—a very different costume from the Maya and Mexican. He is shown sitting on a raft, propelled by four swimmers wearing floats at the waist. These, as well as the ropes by which they tow the raft, are plastically represented. The static pose of the grim chieftain is contrasted by the buoyant figures in the water, and the fish, only painted, retreat into the depths on a different plane.

All four pieces on *Pl. 153* also belong to the Mochica culture. *Fig. a,* nearly 10 inches high, presents a quite different shape. The warrior on top is modeled with realism, and the painted figures below him serve to carry out the martial scene. Interesting are the fernlike plants scattered about the design.

A graphic presentation of a group of soldiers driving bound and humiliated captives before them is given in *fig. b,* a vase with a flaring mouth. The suggestion of landscape—hills and desert vegetation—in the background is unusual. Such an aptitude for recording could have been successfully applied to the illumination of manuscripts had the culture reached for it.

An open pavilion is modeled on the top of *fig. c,* with people seated inside. Others climbing upward on the body of the vessel are depicted in paint, and a small figure near the stirrup, posed as if making his entrance into the pavilion, connects the flat scene with the plastic.

In *fig. d* there is no plastic decoration and the stirrup is placed not at the side but on the top as an integral part of the composition. It is nearly 12 inches high and has a design painted in brick-red on the white body. The fantastic headdress of the seated figure represents some spotted animal and has a feather "fan" behind, similar in shape to the plastic headgear of the others. His waist is bound by a snake. The step design across the shoulders of his shirt will be seen in textiles later (see *Pl. 191*). In his left hand he holds an axe, and with his right is strangling a monster pictured with a fierce human head and arms raised in conflict. On the other side the same scene is repeated. The design is clear and well divided, but angular, and in concept unsubjective. The fine outlines of this drawing, which uses much of the natural background as body of the subject, reminds us of the pottery of archaic Mediterranean cultures. Mochica pottery is painted generally in red on white, with the rare use of black. The effects are gained by modeling and careful drawing rather than by shading and color contrasts.

The plastic vessels in *Pl. 154,* all Mochica, show a lively talent for observation in the depiction of characteristically human gestures and attitudes. In each of the four figures a different pose of the body and a different modeling of the eyes are used for each moment portrayed.

In the smoothly finished vessel of *fig. a,* we see a seated figure, his hands resting on his knees. The main concentration is given to the face, which has an attentive, somewhat questioning expression. Incised marks designating tattoo are visible, and other lines across the head give a glimpse of the haircut of those days. A loincloth is suggested in paint. The details of the profile—low forehead, overhanging brows, aquiline nose, protruding lips, and receding chin—make *in toto* a powerful portrayal.

Fig. b, 9¾ inches high, shows another seated man, in this case apparently asleep. In the tilted head and relaxed features his unconscious state is definitely expressed. The crossed arms and clasping hands are taken from life.

The fragment (*fig. c*) is 12½ inches high. Despite the missing parts, the head and the intact hand testify to the modeler's ability. Here again the emphasis is on the gesture. He sits alert, his arm in action, his eyes wide open, and his expression tense. Compare him with the figure above him, whose narrowed eyes are focused in attention yet whose pose is inert. Paint, now in a bad state of preservation, must have added considerably to the effect; note the white eyeballs with their round staring pupils and the whitened finger nails. A brown shirt with light stripes is faintly visible.

In the last jar (*fig. d*), not quite 8 inches high, a man is shown offering a prayer or incantation over a lifeless form. The position of the hands is a natural one to us. The absorbed expression of the face, in spite of the closed eyes, contrasts interestingly with that of the sleeper in the piece above, as well as with the wasted body in front of him. Here the color is an important part of the composition.

The pieces on the next two plates come from the same region, but the majority of them are later in date, stylistically referred to as Chimú, or, frequently, Late Chimú. Here scenes from everyday life—documents of a people about whom we know far too little to accord them the appreciation they deserve—are modeled with an arresting display of talent.

The first (*Pl. 155, fig. a*), a double whistle jar in polished black ware, about 8 inches long and 10 high, shows two persons carrying a third in a hammock suspended from a pole, while a smaller figure, perhaps a child, walks beside it. The faces, all very much alike, are not expressive, but the plodding movement in the whole group is well conveyed. We feel that here the stress was not on the individual but the event. In other very similar vessels, the object carried is clearly a mummy.

In *fig. b* the action spreads over both flattened jars of the double vessel. On the right one stands a man with a jug bound to his back in typical Indian manner, his hands grasping a thick twisted rope by which he drags at an animal—a llama or alpaca—on the other jar. This rope is disproportionately heavy, for it also serves as handle.

Somewhat more individual expression is found in *fig. c,* a Mochica piece, on which a flat surface again offers a stage but this time with a hint of setting. The spout of the vessel is shaped to form steps that end in an animal head, and the characters are grouped at the rear as if facing an audience. The tallest is playing on a vertical flute, while a child on either side holds on to him with one hand. The boy is carrying a package strapped to his back, and over the girl's shoulder a doll is looking out from a knapsack. One can still make out the painted pattern of the man's shirt in places. As in some of the other scenes, the staring eyes bring in a pathetic touch, doubtless not intended.

Fig. d shows a single jar about 12 inches high. The figure modeled on its rounding top wears oversize earplugs and a tall headdress with drooping feathers. He holds an instrument before his mouth with one hand and leads a doglike animal on a leash with the other. The maturely balanced shape of the vessel augments the effect of the figural decoration.

In all four of these vignettes of Mochica and Chimú life, an unquestioned ability in modeling is displayed. Always the *genre* seems to have been the aim, and it is communicated in this new language with the charm and immediacy of marionettes. Without doubt these pottery pieces were for these people a means of articulation and communication; they had no written language and often expressed through form and color much that we convey in words.

Water jars from the Mochica and Chimú cultures with animal subjects as the principal decoration are displayed on *Pl. 156.* In *fig. a,* slightly over 7 inches high, a little monkey sits on a fruit-shaped vessel in a droll position that shows what keen observers of nature these modelers in clay were. Beside it (*fig. b*), an apelike couple is engaged in lively gesticulation. A small animal perched behind the spout, a frequent addition to this type of pottery, attests to the ever-present urge and talent for decoration. The rounded jar in *fig. c,* nearly 9 inches high, is made of shiny black ware and carries low relief as well as ornament in the round. An appealing little monkey clings to the stirrup, and two bird heads look up from its base. The central band with bird shapes was probably applied by the use of a stamp. All three vessels are Chimú. It is noteworthy that similar shapes have been found executed in silver, showing the broad application of the talent of these people.

The llama jar (*fig. d*) belongs to the Mochica culture and makes use of color, some of which has peeled off. Here the vessel itself has the shape of the animal, an idea spectacularly developed in the portrait heads that will follow. On it, riding backward, lies a human figure, apparently asleep, with his head on the llama's rump and the guide rope coiled about his hand. Again the story is more in evidence than the portrayal of an individual. Although the llama is a highland animal, it makes trips to the coast today and doubtless did also in the past.

In *fig. e,* a Mochica double jar, the larger section is fashioned into the body of a parrot. Its staring eyes and brilliant variegated coloring are well conveyed by the lines on face and wings.

On *Pl. 157* are pictured some of the most naturalistic animal shapes from various regions. The kitten-like creature (*fig. a*) is Mochica. Its open mouth and glaring eyes, the feline posture, and tail curled tightly to the body are all features that are familiar. The naturalistic is not in the least disturbed by the stirrup spout in its head and back.

Fig. b comes from Ecuador. This northern neighbor of the Inca, so excellent in metal-work as we shall see, had also its masters in pottery. The vessel pictured here represents a dog in playful pose. The opening is in the head. As has been mentioned before, this animal was fattened for food in many regions of medieval America, and the fleshy body of this little creature would indicate for him such an end. The cumbersome form, with the short legs and slit eyes of a pig, is well conveyed.

The Chimú fish (*fig. c*) has corduroy sections as decoration in the center and on the tail and fins; the ubiquitous monkey appears on the handle. In its modeling the piece has the substantial character of a bronze.

Fig. d is a fragment representing the head of a puma. The combination of the plastic with painting, a characteristic of the Mochica, is masterly. Mouth, teeth, nose, eyes, and ears are modeled with realism, and a bold application of paint brings out the whiskers, dilated pupil, and muzzle. But the most telling detail is the broadening stroke down the cheek that accents the eye and jaw and makes the face powerful and ferocious.

The Mochica vessel (*Pl. 158, fig. a*), a little over 10 inches high, is a representation of the "potato mother." An autochthonous South American plant, the potato played a major rôle in the nourishment of the people of the Andean Area. Here it is personified, the vegetable form complicated with a woman's face emerging from one end; a second face in profile, visible on the side, symbolizes a new sprout. The dull earth-brown paint on the plant is a good foil for the highly polished dark red of the faces.

Fig. b is a Chimú black-ware double jar with pressed relief design. Animal figures are composed against a spotted matt background with a good sense of placement and proportion. Both parts of the vessel have the roundness of a gourd or vegetable shape, and the neck of one is ingeniously fashioned into a plastic bird's head.

Fig. c, 6½ inches high, may be a gourd. Strikingly fine execution is evident in the shapely form and in the incision work denoting the rind, its only decoration. No paint was needed to convey the subject.

The black-ware piece (*fig. d*) has the meticulous detail work of a still life. It represents a section of maizelike stalk with fruit. The balance in the piece and the reticence in decoration show superior artistry. These last two specimens come from northern coastal districts and belong to a late period, probably Chimú.

The Mochica culture, which was one of the earliest and richest in all pre-Columbian America, achieved an excellence in the modeling of human heads unsurpassed elsewhere. Hundreds of portrait jars have been excavated during the centuries and many museums possess fine examples. In spite of the number, however, each has some detail which makes its study worth while. This genius for portrayal, developed so eloquently, is a manifestation peculiar to this region, and despite the ceramic skill displayed in other parts of the Andean Area, the palm must be awarded to the Mochica potter. His all-roundness, always sensitive approach to the subject, his touch of humor, and complete control of techniques required, not only in the construction of the jar but in bringing out facial expression, are unique. It is possible that some of the portrait jars were made by means of molds, as various other types of pottery were quite commonly produced by this method on the North Coast.

The portrait vessel in *Pl. 159, fig. a,* about 12 inches high, is modeled with strong and characteristic features. The desire of the potter to make a utilitarian shape of the head complicated his task, but even so no hesitancy is noticeable in the execution. Every detail is sharp, and he seemingly had no difficulty in keeping within the given contours. The use of paint on the head covering, as frame and contrast to the face, is a studied artistic addition.

Fig. b presents a tattooed head with still more forceful details, if that is possible. This piece is only 5 inches high and was attached to the neck of a large vase. Eyes, cheeks, nose, and mouth—even the ears—are done with great facility and complete realism, which, however, is far from being boiled down to a stereotyped representation. The incised tattoo marks alienate us somewhat, but, like the wrinkles designated by deeply cut lines, have decorative as well as realistic value.

Pl. 160 presents two more heads from the same cultural circle. The modeling in *fig. a* is on the customary high level, though not as unusual as in those just seen. The detailed headdress lends special interest to the piece, as a recording on pottery of the geometric pattern-world that appears also in weaving, carving, and embossing.

For *fig. b,* the head has been photographed at an angle to make it most understandable to our *l'art pour l'art* perception. In this romantic position, it could be taken for a troubadour of the 13th century or a Florentine prince of the 14th —proof of its supercontinental appeal. The noble profile, the melancholy and intellectual expression speak a universal language.

These faces have nothing either cruel or exaggerated about them. In their physical build-up as well as in their artistic expression, they document great differences between the South American and Middle American cultures.

The Mochica also applied their skill to the depiction of the grotesque and the ill. On *Pl. 161, fig. d,* the two seated individuals with disfigured faces are gruesome reminders of the bodily shortcomings that existed among these people. Some of the examples of this type seem to show mutilation, some congenital defects, and others the inroads of disease. The depiction here of the wasted nose and lips and other repulsive details are strong marks of a general talent, both for observation and realistic delineation, whether of beauty or ugliness. The pieces are about 7 inches high.

The stunning art of portrayal naturally had an influence on the neighboring districts. In *fig. a* modeling ability is still apparent although somewhat stereotyped. The face has a certain dignity. Eyes, nose, and mouth are plastically executed, and the body of the jar carries incised decoration and a painted band. In this section a kind of freezing of the expression can be noticed. Mention should be made of the false drawing of the right hand with its backward-turned fingers.

Fig. b, about 8 inches high, introduces the work of a more southern region, where the culture known as Nazca expressed itself in a characteristically different style. When compared to the great Mochica portraits and the black-ware *genre* scenes, both of which achieved their effect by sheer form and with only two colors, the completely different approach of the Nazcas is at once apparent. They use commonly five or six colors on a single piece. The vessel illustrated shows a minimum of modeling; both face and body of the woman depend chiefly on paint for their expression and decoration. The body is stiff and toylike, the face a painted mask. The figure has charm for us through its fantasy element, not through its realism. The domination of textile patterns in the art of this folk is noticeable in the way the hands are forced into the vertical and in the monster design on the skirt, a familiar one in their embroideries (see *Pl. 177, fig. b*).

The laughing old man in *fig. c,* also Nazca, is an example of what these people could do in the way of characterization if they wished. However, the talent lies again primarily in the painting, not in the plastic. The body retains the rounded outline of the jug and the four-fingered hand shows again textile influence. Much of the attraction is derived from the painted clownlike exaggeration of the features and the bold stripes on the garment.

The Mochica and Nazca cultures, so dissimilar in the style of their art, flourished at the same time, separated by about three hundred fifty miles.

Pottery from the South Coast, imposing in both shape and patterns, is shown on the four plates that follow. *Pl. 162, fig. b,* a mug from the Atacameña culture in Chile, is an exception, which, with its form and the spiral decoration similar to Southwestern pottery, furnishes an interesting example of parallel development. Remote from the direct influence of the great Andean cultures, its makers apparently followed their own artistic impulses.

Figs. d, e, and *f* are identified as Nazca [8] and show characteristic use of human, plant, and animal motifs. Attention should be drawn to the mask on the center band in *fig. d,* reminiscent of the doll-like face of the Nazca woman. In *fig. f* small mouselike creatures run in delightful countermovement to the large feline animals in the center.

Fig. a comes from the Chincha Valley and *fig. c* from the Ica. Their diminutive patterns are closely related, featuring the characteristic textile motifs of the Ica, or Late Nazca, period.

Absolutely flat decoration appears on the two Nazca plates with fish patterns (*Pl. 163, fig. b*). The skillful hand that placed the motif on the first pulled the tail around so boldly that the figure fills the circle with highly decorative effect. In the second, the fish are rather suspended, floating stomach to stomach and facing in opposite directions. A wide dark margin furnishes good contrast. Here, as is so often the case, simplicity is the reason for the universal appeal of the pattern.

In *fig. d* a highly stylized drawing covers the surface of a typical Nazca shape, a spherical jug with two spouts. The design is executed with genuine feeling for space and suggestion of movement. The eyes of the fish are out of proportion and out of place, but aid with their rhythmic repetition the fluent and attractive pattern. There is something about the piece that suggests a neo-primitive drawing of a goldfish bowl.

With the 9th century the influence of the Tiahuanaco culture from the highlands becomes apparent on the coast. Its pattern language mingles with local traits to produce a style called Coast Tiahuanaco. Examples with modeled details from the Nazca region are pictured in *figs. a* and *c.* The former presents an unusual scene, masterly in execution: a condor plucking at the head of a dead man. The piece is only 4 inches high, and its small size may be responsible for the restraint in painting. Every brush stroke is in place. Painted details on the bird are inventively stylized; a single row of eyelashes succinctly expresses the dead eyes. The gesture of picking is realistic, and the claws extending over the eyebrows is a cruel but effective touch. (Compare *Pl. 97, fig. a.*)

In *fig. c* painting predominates. The many colors used can be distinguished in the illustration. The vessel, about 7 inches high, modeled in two bulky sections, represents a double-headed serpent swallowing frogs. On the neck we find the frequently recurring animal-mask of Tiahuanaco style, in this case also double-headed. For a different presentation of a similar subject in the same medium, see *Pl. 116, fig. c.*

POTTERY

Figs. b, c, and *d* on *Pl. 164* show the favorite beaker shape of the Nazca, on which Tiahuanaco designs rarely occur. The figure in the first (*fig. b*) has lost certain iconographical elements which might make it more distinct; in comparison with other examples with figural representation, it is vague and inexpressive. The decoration of the piece below it (*fig. d*) consists of conventionalized heads that suggest different kinds of fish, painted within encircling bands. The lowest section also pictures heads, this time human and so designed as to form a cover of overspreading masks. In contrast, *fig. c* has only one motif, a painted stylized bird. A much more dashing hand arranged this single element and it fills the surface with incomparably more vigor than the lifeless motifs in the vase beside it. The pattern is strongly suggestive of the one on the Coclé bowl (see *Pl. 146, fig. d*).

The cold, flat, and diagrammatic style which had a certain lucidity in the highlands loses it on the tropical Pacific shores and becomes a crammed condensation of an ideological world not too completely digested. The jar with handles (*fig. a*), nearly 12½ inches high, shows its kinship to the Tiahuanaco in its rigid decorative motifs as well as in its shape. With the exception of the plastic head, the design is purely two dimensional, and it is clear that strong local artistic traditions are preserved in it.

Fig. a on *Pl. 165,* a ceremonial urn from Pacheco in the Nazca region, is about 24 inches high. Its style is distinctly Coast Tiahuanaco, sometimes called Epigonal. The main figure is identified as Viracocha by the weeping eyes that look like semaphores (symbolizing the rain-tears of the god), by the radiating aureole of animal heads and plant forms, and the belt with condor beaks. The personification of the idea is still more involved than on the Gateway at Tiahuanaco (see *Pl. 46*). The maker seems to have been so intent upon including all the symbolic and traditional trappings that little time was given to the elaboration of pattern.

The pottery urn (*fig. b*), about 18 inches high, shows the same stylistic characteristics and presents the winged man carved on the Gateway of the Sun. Technical analysis, however, has proved that the piece is not of ancient origin.

The oft-repeated figures of Tiahuanaco art are not particularly ingratiating to our eyes, but it is clear that a powerful concept lies behind them. The certainty of the design and the fastness of color are admirable; the excellent quality of the pottery and the fine polish make the work striking. Even though the ideas behind the representations are obscure to us, it is evident that those who fashioned such pieces knew what they wanted and were without question able to express it with good decorative feeling.

At the site of Tiahuanaco itself, we find greater ease in dealing with highly conventionalized figures. Although strongly stylized, the design seems to bear more relation to the shape of the vessel upon which it is placed, and more breeziness is apparent in its placement. Here animal and human representations are sometimes simplified to a design easily repeated, sometimes combined or blended, producing an involved scheme difficult to disentangle. The shapes themselves have more grace than those of the preceding plate.

The bowl in the upper right of *Pl. 166, fig. a* shows a four-footed animal, comparatively naturalistic—probably a llama—while the one in the upper center presents a kind of griffin, with wings, a beak, and mighty paws. The complete break-up of the subject into an all-over pattern, very decorative, is seen in the upper left, where eyes, nose, and mouth are separated and treated as single units in the design, in much the same manner as was frequently used in the textiles of the region (compare *Pl. 178, fig. a*).

In *fig. b* the center and left-hand vessels both illustrate the adaptation of geometrical motifs to a rounded surface, a talent in which the Southwest also excelled. The vase at the right features a condor as it repeatedly appears, either blocked or painted, on woven fabrics. These three, with the central bowl above, represent the Classic Tiahuanaco style, while the other two are classified as Decadent. It is noteworthy that virtually all Tiahuanaco pottery has a red slip as base, with the designs usually outlined in black or white or both. Black and white on red is one of the basic diagnostics of Tiahuanaco pottery; yellow, brown, or gray may be used to fill in the design.[8]

Although in each region of the Andean Area certain original trends were preserved, outside influences and modifications of pattern produced an overwhelming variety in pottery. On this account, and also because of the vast amount of highly artistic material on hand with scant data, there is still much left to be worked out in the stylistic classification. Certain strains, nevertheless, can be traced. The metamorphosis of one basic shape from a primitive utilitarian vessel to a most civilized and distilled form is presented in our last two plates of this chapter. The jars shown on *Pl. 167* have much in common. All have handles, three of them well down the sides, and all have flaring necks and a sharp demarcation around the middle below the main design.

Fig. a, a simple shape with a simple decoration, comes from the site of Tia-huanaco, but it is so universal in character that it could belong to other early cultures, either medieval American or even Near Eastern or Chinese. *Fig. b,* 10½ inches high, is from Pachacámac, a site of the Central Coast near Lima. It carries conventionalized frogs, painted in red with black outline, which have evolved into pure ornament without any consideration for realism. Its style is Late Coast Tiahuanaco. *Fig. c,* from Chincha, is rounder and more regular in shape, and its neck is utilized to depict a human head. The widely spaced painted design suggests a textile motif and is characteristic of Ica.

Fig. d, of the same provenience and period, seems more closely related to the first two than the one beside it, but actually it is moving away from all three toward the type seen in its perfected form on the following plate. The shape is elongated and a positive refinement is evident. The lines of the piece have become more graceful, and its proportions demonstrate a more mature artistic taste. The painted decoration, with its alternating color scheme, is more varied in interest and tends toward a design composed of smaller elements. This tendency becomes still more marked in the Inca period, when patterns that originated as fish, birds, and other figures are reduced to the smallest scale, far removed from the ideas which they once expressed.

The last centuries before the Conquest in the Andean Area fall under the sign of Inca domination. Smaller political units, which had already evolved an art of their own, were exposed to the centralizing force of a well-organized government, and the administrative changes that followed naturally had their effect on the mental and artistic life of the people. The carefully integrated, protected, even luxurious regime of the Empire disseminated an art, which, although utilizing traditions of the past, carried in itself a certain preciosity in shape and design and standardized its output on a high artistic level.

Nothing could better illustrate this development than the aryballos, 44 inches high, on *Pl. 168.* In comparison with any other pre-Columbian ceramic form, its refinement is outspoken. The Greek term, with its connotation of the beautifully shaped and delicately ornamented vessels of Hellas, is fittingly applied to this type of Inca pottery.

A diminutive animal head, little more than a protuberance at the base of the neck, is the only survivor of naturalism in the decoration. The shape is difficult to fashion, fragile to handle. In the design the three elements are subtly arranged and applied, separated by stripes of varying widths and spacing that give the whole a vertical character. The little unevenness that can be observed in the pattern is just enough to keep the piece lively and to avoid coldness.

Marking the end of a long road of evolution, the jar is in no way decadent; it is rather the balanced expression of a civilized people. Although their mental life and artistic temperament may have been considerably different from that of their distant relatives to the north, in quality of workmanship and richness of expression their pottery attained a level unsurpassed by any other culture of medieval America.

ILLUSTRATIONS

a

b

PLATE 1. ©. *a*) Rito de los Frijoles, New Mexico. Talus-houses, with community dwelling in the foreground. *b*) Mesa Verde, Colorado. Spruce Tree House.

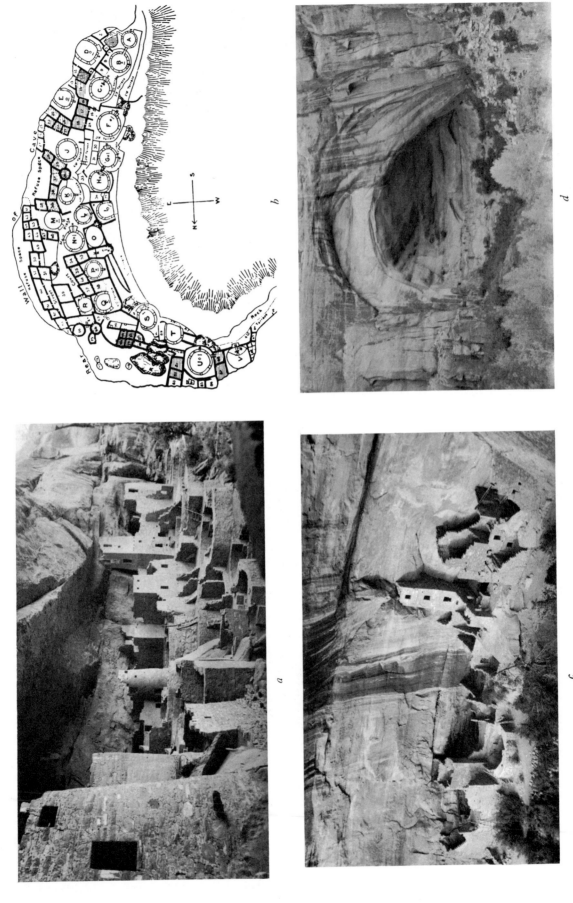

PLATE 2. ⓒ. *a* and *c*) Mesa Verde, Colorado. Cliff Palace and Square Tower House. *b*) Ground plan of Cliff Palace. *d*) Betatakin Ruin, Navaho National Monument, Arizona.

PLATE 3.   ©.   Canyon de Chelly, Arizona.   White House.

a

b

PLATE. 4 ©. Pueblo Bonito, Chaco Canyon, New Mexico. *a*) View from rear. *b*) Theoretical reconstruction. View from front.

a

b

PLATE 5. ©. *a*) Chetro Ketl, Chaco Canyon, New Mexico. Great kiva. *b*) Aztec Ruin, New Mexico.
Interior of reconstructed kiva.

a

b

PLATE 6. ©. *a*) Walpi, Arizona. A Hopi village. *b*) Taos, New Mexico. Five-story community dwelling.

a

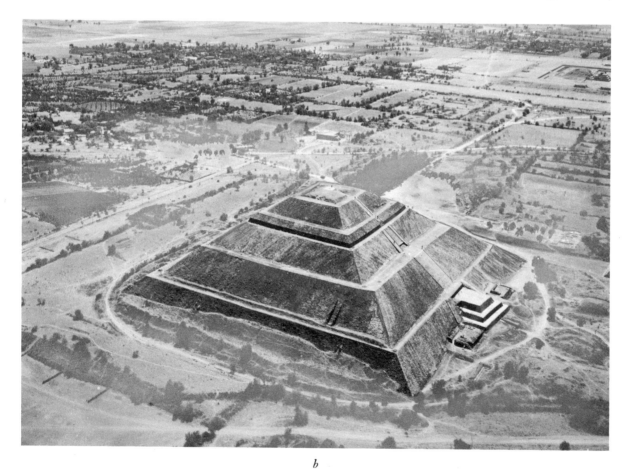

b

PLATE 7. ©. Teotihuacán, Mexico. *a*) General view. Inset: section of the Citadel.
b) Pyramid of the Sun.

a

b

PLATE 8. ©. Teotihuacán, Mexico. *a*) Temple of Quetzalcóatl. *b*) Detail.

a

b

PLATE 9. ©. Xochicalco, Mexico. *a*) Temple-base. *b*) Detail.

PLATE 10. ©. Malinalco, Mexico. *a*) Monolithic temple. *b*) Near view of entrance. *c*) Interior of temple. *d*) Calixtlahuaca, Mexico.

a

b

c

PLATE 11. ©. Tenayuca, Mexico. *a*) Temple-base. *b*) Detail of early stairway. *c*) Fire Serpent, with section of temple-base.

a

b

c

PLATE 12. ©. *a*) El Tajín, Papantla, Mexico. *b*) Stairway. *c*) Airview.

a

b

c

PLATE 13. ©. Monte Albán, Mexico. *a*) View of the Great Plaza, looking north. *b*) Archway, Monticle J. *c*) Monticle M.

a

b

PLATE 14. ©. Monte Albán, Mexico. *a*) View of the Great Plaza, looking south. *b*) Ball Court.

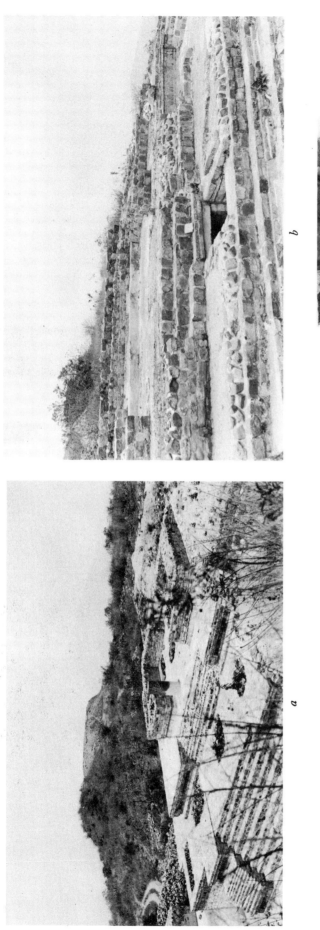

a

b

c

d

PLATE 15. ©. Monte Albán, Mexico. *a*) North end of the Temple of the Tiger. *b*) Entrance to fabulous Tomb 7. *c*) Entrance to Tomb 125. *d*) Entrance to frescoed Tomb 104.

a

b

PLATE 16. ©. Mitla, Mexico. *a*) Palace II. *b*) View from southwest.

PLATE 17. ©. Mitla, Mexico. *a*) Profile of Palace II façade, looking west. *b*) Inner court. *c*) Inner chamber.

a

b

PLATE 18. ©. Mitla, Mexico. *a*) Court of the Tombs, north section, showing tomb entrance.
b) Interior of east tomb.

a

b

PLATE 19. ©. Uaxactún, Guatemala. *a*) Airview of temple-base (Structure E-VII). *b*) Near view.

b

a

d

c

PLATE 20. ©. Copán, Honduras. *a*) Great Plaza. *b*) Model of site. *c*) Reviewing Stand. *d*) Ball Court.

a

PLATE 21. ©. Copán, Honduras. *a*) Hieroglyphic
Stairway. *b*) Detail of balustrade.

b

a

b

PLATE 22. Ⓒ Copán, Honduras. *a*) Temple of the Sculptured Doorway (Structure 22).
b) Entrance.

a

b

c

PLATE 23. ©. Copán, Honduras. Views of the sculptured doorway.

PLATE 24.   ©.   Tikal, Guatemala.   View from Temple I, looking toward temples II, III, and IV.

a

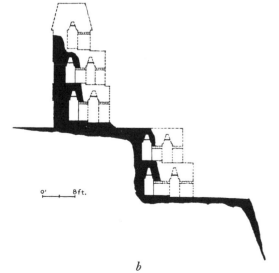

b

PLATE 25. ©. Tikal, Guatemala. *a*) Rear section of the Palace of the Five Stories (Structure 10). *b*) Cross-section of same.

a

b

PLATE 26. ©. Palenque, Mexico. *a*) General view of the Palace Group. *b*) House A from court.

a

b

PLATE 27. ©. Palenque, Mexico. *a*) Temple of the Cross. Note the inner vaulting revealed by
the collapsed façade. *b*) Model of theoretical reconstruction.

a

b

PLATE 28. ©. Río Bec B, Mexico. *a*) Building 1. *b*) Model.

a

b

PLATE 29.   ©.   Tulum, Mexico.   *a*) Castillo group, showing natural seawall.   *b*) Castillo viewed from court.

a

b

PLATE 30. ©. Tulum, Mexico. *a*) Temple of the Frescoes. *b*) Model.

a

b

PLATE 31. ©. *a*) Sayil, Mexico. Palace. *b*) Uaxactún, Guatemala. Present-day house.

a

b

PLATE 32.   ©.   Labná, Mexico.   *a*) Gateway.   *b*) Detail of Great Palace (Structure I).

a

b

c

d

PLATE 33. ©. Yucatan, Mexico. Flying façades: *a*) Structure XI, Labná; *b*) temple, Sabacche; *c*) Red House, Chichén Itzá; *d*) model of Red House, showing cross-section.

a

b

PLATE 34.   ©.   Kabah, Mexico.   *a*) Palace I from southwest.   *b*) Detail.

a

b

PLATE 35. ©. Uxmal, Mexico. *a*) Temple of the Dwarf and corner of the Nunnery. *b*) Palace of
the Governor, House of the Turtles, House of the Doves.

a

b

c

PLATE 36. ©. Uxmal, Mexico. *a*) Façade of Palace of the Governor. *b* and *c*) Details, inner court
of the Nunnery.

a

b

PLATE 37. ©. Uxmal, Mexico. *a*) The Nunnery complex from the Palace of the Governor. *b*) East building of the Nunnery from the inner court.

a

b

PLATE 38. ©. Chichén Itzá, Mexico. *a*) The Nunnery. *b*) East end.

a

b

PLATE 39. ©. Chichén Itzá, Mexico. *a*) The Observatory, or Caracol. *b*) Temple of the Three Lintels.

a

b

PLATE 40. ©. Chichén Itzá, Mexico. *a*) Temple of the Tigers. *b*) Ball Court.

PLATE 41. ©. Chichén Itzá, Mexico. El Castillo.

a

b

PLATE 42.   ©. Chichén Itzá, Mexico.   *a*) Frontal view of the Temple of the Warriors.
b) Southwest corner of upper building.

a

b

PLATE 43. ©. Chan-Chan, Peru. *a*) Walls with stucco-like decoration. *b*) Hall of the Arabesques.

PLATE 44. Ⓒ. Paramonga, Peru. La Fortaleza.

a

b

PLATE 45.   ©.   *a*) La Centinela, Chincha Valley, Peru.   *b*) Adjoining palace.

a

b

PLATE 46.   ©.   Tiahuanaco, Bolivia.   *a*) Gateway of the Sun.   *b*) Detail.

a

b

PLATE 47. ©. *a*) Pirapi, Bolivia. Burial towers, or *chulpas*. *b*) Sillustani, Bolivia. Burial tower.

a

b

PLATE 48. ©. *a*) Cuzco, Peru. Street showing Inca masonry. *b*) Ruins at Tampumachay, near Cuzco.

a

b

PLATE 49. ©. Sacsahuamán, Peru. *a*) Fortress. *b*) Throne of the Inca.

a

b

PLATE 50. ©. *a*) Tampumachay, Peru. Ruins with fountain. *b*) Ollantaytambo. Hall of the Niches.

a

b

PLATE 51. ©. Pisac, Peru. *a*) Semicircular ruins of "garrison." *b*) Section of temple group.

a

b

PLATE 52. ©. Pisac, Peru. *a*) Entrance to Sundial, or *Intihuatana*. *b*) Rear view.

PLATE 53. ©. Machu Picchu, Peru. General view in morning mist.

a

b

PLATE 54.   ©.   Machu Picchu, Peru.   *a*) Semicircular tower.   *b*) Section with three windows.

a   *b*

c

PLATE 55. ©. Machu Picchu, Peru. *a*) Masonry combined with carved living rock.
b) So-called Sundial or microcosmos altar. *c*) View of tower.

a

b

PLATE 56. ©. Machu Picchu, Peru. *a*) View across gorge. *b*) Ruins of terraces.

b

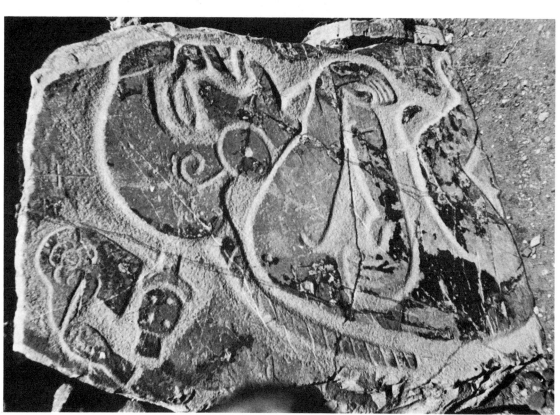

a

PLATE 57. ©. Sculptured stone slabs, Monte Albán, Mexico.

a

b

PLATE 58. ©. *a*) Zapotec stone relief. *b*) Aztec stone relief.

c

b

a

PLATE 59. ©. *a*) Huaxtec figure. *b*) Aztec "pulque vessel." *c*) Aztec Goddess of Agriculture.

a

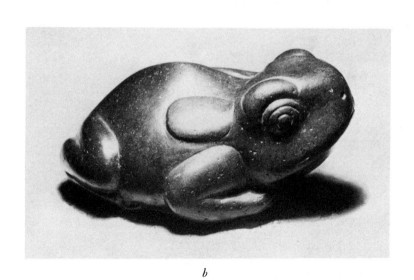

b

c

PLATE 60. ©. Aztec animal figures: *a*) rattlesnake; *b*) toad; *c*) "dog."

a

b

PLATE 61. ©. *a*) Aztec seated figure. *b*) Recumbent anthropomorph, Vera Cruz?.

a

b

a

b

c

PLATE 63. ©. *a*) Stone relief from Ball Court, El Tajín, Papantla, Mexico. *b*) Relief in fired clay, southern Mexico. *c*) Eagle stone relief, Chichén Itzá, Mexico.

a

b

PLATE 64. ©. *a*) Totonac yoke. *b*) Detail of one end.

a

b

c

PLATE 65.   ©.   Details of three Totonac yokes.

b

a

PLATE 66.   ©.   Two Totonac axe-shaped stone heads.

PLATE 67. ⓒ. Three Totonac *palmas.*

PLATE 69. ⓒ. *a*) Totonac stela, Tepetlaxco, Mexico. *b*) Carved stone disk, southeastern Mexico. *c*) Maya stela, Tenam, Mexico.

PLATE 70. ©. *a*) Stela 16. Tikal, Guatemala. *b*) Stela 10, Xultún, Guatemala.

c

b

a

PLATE 71. ©. *a*) Stela H, Copán, Honduras. *b* and *c*) Detail and north side of Stela D, Quiriguá, Guatemala.

c

b

a

a

b

PLATE 73. ⒸⒸ. *a*) Stela 40, Piedras Negras, Guatemala. *b*) Detail of upper half.

a

b

PLATE 74. ©. *a*) Stela 12, Piedras Negras, Guatemala. *b*) Detail of lower third.

c

b

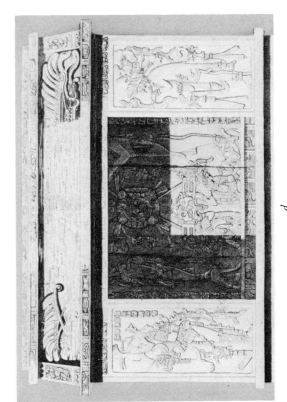

d

a

PLATE 75. ©. *a*, *b*, and *c*) Sculptured stone tablets from the sanctuary, Temple of the Sun, Palenque, Mexico. *d*) Drawing by F. Catherwood, showing their original position.

PLATE 76. ©. *a*) Lintel 53. *b*) Lintel 15. Yaxchilán, Mexico.

a

b

PLATE 77. ©. *a*) Lintel 1. *b*) Lintel 3. Piedras Negras, Guatemala.

b

a

PLATE 78. ⓒ. *a*) Fragment of stone relief, Piedras Negras, Guatemala. *b*) Fragment of stone relief, Jonuta, Mexico.

b

a

PLATE 79. ©. Figures in stucco relief, Palace Group, Palenque, Mexico.

c

b

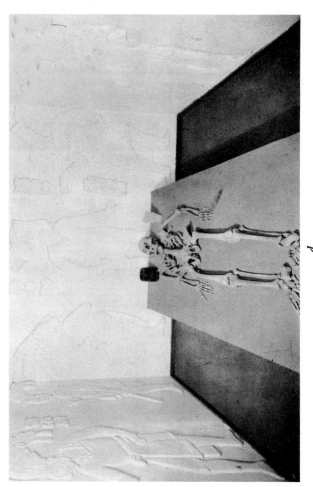

d

a

a

b

PLATE 81. ©. *a*) Stone tablet from Palenque, Mexico. *b*) Maya astronomer seated
on a hieroglyph, Chiapas, Mexico.

a

b

c

PLATE 82. ©. Round stone reliefs: *a*) **Ball**-court marker, Copán, Honduras; *b*) small altar, Tonina, Mexico; *c*) Ball-court marker, Chinkultic, Mexico.

a

b

c

PLATE 83.   ©.   Sculptured profiles: *a*) Piedras Negras, Guatemala;   *b*) Copán, Honduras;
c) El Tajín, Papantla, Mexico.

b

a

PLATE 84. ©. *a*) Detail of Maya lintel, El Chicozapote, Mexico. *b*) Zapotec sculptured stone, Zachilla, Mexico.

b

a

PLATE 85. ©. *a*) Head of a monster. *b*) Maya head. Copán, Honduras.

PLATE 86. ©.   Stucco heads: *a*) Palenque, Mexico;   *b*) Piedras Negras, Guatemala;   *c*) Uxmal, Mexico;
d) Louisville, British Honduras.

PLATE 87. ©. Human figure of stone from the Hieroglyphic Stairway, Copán, Honduras.

PLATE 88. ©. Stone heads: *a*) Copán, Honduras; *b*) Quiriguá, Guatemala; *c*) provenience unknown; *d*) Copán.

PLATE 89. ©. Two Maize-god-type sculptures, Copán, Honduras.

PLATE 90. ©. Bust of the Maize-god, Copán, Honduras.

b

d

a

c

PLATE 91. ©. Plastic decorations on the bases of buildings, Mexico: *a*) Palenque; *b*) Monte Albán; *c*) Acancéh; *d*) Chichén Itzá.

PLATE 92. © . *a*) Detail of mural, showing warrior seated on jaguar throne, Temple of Chacmool, Chichén Itzá, Mexico.
b) Jaguar throne from inner temple, El Castillo, Chichén Itzá.

a

b

a

b

PLATE 93. ©. *a*) Atlantean columns, Chichén Itzá, Mexico. *b*) Chacmool from Chichén Itzá.

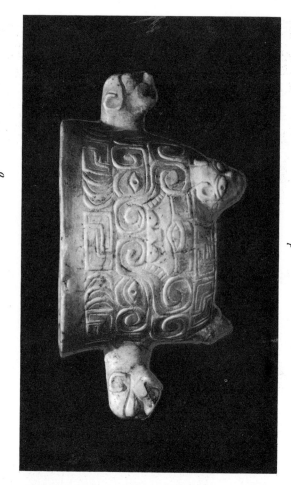

a

b

c

d

PLATE 94. *a*, *b*, *c*, Sculptured marble vases, Ulúa Valley, Honduras. *d*, ...

a

b

PLATE 95.   ©.   Sculptured marble vases, Ulúa Valley, Honduras.

PLATE 96. ©. Seated stone figures: *a*) Chichicastenango, Guatemala; *b*) Río Frío, Costa Rica.

a   *b*

c   *d*

PLATE 97.   ©.   *a* and *b*) Sculptured "axes," Guatemala.   *c* and *d*) Stone figures, Costa Rica.

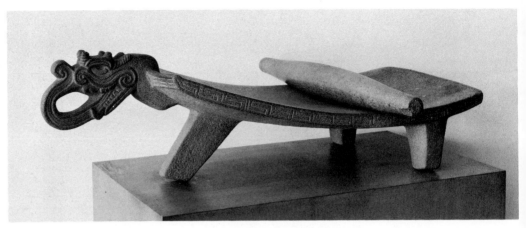

a

b

c

PLATE 98. ⓒ. Sculptured *metates* (grinding stones):   *a*) Guatemala;   *b*) Costa Rica;   *c*) Nicaragua.

a   b

c

PLATE 99.   ©.   a) Monolith E, Cerro Sechín, Peru.   b) Stela Raimondi,
Chavín de Huántar, Peru.   c) Giant statue, Tiahuanaco, Bolivia.

a

b

PLATE 100. ©. Carved stone bowls: *a*) Chavín; *b*) Highland Inca.

a

b

c

d

e

PLATE 101. ©. Pottery shapes from Arizona.

a

b

c

PLATE 102.   ©.   Water jars, or *ollas*:   *a*) Arizona;   *b*) Colorado;   *c*) New Mexico.

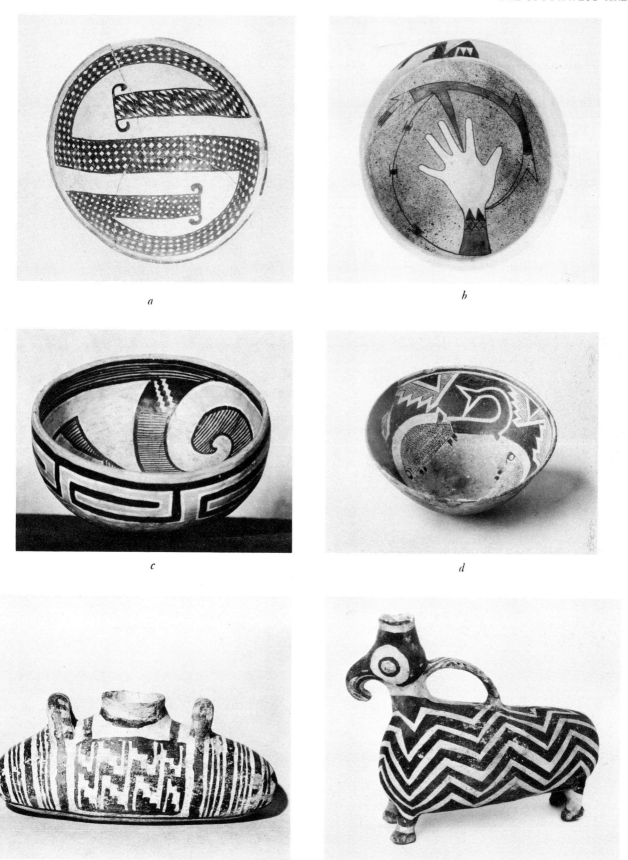

PLATE 103. ©. Various painted pottery: *a, b, c,* and *f*) Arizona; *d*) New Mexico; *e*) Colorado.

PLATE 104.   ©.   *a*) Three Pueblo mugs, Navaho Canyon, Arizona.   *b*) Double jar, Mesa
Verde, Colorado.   *c*) Pottery dipper, New Mexico.

a

b

c

d

PLATE 105.   ©.   Various types of black-and-white and colored ware: *a*) New Mexico;   *b*) Colorado;   *c*) Arizona;   *d*) northern Mexico.

c

f

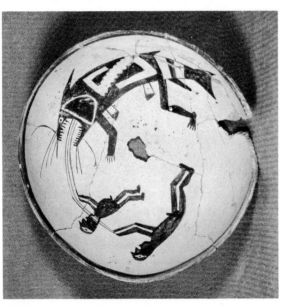

b

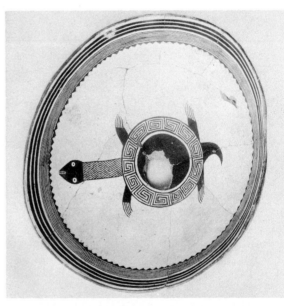

e

a

d

PLATE 106. ©, Mimbres bowls, New Mexico.

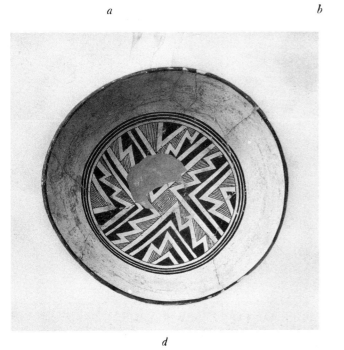

PLATE 107.   ©.   Mimbres bowls, New Mexico.

a

b

c

d

PLATE 108. ⓒ. *a* and *b*) Painted water bottles, Arkansas. *c*) Incised bowl, Louisiana.
d) Burial urn with stamped decoration, Georgia.

a

b

c

d

PLATE 109. ©. *a*) Precipitation jar, Missouri. *b*) Black-ware bottles, Arkansas. *c*) Horned
snake effigy bowl, Arkansas. *d*) Incised brown-ware bottle, Louisiana.

a

b   *c*

PLATE 110. ©. Early pottery shapes: *a*) Monte Albán; *b* and *c*) Teotihuacán.

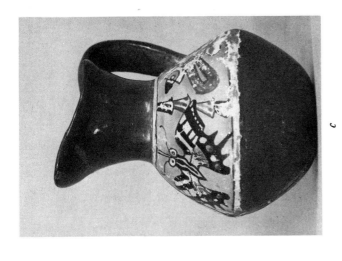

c

b

a

f

e

d

PLATE III. ©. Pitchers: *a*) Toluca Valley; *b*) Oaxaca; *c*) Puebla. Tripods: *d*, *e*, and *f*) Oaxaca.

a

b

c

PLATE 112. ©. Tarascan figures in clay.

a   *b*

c

d   *e*

PLATE 113. ©. *a*) Tarascan mother and child. *b*) Miniature warrior. *c*) Figure on couch, northwest Mexico. *d* and *e*) "Pretty ladies," Valley of Mexico.

POTTERY

b

a

c

d

PLATE 144 © Pottery types. Colima

PLATE 115. ©. *a* and *b*) Tarascan warriors. *c*) Small standing figure, Chiapas.
d) Seated figure, central Vera Cruz.

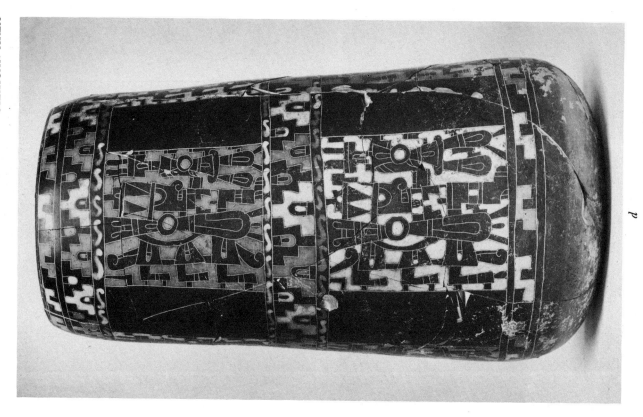

d

b

a

c

PLATE 116

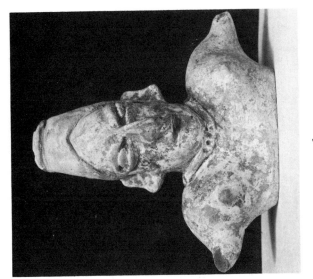

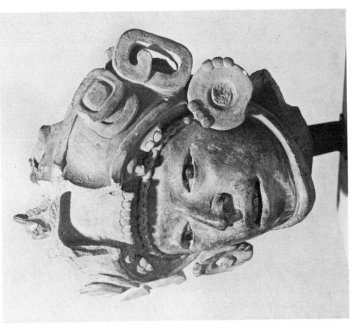

c

e

b

a

d

PLATE 117. ©. Clay heads from different cultures:
a) Zacatenco, D. F.; *b*) Vera Cruz?; *c*) Guadalajara,
Jalisco; *d*) Vera Cruz; *e*) Vera Cruz?.

a

b

c

d

PLATE 118. ©. *a*) Figurine, Tempoal. *b*) Masquette of moan bird. *c*) Pottery whistle. *d*) Bat head. Vera Cruz.

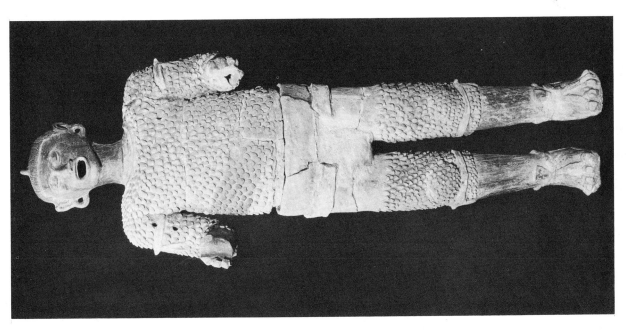

a

b

PLATE 119. © . Large Aztec terra-cotta figures.

PLATE 120. ©. Zapotec Messenger Dogs of the Gods, Oaxaca.

a

b

c

PLATE 121. ©. Effigy funerary urns and incense burner, Oaxaca.

a

b

c

d

PLATE 122.   ©.   Zapotec incense burners, Oaxaca.

a

b

c

d

PLATE 123. ©. Representations of human figures, Oaxaca.

a

b

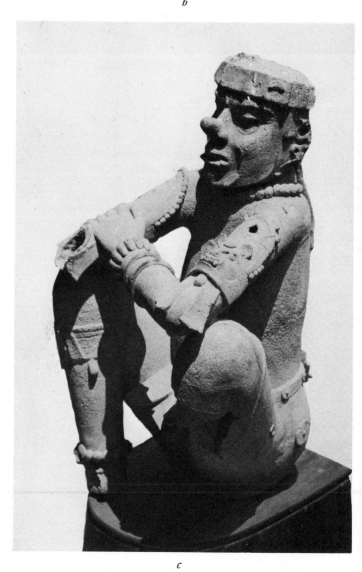

c

PLATE 124. ©. *a*) Standing figure. *b*) Vessel with carved medallion. *c*) Large seated statue. Oaxaca.

a

b

c

PLATE 125. ©. *a*) Incense burner, Puebla, Mexico. *b*) Incense burner, Guatemala. *c*) Large
vessel, Guatemala.

a

b

c

PLATE 126. ©. *a*) Undecorated vessels, British Honduras. *b*) Polychrome funerary jar, Chiapas, Mexico.
c) Painted beaker, Vera Cruz, Mexico.

a

b

c

d

PLATE 127. ©. *a* and *b*) Effigy vases, Kaminaljuyú, Guatemala. *c*) Brownish tripod vessel with lid, Kaminaljuyú. *d*) Black-ware effigy, Uaxactún.

By special permission of Carnegie Institution of Washington.

a   *b*

c

PLATE 128. ©. *a* and *c*) Stuccoed tripod vessel with calligraphic decoration, Uaxactún, Guatemala, and unrolled design. *By special permission of Carnegie Institution of Washington.* *b*) Stuccoed tripod vase with painted decoration, Kaminaljuyú.

a

b

c

PLATE 129. ©. *a* and *c*) Cylindrical vase with painted decoration, Uaxactún, Guatemala,
and unrolled design. *b*) Interior design of painted tripod bowl, Holmul.

a

b

c

d

PLATE 130. ©. *a* and *c*) Painted vase with warriors, Chamá, Guatemala, and unrolled design. *b* and *d*) Painted vase with dignitary borne on a journey, Ratinlixul, and unrolled design.

a

b

c

d

PLATE 131. ©. Polychrome vases of different shapes: *a*) Nebaj district, Guatemala; *b*) Chamá, Guatemala; *c*) Copán, Honduras; *d*) El Salvador?.

PLATE 132. ©.   Vases representing human heads, Guatemala: *a*) Quiriguá;   *b*) Kaminaljuyú.

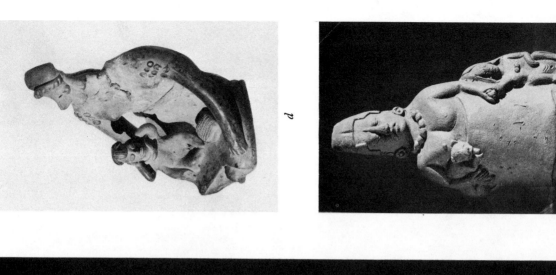

d

e

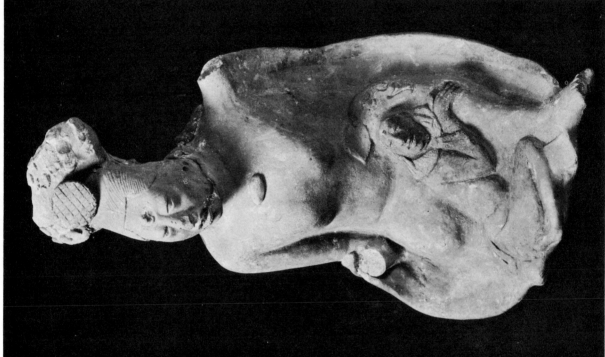

c

a

b

PLATE 134. ©. Variations on a theme: *a*) Cuernavaca, Mexico; *b*) Solcajá, Guatemala; *c*) Campeche, Mexico; *d*) Tarascan

a

b

c

PLATE 135. ©. Vases with incised figural decoration: *a*) Yucatan?, Mexico; *b*) Zacualpa, Guatemala; *c*) Asunción Mita, Guatemala.

a

b

c

PLATE 136, ©. Relief vases from Guatemala: *a*) Uaxactún; *b*) Zacualpa; *c*) Kaminaljuyú.

a

b

PLATE 137. ©. Relief vases from Mexico: *a*) Yucatan?; *b*) Peto, Yucatan.

PLATE 138. ©. *a*) Sculptured bowl, San Agustín Acasaguastlán, Guatemala. *b*) Tall relief vase, Ataco, El Salvador.

a

b

c

d

PLATE 139. ©. *a*) Beaker with relief decoration, Guatemala?. *b*) Beaker with relief, incision, and
painted decoration, Jutiapa, Guatemala. *c*) Buff beaker with glyphs in relief, Tonacatepeque, El Salvador.
d) Jar with incised glyphs and painted decoration, Ulúa Valley, Honduras.

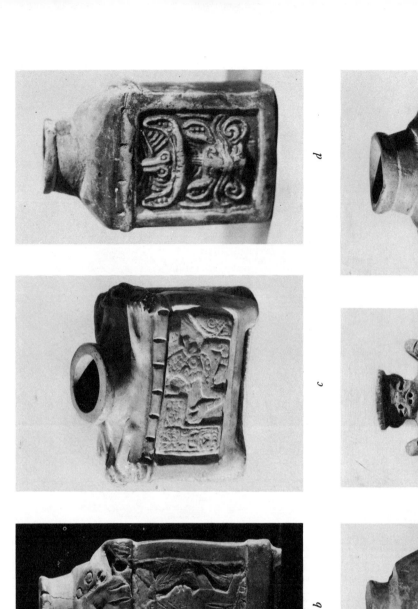

PLATE 140. ©. Small flasks: *a*) Honduras; *b*, *c*, and *d*) El Salvador; *e*) Yucatan, Mexico; *f*, *g*, and *h*) El Salvador.

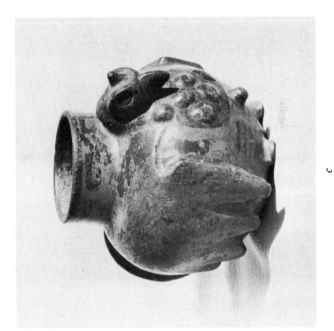

a

b

c

d

PLATE 141. ⓒ. Various shapes from the Guatemalan highlands: *a*) Kaminaljuyú; *b*) Sololá?; *c*) Zacualpa; *d*) Nebaj.

a   b   c

d   e

PLATE 142. ⓒ. *a* and *b*) Cylindrical jars with painted decoration, El Salvador. *c*) Vessel with painted decoration, Coclé, Panama. *d* and *e*) Mayoid painted vases, El Salvador and Ulúa Valley, Honduras.

c

b

a

PLATE 143. ©. Cylindrical vessels with animal handles, Honduras.

a

b

c

PLATE 144. ©. Incense burner lids: *a*) Guatemala; *b*) Nicaragua; *c*) Costa Rica.

a

b

c

d

PLATE 145. ©. *a*) Animal effigy pot with negative painting, Nicoya, Costa Rica. *b*) Negative painted jar with rattle base, Costa Rica. *c*) Polychrome tripod bowl, Nicaragua. *d*) Animal effigy jar with polychrome decoration, Zacualpa, Guatemala.

c

e

b

d

a

a

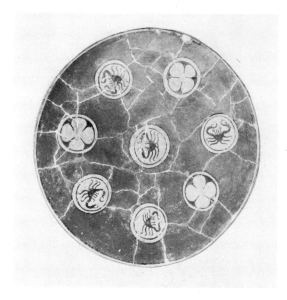

b

c

d

e

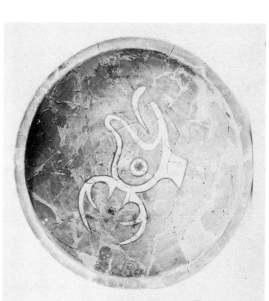

f

PLATE 147. ©. Plates, Coclé, Panama. *All examples on these two pages, except for fig. a on the first, are reproduced by special permission of Peabody Museum of Harvard University.*

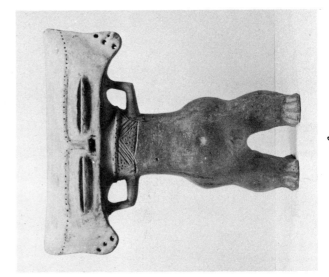

a

b

c

d

e

f

a

b

c

d

PLATE 149. ©. *a*) Tripod bowl with monkey figures, Panama. *b*) Clay stool, Panama. *c*) Tripod with monkeys, Costa Rica. *d*) Bottle with animal decoration, Brazil.

PLATE 150. ©.   *a* and *b*) Vessels with human figures, Colombia.   *c* and *d*) Alligator-ware jars, Brazil.

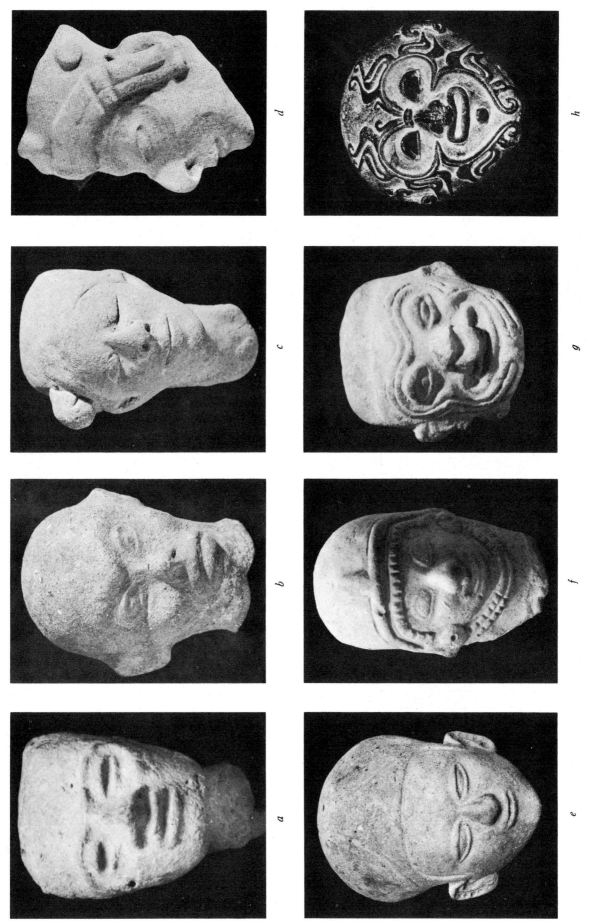

PLATE 151. ©. Small pottery heads: *a*) Venezuela; *b-h*) Ecuador.

a

b

a

b

c

d

PLATE 153. ©. Mochica vessels with story-telling decoration.

a

b

c

d

PLATE 154. ©. Mochica effigy vessels showing striking poses.

a

b

c

d

PLATE 155.   ©.   Scenes of Mochica and Chimú life.

c

b

a

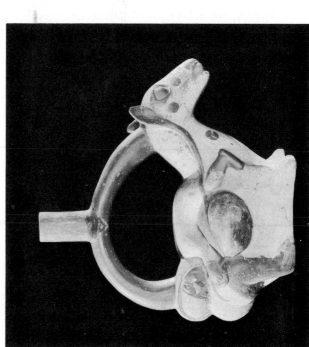

PLATE 156. ©. Mochica and Chimú water jars with animal subjects.

a

b

c

d

PLATE 157.   ©.   Animal representations, Peru and Ecuador.

PLATE 158. ©. *a*) Mochica Potato Mother. *b*) Chimú double jar with pressed relief. *c* and *d*)
Chimú shapes of a vegetable and fruit.

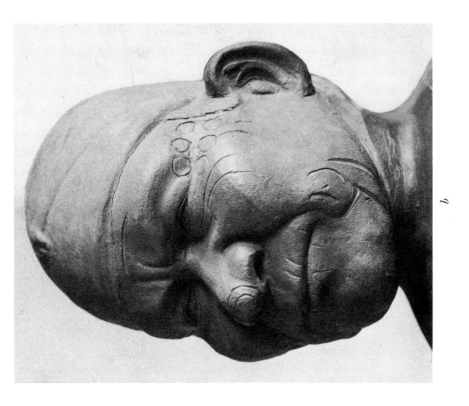

PLATE 159. © Mochica portrait vessels.

b

a

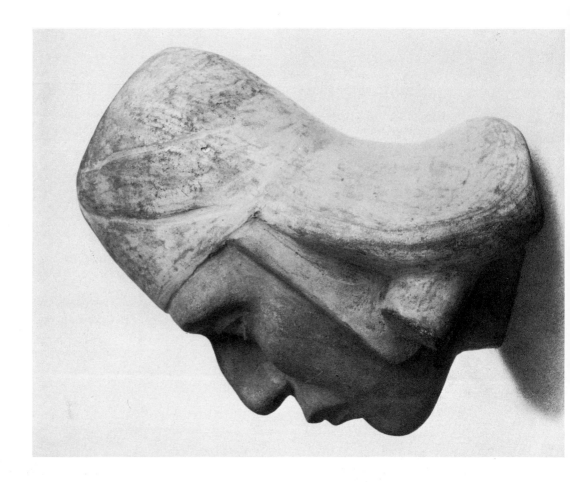

a

PLATE 160. © Mochica portrait vessels.

c

b

a

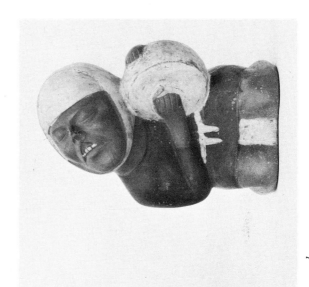

d

PLATE 161. ©. *a*) Mochica effigy jar. *b* and *c*) Nazca effigy jars. *d*) Mochica effigies, depicting ravages of disease.

c

f

b

e

a

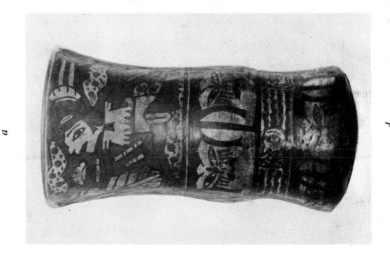

d

PLATE 162. Ⓒ Various shapes from South Coast of Peru and Chile

PLATE 163. ©. Painted ware: *a* and *c*) Coast Tiahuanaco; *b* and *d*) Nazca.

a

b

c

d

PLATE 164. ©.   *a*) Painted jar with handles, Coast Tiahuanaco.   *b, c,* and *d*) Painted jars, Nazca.

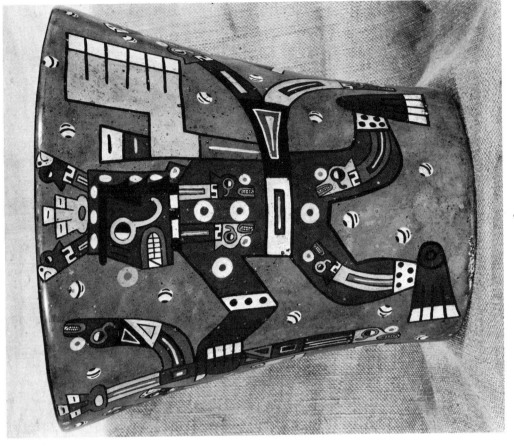

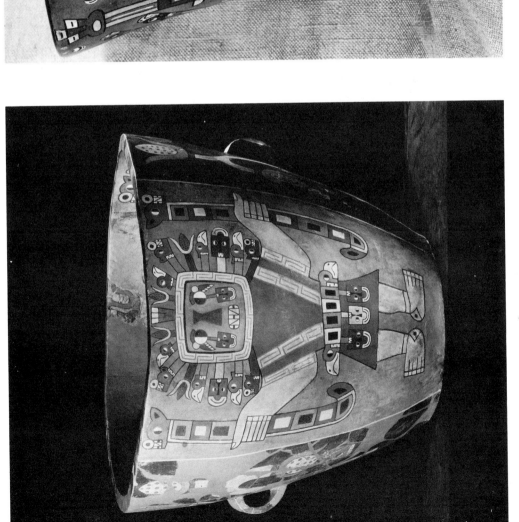

a

b

PLATE 165. ©. Large ceremonial urns in Coast Tiahuanaco style: *a*) Nazca region; *b*) South Coast of Peru.

a

b

PLATE 166. ©. Bowls and jars in Classic and Decadent Tiahuanaco style, Tiahuanaco, Bolivia.

a   *b*

c   *d*

PLATE 167. ©   Modulations of a basic shape: *a*) Decadent Tiahuanaco; *b*) Late Coast Tiahuanaco; *c* and *d*) Ica.

PLATE 168. Ⓒ. Inca aryballos.